INTOXICATION

INTOXICATION

An Ethnography of Effervescent Revelry

Sébastien Tutenges

Rutgers University Press
New Brunswick, Camden, and Newark,
New Jersey, and London

Library of Congress Cataloging-in-Publication Data

Names: Tutenges, Sébastien, author.
Title: Intoxication : an ethnography of effervescent revelry / Sébastien Tutenges.
Description: First Edition. | New Brunswick, New Jersey : Rutgers University Press,
[2023] | Includes bibliographical references and index.
Identifiers: LCCN 2022008966 | ISBN 9781978831209 (Paperback : acid-free paper) |
ISBN 9781978831216 (Hardcover : acid-free paper) | ISBN 9781978831223 (epub) | ISBN
9781978831230 (pdf)
Subjects: LCSH: Drinking of alcoholic beverages. | Intersubjectivity. | Social interac-
tion. | Emotions—Sociological aspects. | Rites and ceremonies.
Classification: LCC GT2884 .T88 2023 | DDC 394.1/3—dc23/eng/20220519
LC record available at https://lccn.loc.gov/2022008966

A British Cataloging-in-Publication record for this book is available from the British
Library.

References to internet websites (URLs) were accurate at the time of writing. Neither the
author nor Rutgers University Press is responsible for URLs that may have expired or
changed since the manuscript was prepared.

Cover image: Sebastian Matthes

♾ The paper used in this publication meets the requirements of the American National
Standard for Information Sciences—Permanence of Paper for Printed Library Materi-
als, ANSI Z39.48–1992.

www.rutgersuniversitypress.org

Manufactured in the United States of America

CONTENTS

INTOXICATION

CHAPTER 1

INTRODUCTION

My research on intoxication had a desultory beginning in 2001. I was studying anthropology at the University of Copenhagen in Denmark and preparing to conduct fieldwork at a Buddhist monastery in India as part of my master's thesis project. On the side, I had a job as a student assistant on a research project about young people and their use of tobacco, alcohol, and illicit drugs in a provincial town called Ringsted. So I spent my weekdays reading lengthy books on Buddhism, and on weekends, I went to bars and nightclubs to observe young people having fun. But I could find no funding for my fieldwork in India. Moreover, as time went by, I grew more and more fascinated with the Ringsted youth. In particular, I was intrigued by the ritualistic character of their substance use and their determined efforts to derange their senses and experience altered states.

One of the first people I got to know in Ringsted was a seventeen-year-old named Sofie. I met her at Lion Bar one quiet Thursday evening as she was sitting with a friend looking at pictures of themselves and waiting for something to happen. She invited me over and asked me to evaluate the pictures and tell my story. This would become the general tone of our conversations. She joked and asked complicated questions, and I tried to reciprocate. It turned out that she was an ambitious student, active in local politics, and popular among friends. She was also in a relationship with a nice boyfriend and living with her parents in a big house. However, she described her life until recently as dull. Something had been missing, she said, but this changed after she started drinking alcohol. She made it sound like alcohol had flung open the doors to a brand new world full of interesting people, wild parties, sex, and occasional experimentation with cannabis. She wanted to be wild and try out everything that she had not tried before. Alcohol was central to these pursuits because it made her more courageous and carefree. Sometimes she became so drunk that she could hardly stand on her feet, but this was fine, she said. "Crazy stuff" always happened when she got "wasted," and this was fun because it gave her new experiences and great stories that she could share with friends.

I met many other people in Ringsted with this urge for wild intoxication. Where did it come from? What purpose did it serve? Why run risks when life is so new and wide open? As my Ringsted fieldwork progressed, myriad questions were spreading across the pages of my field diary. I realized that I was spending much more time pondering them than my books about Buddhism. So I gave up my plans to study the monastic life and decided instead to write my master's thesis on the Ringsted youth. As it turned out, though, the difference between the monks and the merrymakers was not as enormous as I had imagined. Partying youths, I discovered, are also seeking something akin to a religious experience.

My supervisor, the anthropologist Michael Jackson, supported my new initiative and gave me some lasting advice. He recommended that I approach the revelers with an open mind and that I not—as often happens in studies of substance use—focus narrowly on the adverse effects of drugs or on possible solutions to the "drug problem." He prompted me to concentrate on getting close to the youths in order to shed light on their experiences, stories, and perspectives.

The result has been two decades of studying people fifteen to thirty-five years old in a variety of nightlife environments, including pubs, bars, nightclubs, strip clubs, music festivals, drug dens, drug markets, dance parties, and seaside resorts in Bulgaria and Spain. My research has covered many different themes, but looking back, I can see that it has always revolved around one fundamental question: Why intoxication? In this book, I examine this question, guided by Durkheim's concept of "collective effervescence." This concept, though originally developed to explain religious rituals, is essentially about group intoxication. It is not concerned with the intoxication of singular individuals who achieve altered states all by themselves, such as through solo drinking or solo dancing. Rather, what collective effervescence refers to, and what this book is about, are forms of intoxication that involve and affect at least two individuals who are gathered in the same place.

History of the Concept of Collective Effervescence

Anthropologists Marcel Mauss and Henri Beuchat laid down some of the early foundations of the concept of collective effervescence in their masterly monograph on the Inuit from 1904 to 1905. The term *effervescence*—or to be exact, "a chronic state of effervescence"—is mentioned only in passing in the book, but it is used in a key passage that describes how the otherwise dispersed Inuit families gather during the winter season to live close together and engage in a range of social activities including feasting, dancing, singing, having sex, reciting myths, and performing ceremonies (Mauss and Beuchat 2008, 470). For the Inuit, the winter season is like one long festival and is of such intensity that it makes their emotions effervesce and spill over so that the entire community is permeated by the same state of excitement. Mauss and Beuchat argue that this cyclical rhythm of life, the alternation between periods of dispersal and periods of intense communion, is found in many societies other than the Inuit and that this rhythm has profound influence on all aspects of life.

Émile Durkheim also began to use the concept of "collective effervescence" in his writings and lectures from around 1900, but it was in 1912 with the publication of his masterpiece *The Elementary Forms of Religious Life* that the concept found full-blown expression (Pickering 2009, 382). The book is a case study of totemism among Australian Aborigines and ambitiously aims to elucidate the cross-cultural foundations of religious experiences, beliefs, and institutions. Echoing the analysis of his collaborators Mauss and Beuchat, Durkheim writes that the life of the Aborigines alternates between two contrasting phases: times when the population is scattered in small groups and life is centered around work activities, such as hunting and fishing, and times when the population assembles for religious celebrations. It is during these celebrations, when people convene in the same place, that states of effervescence can occur. Durkheim explains,

> The very act of congregating is an exceptionally powerful stimulant. Once the individuals are gathered together, a sort of electricity is generated from their closeness and quickly launches them to an extraordinary height of exaltation. Every emotion expressed resonates without interference in consciousnesses that are wide open to external impressions, each one echoing the others. The initial impulse is thereby amplified each time it is echoed, like an avalanche that grows as it goes along. And since passions so heated and so free from all control cannot help but spill over, from every side there are nothing but wild movements, shouts, downright howls, and deafening noises of all kinds that further intensify the state they are expressing. (1995, 217–218)

Such a fervent description was unusual for Durkheim, who wanted to establish sociology as a respectable science on par with the natural sciences and thus normally wrote in a measured tone, exuding scientific expertise. Yet *The Elementary Forms* contains several passages about rituals that radiate such vitality that the reader can almost sense the charged atmosphere of the events. The theme of the book was also unusual for Durkheim. He had made his name writing on topical issues, such as the suicide rates among Protestants and Catholics. Then—at the peak of his career—he devoted year after year to studying so-called primitive peoples and their religions. He even had the audacity to argue that the religion of the Aborigines is based on an experience that forms the foundation of all religions, including the Christianity in his own home country: namely, the experience of collective effervescence, of being taken outside of oneself and merging with a larger whole.

Durkheim's book sparked much controversy when it was published, but it also received massive praise and became a source of inspiration for researchers around the world (Smith 2020). Indeed, the book has been called Durkheim's very best and "*the* classic in the sociology of religion" (Pickering 2009, xix). In France, the notion of collective effervescence soon came to play an important role among Durkheim's followers. In the 1930s, dissident surrealist Georges Bataille was among the founders of the Collège de Sociologie and the secret society Acéphale, two groups that were so inspired by collective effervescence that they did more than read and write about it; they also organized and participated in rituals that they believed could unleash effervescent forces and help revitalize themselves and society, which they regarded as becoming increasingly fragmented, morose, and dangerously close to being overtaken by the Fascists.

Since the late 1970s, sociologist Michel Maffesoli and his followers at the Sorbonne have conducted research along similar lines. A substantial number of the publications presented by his group employ the notion of effervescence—whether in studies of specific phenomena, such as rock concerts, or more abstract subjects, such as the times in which we live. For the Maffesolians, our present postmodern age shares many characteristics with the high-intensity periods of the Inuit and the Aborigines as described by Mauss, Beuchat, and Durkheim. In their view, contemporary life is highly focused on assembling people together—or trying to assemble them—in order to pump up the collective energies, for instance, at parties, political rallies, sports events, and religious ceremonies. Even after COVID-19 emerged and its deadly consequences were clear, many people continued to throng together in large numbers at the expense of personal and public health. The desire for collective effervescence is simply too strong and essential for human well-being—especially in our age, which, according to Maffesoli, is ruled not by rational Apollonian urges but by those embodied in Dionysus, "the god of versatility, of play, of the tragic and the loss of the self" (1996a, 61).

Outside of France, the concept of effervescence was long absent from social science literature, even in studies drawing on *The Elementary Forms*. This has changed over the last few decades, however, during which numerous studies have applied and elaborated on the concept (Allen, Pickering, and Miller 1998). The tradition of microsociology, spearheaded by sociologist Randall Collins, has been particularly prolific, offering an original reading of *The Elementary Forms*, a new theoretical model for understanding human interaction, and a range of empirical studies on topics as diverse as sex, thinking, sports, violence, and religion. The centerpiece of this neo-Durkheimian microsociology is Collins's *Interaction Ritual Chains*, which presents collective effervescence as "a process of intensification of shared experience . . . a condition of heightened intersubjectivity" that emerges out of successful interaction between individuals who are copresent (2004, 35). This can happen in large crowds, such as when a group of fans is cheering at a stadium, or between a few people, as in the case of engrossing dinner conversation. This kind of intense intimacy, which we need just as much as we need food and sleep, strengthens social bonds and gives us the emotional energy needed to survive the vicissitudes of life (373).

Cultural sociology is another tradition that draws heavily on *The Elementary Forms* and in which the concept of effervescence is put to work, although more sporadically than in microsociology (Alexander, Jacobs, and Smith 2012). The main focal point in cultural sociology—as well as cultural psychology (Valsiner 2012) and cultural criminology (Ferrell, Hayward, and Young 2015)—is the process of meaning making. Scholars in this diverse tradition posit that we humans are "compulsive meaning makers" with a fundamental need to make sense of whatever we encounter in our lives, from our personal mood swings to events in the outer world (Valsiner 2014, 1). Effervescent events play vital roles in how we make meaning because they alter the way we experience ourselves and our connections with other people. Take as an example the terrorist attacks on the World Trade Center and the Pentagon on September 11, 2001. These attacks were broadcast worldwide and led to innumerable effervescent gatherings—in front of televisions, on streets, in legislative bodies, and far beyond—that changed the way people thought and felt about themselves and the world: narratives of doom started spreading, the lines between friend and foe were drawn anew, nations were reclassified in terms of good versus evil, and do-or-die sentiments surged (Smith 2005, 158).[1] What followed was war. Cultural scholars have forged tools to understand such processes of collective meaning making and the way these processes shape subjective experiences and drive social action (Spillman 2020).

Émile Durkheim, Georges Bataille, Michel Maffesoli, and Randall Collins—these are names that will appear many times throughout this book along with those of Michael Jackson and various cultural scholars. These diverse scholars and scholarly traditions are all influential to my interpretation and application of collective effervescence. In other words, this book is not strictly or solely Durkheimian. The primary aim is not to decode what the grandmaster originally wrote and said but rather to use and expand his analytical framework in order to clarify why humans so eagerly intoxicate themselves.[2]

COLLECTIVE EFFERVESCENCE DEFINED

Durkheim does not give a precise definition of collective effervescence in *The Elementary Forms*, although it is key to his religious theory. He does, however, give many examples of situations that supposedly involve effervescence, including the French Revolution, the Crusades, the St. Bartholomew's Day massacre, the Dreyfus affair, and as we have seen, the religious gatherings among Australian Aborigines. So for Durkheim, collective effervescence is a broad phenomenon that may erupt in both religious and nonreligious contexts, and it can be a defining feature of an entire era as well as of specific, small-scale ritual gatherings. This has led critics to ask what differentiates collective effervescence from other types of excitement, such as those of falling in love, watching a good movie, or going on a shopping spree (see, e.g., Richard 1994, 247). Indeed, as sociologists Chris Shilling and Philip A. Mellor point out, Durkheim's notion of effervescence is "open to competing interpretations and applications" (2001, 50).

In this book, I operate with the following definition of collective effervescence: It is an altered state of heightened intersubjectivity marked by intense, transgressive, and yet mutually attuned actions and emotions among individuals who are gathered in the same place. This state may be divided into five experiential components. First, and most importantly, there is a powerful feeling of connectedness, of being part of a community, a common body. Second, there is an intense rush of emotions that carries people outside of themselves and makes them forget the humdrum and stresses of everyday life. Third, transgressive urges emerge that make people do what they would not normally do, ranging from innocent breaches of etiquette to lawbreaking. Fourth, some of the collective energies of being assembled, interactively engrossed, and transgressive are channeled into symbols (e.g., songs, photos, and stories) that come to stand for the people who invested them with their energies. Finally, there is a sense of purpose, vitality, and solidarity that makes life worth living.

My definition of collective effervescence differs from Durkheim's original conception on two main points. First, in my understanding, collective effervescence refers exclusively to states of heightened intersubjectivity among individuals who are present in the same specific time and place. It does not encompass the kind of social ebullience that defines entire eras, such as the years around the French Revolution. This is not to deny that eras can be marked by high levels of collective effervescence, but as an ethnographer, I am not comfortable with studying and making generalizations about the mechanisms behind such prolonged and far-flung bursts of energy. I, therefore, opt for a definition that focuses narrowly on experiences that come from instances of human assembly occurring in a specific location for a limited or defined duration of time.

Second, Durkheim mainly reserved the concept of collective effervescence to designate social events of such magnitude that they touch the very heart of a society. He held that those partaking in an occasion of full-blown effervescence will be so affected by it that they, and possibly also their predecessors, will feel a need to repeatedly commemorate it through ritual performances and reenactments. As sociologist W. S. F. Pickering puts it, Durkheim understood collective effervescence as belonging to "the serious side of life" (2009, 408). So Durkheim himself would perhaps have been hesitant to extend the concept to some of the activities that this book addresses (e.g., engrossing conversation and casual sex). But again, the primary aim here is not to write an exposition of Durkheim's pronouncements, nor is it to follow his original argument as closely as possible and in all aspects. Rather, the aim is to elaborate, and empirically substantiate, an analytical framework that can help us understand why so many people around the world so thoroughly and tenaciously intoxicate themselves during their leisure time.

Collective Effervescence Typologized

Durkheim employs the concept of collective effervescence in a very broad sense, without specifying how it varies across types of gatherings. For instance, as mentioned, he uses the concept to describe the psychosocial arousal of religious gatherings, revolutions, and massacres. But what, one may ask, are the differences between the types of arousal emerging in these very different situations? Durkheim is not clear on this, nor are most of his followers—including Collins, whose work I will discuss in the next section. The focus is more on what effervescent situations have in common than on what sets them apart. I, therefore, agree with Pickering's argument that there is a need to refine Durkheim's concept and build "some kind of internal classification of types of collective effervescence" (2008, 451).

Pickering identifies two basic "types or functions" of collective effervescence from the work of Durkheim. First, there is "creative effervescence," which refers to aroused assemblies "where the level of feeling is of a most intense kind, where the final outcome may under certain circumstances be uncertain and where it is possible that new ideas emerge" (Pickering 2009, 385). Second, there is "re-creative effervescence," which refers to aroused assemblies "where the level of excitement is intense, but where those gathered together feel a bond of community and unity (as in the function mentioned above), and where as a result the members feel at the end morally strengthened" (2009, 385). The main difference is that the first type may lead to new ideas and practices, whereas the second one merely reproduces and strengthens the status quo. The distinction between creative and re-creative effervescence is important to have in mind, especially when assessing the short- and long-term outcomes of effervescent events. However, in this book, I consider not only the outcomes of effervescence but also the interactions that lead up to and create effervescence (chapter 2) as well as, most comprehensively, the phenomenological characteristics of lived effervescent experiences (chapters 3–7). I therefore propose a different and distinct typology that is more detailed than Durkheim's broad approach or Pickering's two-pronged classification.

I consider *collective effervescence* to be an umbrella term that covers a variety of subtypes, and in this book, I distinguish between the following six:

drunken effervescence, psychedelic effervescence, melodramatic effervescence, violent effervescence, compassionate effervescence, and sexual effervescence. These subtypes are the ones that I have observed and heard about most frequently during my fieldwork among revelers, but the typology is not exhaustive. With more data from other populations and settings, it would have been possible to expand the typology with more subtypes and sub-subtypes. For instance, *violent effervescence* is in itself a broad term that may be divided into its own subtypes, such as nihilistically violent effervescence, politically violent effervescence, and sexually violent effervescence.[3] However, the six-pronged typology that I am here advancing is elaborate enough for my present purposes of examining the human propensity for intoxication. Let me briefly outline the defining characteristics of each of the six subtypes.

Drunken effervescence is by far the most common variant of collective effervescence in the nightlife settings that I have studied. The term refers to a state of intoxication that involves impaired mental and physical coordination reflected in symptoms such as staggering, stumbling, vomiting, slurred speech, and irrational decision-making. It is essentially a clumsy form of effervescence, although some people feel that it enables them to perform complicated tasks such as seducing strangers and climbing between balconies. Episodes of drunken effervescence are generally characterized by initially high levels of energy that drop into a state of drowsiness or stupor in the final stage. Drunken effervescence is driven by, and focused mainly on, alcohol consumption, but it may also involve other stimulants such as music and cocaine.

Psychedelic effervescence is a more rare form of collective effervescence in which the world, the self, and other people appear in new, unexpected forms. Reality loses its self-evidence; the familiar becomes enigmatic. Some variations include hearing voices, having surrealistic visions, and receiving spiritual revelations. This altered state is closely associated with psychedelic drugs such as mushrooms and LSD, but it may also be generated by means of what Mauss calls "body techniques" such as yogic respiration exercises, rhythmic dancing, and whirling (Mauss 1979; Gell 1980).

Melodramatic effervescence is a largely understudied but common phenomenon in nightlife environments (see, however, Grazian 2008).[4] It is a condition of heightened intersubjectivity with a strong histrionic component. It is generally triggered by deliberately daring or mischievous acts that are aimed at creating strong emotional reactions and drama. A typical example of this is when a person feigns an interest in someone and tries to seduce him or her, only to walk away when the seduction is accomplished. Another example is the exchange of dares within friend groups. This occurs when group members compete in risky or risqué undertakings such as removing one's pants in front of a crowd or kissing a police officer. Alcohol, drugs, and violence may fuel and amplify melodramatic effervescence, but these elements are not always present. Daring and mischievous acts per se can stir up lots of emotional turbulence and in-group solidarity.

Violent effervescence is a variant of effervescence marked by varying degrees of tension, fear, and confusion (Collins 2008). When violent confrontations erupt, they create a strong emotional field that affects not only the opponents but also bystanders, infusing everyone with energy and making them more prone to behaviors outside their normal code of conduct. Hence people who are involved in violence tend to speak or act in ways that they regret afterward, such as squealing, spitting, freezing, or hitting the wrong person. Some revelers deliberately seek out violent confrontations because they enjoy the emotional rush. Most, however, find violence to be distinctly unpleasant and emotionally corrosive.

Compassionate effervescence is a condition of heightened intersubjectivity characterized by an overflow of sympathy, solidarity, and love, typically toward friends who are in physical proximity. This condition may manifest itself as an almost compulsory need to touch people, hold others close, show signs of affection, or make others feel well. An example of this is the practice of forming "cuddle puddles" during or immediately after electronic dance music events; revelers snuggle up, sometimes in very large groups, to hug, caress, massage, and kiss each other (Holmquist 2006, 118–119; Kavanaugh and Anderson 2008). This sometimes progresses in a sexual direction, but often compassionate effervescence stays focused on the immediate gratifications of sharing intimacy and mutual caring. Compassionate effervescence may not be particularly turbulent and action-oriented, for its intensity generally comes from a powerful sense of oneness.

Sexual effervescence is based on the interactions of persons—typically two—who stimulate each other sexually, with or without penetrative acts. This experience involves a strong sense of being together or inside each other, while rhythmically moving toward sexual climax (Collins 2004, 231). The outcome of sexual effervescence is moral commitment and solidarity between the sexual partners, although this may be rather short-lived in cases of one-night stands. The condition of sexual effervescence may emerge in nightlife venues—for instance, among revelers who touch and grind against each other on the dance floor. However, full-blown sexual effervescence usually occurs in more intimate settings that are secluded from the public eye.

Experiences of group intoxication tend to be complex and changing, so the above typology should not be taken too rigidly. For example, an experience of drunken effervescence may have certain psychedelic aspects (drunken individuals sometimes hallucinate). Similarly, over the course of a night, individuals may shift between moments of, say, drunken effervescence, violent effervescence, and compassionate effervescence. It is not uncommon to see drunken men have fun together, then fight, and then lovingly hug each other, as if to signal mutual appreciation, peaceful intentions, and perhaps some sort of gratitude for the actions they have just been through.

It should be noted that effervescence occurs not just in different forms but also in varying degrees. At its lowest degree, it is a subtle buzzing of increased interactivity and mutual awareness. At its highest pitch, it is a powerful rush of rhythmically synchronized actions and emotions that involves a sense of being overtaken by a collective force with its own agenda.

A situation of group intoxication may, therefore, be analyzed according to different focal points, including the conditions that produce it, the type(s) of effervescence that it represents, the degree of its manifestation, and the short- and long-term outcomes that may result. But whatever the perspective, the analysis will necessarily be tentative due to the elusive character of collective experiences. We will never have enough data to be assured that we completely know the experiences of another person, to say nothing of the experiences of an entire group. Even if we did, the insurmountable problem would remain of accurately describing those experiences (Bruner 1986). Therefore, the ambition of this book is not to develop a conclusive, positivist theory that predicts and explains intoxication. The emphasis here is not on measurement, causes, effects, theory testing, and logical laws. Rather than utilizing positivism, my philosophical orientation is phenomenological and thus emphasizes embodied understandings and detailed descriptions of human experience (Jackson 1996). Accordingly, the ambition of this book is to find the "least false words" to describe states of intoxication as they are experienced from a first-person perspective (Maffesoli 1996b). The key words that I employ in these descriptive efforts are those of collective effervescence and its subtypes: drunken effervescence, psychedelic effervescence, melodramatic effervescence, violent effervescence, compassionate effervescence, and sexual effervescence.

COLLECTIVE EFFERVESCENCE APPLIED

Collins's book *Interaction Ritual Chains* (2004) has played a major role in making the concept of collective effervescence accessible, applicable, and increasingly popular in the social sciences. Building on a synthesis of Durkheim and Erving Goffman, the book presents a microsociological theory of the social interactions that make up everyday life and hold society together. Collins claims that his theory can account for any type of social interaction—be it conversations at an office meeting, singing at a religious ceremony, nonverbal flirtation on a dance floor, and even the stream of internalized conversations inside a person's mind. Collins argues that the success of all such inter- and intrasubjective interactions depends on how much collective effervescence they generate; low-effervescence interactions are strenuous, whereas high-effervescence interactions are empowering. He therefore uses the term *failed rituals* to denote focused interactions that provide "little or no feeling of group solidarity; no sense of one's identity as affirmed or changed; no respect for the group's symbols; no heightened emotional energy" (2004, 51). People consciously or unconsciously try to avoid rituals that they expect will fail and instead pursue rituals that are likely to fuel them with effervescence. Indeed, Collins writes that "human beings are emotional energy seekers" who are irresistibly drawn to "the most intense ritual charges they can get" (2004, 373, 51). The energy that a person derives from a successful ritual is then invested in the pursuit of the next successful ritual, and so forth. Hence his concept of *interaction ritual chains*.

Collins argues that "four main ingredients or initiating conditions" must combine in order for a ritual to produce collective effervescence (2004, 47). First, there has to be at least two ritual participants who are physically close enough to sense each other's bodily signals. Second, there must be boundaries marking off these participants from perceived outsiders. Third, the participants have to focus their attention on the same object or activity while being mutually aware that they share that attention. Finally, the participants must have a common emotional mood or experience. If any of these conditions are absent, the ritual is likely to fail. If all the conditions are met, the participants will be in a position to engage in the rhythmically coordinated interactions that, eventually, will open them to the experience of collective effervescence.

Collins emphasizes again and again the importance of people being together in the same place—notably, in this central passage: "Bodily presence makes it easier for human beings to monitor each other's signals and bodily expressions; to get into shared rhythm, caught up in each other's motions and emotions; and to signal and confirm a common focus of attention and thus a state of inter-subjectivity. The key is that human nervous systems become mutually attuned" (2004, 64). For Collins, as well as Durkheim and Goffman, assembly is key to human existence. It is through chains of body-to-body encounters that macro-level conventions and institutions come into being. Collins therefore insists that "all macro is composed of micro, and that all micro is surrounded by other micro which thereby makes up its macro context" (1988, 245). In other words, every-thing comes from being together, acting together, and experiencing together (see also Pickering 2009, 345). This has the methodological implication that Collins prioritizes microlevel consideration of embodied interactions and experiences.

In Collins's theory, full-blown collective effervescence is what successful ritu-als feel like. This feeling is one of intense intersubjectivity, which ends as soon as the ritual participants lose their mutual attention or move physically away from one another. However, Collins writes that rituals with high levels of collec-tive effervescence have a number of more long-term outcomes. These outcomes include (1) "a feeling of membership"; (2) "emotional energy [EE]," meaning an individual feeling "of confidence, elation, strength, enthusiasm, and initiative in taking action"; (3) "symbols that represent the group: emblems or other representations (visual icons, words, gestures) that members feel are associated with themselves collectively"; and (4) "feelings of morality: the sense of rightness in adhering to the group, respecting its symbols, and defending both against transgressors" (Collins 2004, 49).[5]

Collins clearly has positivist ambitions. This can be seen from his meticulous discussion of how to measure "emotional energy and its antecedents" through analysis of eye movements, vocal rhythms, hormone levels, and self-reported data (Collins 2004, 133–140). Moreover, he claims that his theory identifies the causes and effects of collective effervescence and that it can be used to predict and explain a great variety of behaviors, from sexual interaction to social stratification to tobacco smoking.

A number of studies have applied, tested, and largely validated Collins's theory. This includes studies on religious practices (Draper 2019), sports events (Cottingham 2012), tourism (Bargeman and Richards 2020), American megachurches (Wellman, Corcoran, and Stockly-Meyerdirk 2014), restorative justice (Rossner 2013), open drug scenes (Grønnestad, Sagvaag, and Lalander 2020), online social interaction (Maloney 2013), livestreamed concerts (Vandenberg, Berghman, and Schaap 2020), vipassana meditation (Pagis 2015), job interviews (Rivera 2015), speed dating (McFarland, Jurafsky, and Rawlings 2013), and much more (Weininger, Lareau, and Lizardo 2018). Based on a review of the literature, sociologist Lasse Suonperä Liebst makes the convincing conclusion that Collins's theory is "the most advanced explanatory account of collective effervescence to date" (Liebst 2019).

However, Collins's interaction ritual theory is not without its critics, who have variously charged that it is overly generalizing and universalizing while ignoring specifics of individual cases. Wellman, Corcoran, and Stockly-Meyerdirk thus observe in a study of American megachurches that "having few barriers to ritual participation actually facilitates successful rituals by increasing the number of participants, thereby amplifying the collective effervescence of the experience" (2014, 654). This contradicts Collins's proposition that having barriers excluding outsiders is a necessary initiating condition for facilitating a mutual focus of attention, a common mood, and eventually, collective effervescence. What this suggests is that rituals are too complex to pin down to simple, universal models like the one presented by Collins. The number and kinds of initiating conditions may vary from ritual to ritual, as may the intensity and types of effervescence at the heart of the ritual. The number and kinds of long-term outcomes are likewise variable. So while Collins's model gives precious advice on where to look, how to look, and what sense to make of ritual interactions, it should not be followed slavishly. Empirical sensitivity is needed, always.

David Boyns and Sarah Luery discuss a related problem in Collins's model, namely, "its one-dimensional conceptualization of emotional energy" (2015,

153). They argue that, for Collins, "emotional energy resides on a continuum that ranges from low to high levels," but that his theory "neither accounts for different *types* of emotional energy, nor specifies the social dynamics that might produce a distinction between positive and negative emotional energy" (2015, 153). Sociologists Anne Heider and Stephen Warner's study (2010) of Sacred Harp singing also points to a lack of nuance in Collins's theory. They observe that rather than sharing a common mood or emotional experience, as Collins would have it, the participants in successful rituals may have very different emotional reactions to what is happening: "Sacred Harp suggests that it is not necessary that everyone present experiences the same emotional response to a given song. A room full of tear-streaked faces is not an index of identical emotions. A text about death may sharpen the grief felt by those who have recently lost a loved one, but others may experience joy at having been healed of a deadly disease. A text about sin may induce an experience of fresh guilt in some singers and forgiveness in others" (Heider and Warner 2010, 89).

These observations call for reconsideration of Collins's and Durkheim's key concepts. Collective effervescence and emotional energy should not be understood as uniform conditions that affect all ritual participants in the exact same way. Rather, these are processual, multifaceted, and ambiguous conditions that affect participants differently, depending on their embodied predispositions. Successful rituals are emotionally moving, but they move people in different ways (Rappaport 1999; see also St John 2018). It is the same with symbols. As David Kertzer puts it, "Symbols can have a strong emotional impact on people, rallying them around the organizational flag, in spite of the fact that each participant interprets the symbols differently" (Kertzer 1989; quoted in Heider and Warner 2010, 89). Indeed, the appeal of many rituals and symbols stems from their ambiguity. It is due to their openness to interpretation that people of different backgrounds so readily engage with them, try to make sense of them, and thereby make them their own.

Unlike Collins, I read *The Elementary Forms* primarily through a phenomenological lens, not a positivist one.[6] Accordingly, the focus of this book is on the experience of group intoxication per se more than on its measurement, causes, and effects. Let me briefly explain what I mean by phenomenology, since this is key to my approach. I use the term *phenomenology* in a broad sense as the scientific study of experience in its lived immediacy (Jackson 1996). The goal in phenomenology is to capture the essence of people's experiences and the essential meanings they attach to them. To do so, it is important to set aside preconceptions and meet people with openness. This is complicated, since our preconceptions are tied up with who we are. They cannot be willed away, but they can be kept in check and prevented from dictating our interpretations.

A central tenet in phenomenology is to avoid explaining phenomena before they have been understood "from within" (Moran 2000, 4). This understanding "from within" requires careful consideration of concrete experiences in all their situated complexity, without rushing to conclusions about why they occurred, what they mean, and what they will lead to. The term *experience* should, in this context, be understood as something we undergo rather than as the stockpile of knowledge and know-how that we acquire over time: "It is something that happens *to* us, and not something accumulated and mastered *by* us" (Henriksson and Friesen 2012, 1). Phenomenology is an invitation to study experience in this sense of the term.

In-depth empirical descriptions have a central place in many phenomenological works, including this book, because this style of writing can bring us close to embodied, emotional, and sensory facets of existence. As Jackson explains, many phenomenologists are skeptical of the "arcane, abstract, and alienating character of much theoretical thought" and, therefore, take care to write "detailed descriptions of lived reality" in order to circumvent "the estranging effects of conceptual models and systematic explanation which, when pushed too far, disqualify and efface the very life one wants to understand, and isolate us from the very life we have to live" (Jackson 1996, 2). Accordingly, I use the concepts of collective effervescence and its subtypes as descriptive tools to illuminate intoxicating experiences "as they exist for the people living them" (Katz 2002, 255). These concepts do not offer any simple explanation of intoxicating experiences but encapsulate some of their essential properties without reducing them to isolated or static states of consciousness.

The way I apply the concept of collective effervescence comes close to the way religious studies scholar Tim Olaveson applies it in his study of rave parties in central Canada. Olaveson sets out to uncover "the nature of the rave experience" (2004b, 13) and finds that its key feature is "an intense sensation of interpersonal and sometimes universal connection between participants, often described as 'connectedness', 'unity' or 'love'" (2004a, 87). He writes that this is a "meaningful and religious experience for many participants" (2004b, 208) and that it can be deeply rewarding and transformative. Having established this, he demonstrates that the rave experience is equivalent to collective effervescence, as defined by Durkheim, because both involve altered states of consciousness that are temporary, irrational, affectively charged, transgressive, potentially healing, and revolving around the powerful feeling of being intimately connected with other human beings. In this book, I extend Olaveson's proposition beyond the rave scene to include a much broader spectrum of intoxicating practices and scenes. In short, my key argument is that the concept of collective effervescence captures some of the essence of what people search for, and what they sometimes experience, when they collectively intoxicate themselves in myriad contexts: rave parties, private parties, concerts, festivals, pubs, bars, strip clubs, or nightclubs. In particular, the concept and its subtypes are powerful tools for understanding and describing intensive forms of group intoxication.

A Sympathetic Approach

Durkheim's approach to intoxication is refreshingly nuanced in comparison to both classical and contemporary research on the topic. Classical crowd scholars such as Gabriel Tarde (2007) and Gustave Le Bon (2001) wrote extensively about intoxication in crowded contexts, but they did so in a distinctly problem-focused manner. They were deeply skeptical of crowds and their alleged propensity for drunken abandon and savagery. Karl Marx did not write much about crowds (Borch 2012, 90), and his treatment of intoxication is mainly depreciative, as illustrated by his famous statement that religion is "the opium of the people" (Marx 2008, 42). Max Weber (1968) *did* write about intoxication in his work on charismatic leaders and their hypnotic powers—and some decades later, Howard Becker (1997) and Mary Douglas (1987) published pioneering work on the sociality and constructive functions of legal and illegal drugs. Of course, other scholars could be mentioned, but the general picture is clear: intoxication is largely neglected or devalued in classical social science research (Shilling and Mellor 2011).

Today, there is a vast number of researchers specializing in alcohol, drugs, and their effects. The great majority of them use quantitative methods and treat intoxication as an individual or social problem. Anthropologist Geoffrey Hunt and colleagues thus assert that contemporary drug research gives primacy to "a discourse of pathology, deviancy, and problems" (Hunt, Moloney, and Evans 2009, 605). The same type of discourse dominates in contemporary alcohol research, leaving little room for the study of the "allure, joy, collective celebrations, and bonding rituals associated with heavy drinking" (Vander Ven 2011, 15). Young people's intoxication is especially framed as a threat in need of regulatory control and intervention. This is partly because the funding of alcohol and drug research comes from sources that work to improve public health and safety (Hunt and Barker 2001). If researchers want to receive funding, they are compelled to formulate study designs that highlight problems and point to solutions. As a result, there is a massive gap between, on the one side, researchers (who emphasize problems) and, on the other side, revelers (who are seeking pleasure). Durkheim's work can help bridge this gap. For although he was a serious, hard-working academic, he had the greatest respect for revelry and intoxication, and he offers constructive advice on how to study these phenomena.

Durkheim presents what may be termed his "sympathetic approach" to religion and other social phenomena in the opening pages of *The Elementary Forms*, where he argues that "it is a fundamental postulate of sociology that a human institution cannot rest upon error and falsehood. If it did, it could not endure. . . . The most bizarre or barbarous rites and the strangest myths translate some human need and some aspect of life, whether social or individual" (1995, 2). Durkheim thus cautions us not to diminish or dismiss other peoples' practices and beliefs. He holds that, in order to understand cultural others, it is necessary to take them seriously, even when they engage in activities that at first glance may appear barbarous or bizarre. In an unprepared speech given at a conference organized by the Union of Free Thinkers and Believers, he pushed this argument even further, insisting that the task of freethinking religious scholars is to tune in mentally and emotionally with the religious person. In line with phenomenology, Durkheim calls for sympathetic research focused on experience as experienced by the experiencer: "In brief, what I ask of the free thinker is that he should confront religion in the same mental state as the believer. It is only by doing this that he can hope to understand it. Let him feel it as the believer feels it; what it is to the believer is what it really is. Consequently, he who does not bring to the study of religion a sort of religious sentiment cannot speak about it! He is like a blind man speaking about colour" (1994, 184).

I will follow Durkheim's sympathetic approach as best as I can throughout this book. This is not because I want to deny the dark sides of intoxication. I have grown up with alcoholism in my family, a sort of effervescence gone wrong, and am acutely aware of the ravages these forces can cause. I firmly believe, however, that if we want to understand these forces and find better ways to deal with them, it is crucial to study them with sympathy.

I acknowledge that hostility, aversion, resentment, anger, condemnation, and fear can be valuable driving forces in research. Such reactive feelings can be productive, for instance, when starting on a research project: an injustice is observed, and research efforts are mobilized to make things right. Reactive feelings have this way of narrowing the mind, focusing the energies, and pushing toward action. However, researchers should always keep reactive emotions in check; otherwise, those emotions may swell and turn into obstacles to understanding. Focusing too intently on injustice easily makes one lose sight of other aspects of life (Nietzsche 1969, 39).

Sympathy can therefore be a good antidote or supplement to the reactive feelings that inevitably emerge in a study such as the present one. In particular, I find sympathy to be important during the phases of data collection and analysis. It can help open the mind, facilitate encounters, smooth interactions, and create attunement between the researcher and those being researched. For example, interviews conducted in an atmosphere of mutual sympathy tend to be more rewarding than interviews conducted in a mist of suspicion, fear, or worse, hostility. Sympathy can obviously be difficult to muster in certain situations and toward certain individuals, but it is generally worth trying.

Let me quote another insightful passage from Durkheim's earlier mentioned speech: "There cannot be a rational interpretation of religion which is fundamentally irreligious; an irreligious interpretation of religion would be an interpretation which denied the phenomenon it was trying to explain. Nothing could be more contrary to scientific method" (1994, 185). The same can be said about the study of intoxication. Anyone who approaches this topic in an overly sober manner is likely to misunderstand it. And just as with the effervescence that emerges at a religious ceremony, so with the effervescence at a dance party: these experiences are difficult to measure and quantify, but they are nonetheless very real and must be studied and described, if not on their own terms, then at least in a manner that does them justice. There has to be some degree of resonance between the researcher and those being researched, a certain degree of sympathy, and the style of writing should be tailored to the subject of study.

This book is written in the sympathetic spirit of the late Durkheim. However, the sympathy is not complete. Complete sympathy is just as impossible as the objective, unbiased approach advocated in the early writings of Durkheim (2017). There will be instances of criticism, but these are aimed less at the revelers in my study than at the commercial venues that seek to exploit their desire for collective effervescence. In the section that follows, I will discuss these venues in detail, in part because they form the main context in which I collected my data and also because they play an important role in the production of collective effervescence today.

Research Settings

This book is based on three major ethnographic field studies of people from Denmark in the fifteen to thirty-five age group. Most of them had working- or middle-class backgrounds and were studying or working full-time. In other words, the book is about ordinary adolescents and adults living in Denmark, which is a welfare country known for having one of the world's highest taxes on personal income but also high levels of income equality, social trust, education, and happiness.

The first field study took place from 2001 to 2003 in Ringsted, a small town located forty minutes by train from Denmark's capital, Copenhagen. At the time of the fieldwork, Ringsted featured one nightclub and two bars that catered to predominantly young crowds. The second field study was conducted between 2007 and 2008 in Sunny Beach, a nightlife resort located on the Black Sea coast in Bulgaria. The resort attracts large numbers of young tourists from Northern Europe who typically come for a week to party intensively, mainly with peers from their home countries. It is strikingly similar to resorts in other parts of the world, such as Ibiza in Spain and Cancún in Mexico: there is an abundance of sea, sun, sand, hotels, shops, restaurants, bars, pubs, nightclubs, and brothels. The third field study was conducted between 2011 and 2013 in the Danish cities of Copenhagen, Aalborg, Nykøbing Falster, and Sønderborg. These cities were selected to represent an array of urban and provincial environments across Denmark.

All three field studies mainly took place in the evening and nighttime inside or in the vicinity of commercial nightlife venues, such as pubs, bars, and nightclubs. These settings are not "free for all" playgrounds where "anything goes," as some commentators would have it. Rather, they are carefully calibrated to give customers an uplifting experience that will make them stay long and spend lots of money, mainly on alcohol. What they offer is a commodified and predominantly drunken form of effervescence on a massive scale.

Consider the example of a youth-oriented nightclub in Copenhagen.[7] When you approach the club, the first things that catch your attention are alcohol advertisements, most of which are banners with promotions and colorful brand logos. At the entrance there are one or two bouncers in charge of diffusing conflicts and admitting the "right mix" of people. Being a woman, well-dressed, and White will facilitate access, whereas being a group of men, poorly dressed, or non-White may lead to rejection. "Members only," the bouncers might say, or "not tonight, lads." Drunkenness may also result in rejection, but only the sort of helpless drunkenness that makes it difficult to walk and spend money in the bar.

Inside the club, there is a dance floor and loud, fast-paced music that calls for forceful bodily responses in the form of dancing, singing, or shouting. Seats are sparse because seated bodies take up more space than standing bodies. People sitting down are also more relaxed and drink slower than people standing up. Tables are also scarce, both to save space and to nudge customers to keep their drinks in their hands, close to their mouths. As for the bar counters, they are centrally placed and bathed in spotlights so that customers are constantly reminded of the possibility to buy more booze. This positioning also allows the bartenders to be in close contact with customers and detect conflicts before they escalate.

The bartenders assist in directing the customers' attention toward the counter and its liquid temptations. They may do this by wearing revealing clothes, mirroring the customers' body language, looking them in the eyes, calling them by their names, flirting with them, teasing those who drink moderately, juggling with bottles, or whooping when somebody places a big order. Tricks like these are transmitted from management to staff and contribute to the nightclub's true purpose: the solicitation and sustenance of high levels of consumer excitement and expenditure. In other words, nightlife venues do not merely comply with people's desire for collective effervescence. They actively stimulate, amplify, and orchestrate these desires to maximize profits.

Recent decades have seen drastic changes in nightlife settings across the world. The general trend in Northern Europe (Hobbs et al. 2003) and elsewhere (Lindsay 2009) has been for the closing of traditional, individually owned community pubs and the opening of themed venues owned by national or international corporations (see also Hadfield 2009). Urban geographers warn that this concentration of ownership has led to a standardization and homogenization of nightlife, leaving revelers with less choice when they go out (Chatterton and Hollands 2003). The venues may be differently themed—such as "Crazy Daisy," "Mona Lisa," and so forth—but the operational format, products on sale, and general atmosphere of these places are much the same. Another consequence of the corporatization of pubs, bars, and clubs has been an accumulation of expertise on how to make customers spend money on these establishments' signature and highly profitable product: alcohol. This is part of the reason that much of the world is now convinced that the best way to live it up is to get drunk.

The experience and meaning of revelry change with the passing of time. Different types of effervescence are associated with different historical epochs and cultural settings. To adapt Simone de Beauvoir's famous assertion, one is not born a reveler but rather becomes one through socialization processes that occur in specific historical and cultural contexts (1949). Commercial nightlife venues are key to these processes because of their popularity and marketing ingenuity. It is in these environments that many youths learn how to be festive together with peers: what and how much to consume, how to navigate a dance floor, how to flirt with strangers, what experiences to pursue, and how to make sense of intoxication. This is not to suggest that commercial forces are in full control of all revelry. Rather, it is to suggest that they significantly influence the cultural repertoire of available meanings, stories, experiences, and behaviors that people draw on in their effervescent situations (Lamont and Thévenot 2000). People carry this ever-changing cultural repertoire with them, even when they are outside the context of commercial, alcohol-focused venues. From this perspective, culture should not be understood merely as the ideas, values, symbols, discourses, and narratives that flow between members of society. Culture is also something within us, like a dynamic set of tools or resources, organizing but never determining how we experience and make sense of our world (Valsiner 2012).

It should be noted that the promotion of drunken effervescence is most pronounced in inexpensive venues that cater to young patrons (e.g., themed chain pubs) and less so in expensive venues with more adult patrons (e.g., wine bars and craft beer bars). It is important to note, moreover, that there are individuals and sectors of society who prefer to drink little or nothing, such as certain members of the rave scene and the straight edge movement. However, in many Western countries, it is notoriously difficult for non- and antidrinking youths to find venues where they can enjoy effervescence without having to deal with aggressive alcohol marketing and swarms of drunken peers (Conroy and de Visser 2014).

Critical awareness is spreading (Hadfield 2015). The alcohol industry is under criticism that its marketing of alcohol is too aggressive. Authorities are being accused that their deregulation of alcohol licensing laws has gone too far and that it is time to reduce the number of drinking venues and their opening hours. The healthcare system and inner-city police forces report that they are

being overburdened during weekends by problems caused by intoxicated revelers. And local residents complain about weekend violence, noise, and littered
streets. Changes may be underway, and the alcohol consumption of adolescents
and young adults has in recent years gone down in many countries, including
Denmark. However, ours is an age of drunken effervescence and will probably
continue to be so for a very long time. Accordingly, the majority of this book is
about this particular subtype of collective effervescence.

ETHNOGRAPHY IN EFFERVESCENT ENVIRONMENTS

Most data in this book were collected with ethnographic methods. They come
from more than two hundred nights of observation and 109 interviews with rev-
ellers, bartenders, bouncers, and tour guides. I also have a large pool of survey
data, but these play only a minor role in this book, since their focus is less on the
lived experience of intoxication and more on the prevalence of various phenomena, such as the number of alcohol units consumed during vacations in Sunny
Beach (Tutenges and Hesse 2008) and the severity of hangovers associated with
continuous drinking over a week (Hesse and Tutenges 2010).[8]

The kind of ethnography that I practice is inspired by the sympathetic
approach of Durkheim (1995) and the phenomenology of Jackson (1996). This
sympathetic phenomenology is useful for dismantling barriers of prejudice,
facilitating intersubjective attunement, and expanding insights into the experiences and situations of other people. However, the approach also poses some
serious ethical and practical challenges when doing fieldwork in effervescent
environments. This became abruptly clear to me during my first field study.

For some months, I had been going regularly to Ringsted on Friday and Saturday
nights, often with other student assistants who were working on the same project,
the Ringsted Project.[9] We usually worked in pairs, going back and forth between
a selected drinking venue, where we made observations, and an office, where we
entered our field notes into computers. This was a procedure that provided us with
lots of detailed notes, but it also disrupted the flow of our nights and made our experiences very different from those of the youths we were trying to understand. Therefore, my colleague Anna Bendtsen and I decided to immerse ourselves more fully in
the field. Our plan was to drink more, cut down on the questioning, and just try to
have a good time like the people we were studying.

One night, we arranged to meet in a bar with Leo and Henning, whom we
had befriended during previous visits. Everything started out well. We talked,
selected songs on the jukebox, and drank beer with shots of schnapps. Anna and
I occasionally scribbled on our notepads, but otherwise, we allowed ourselves to
get carried away by the increasingly drunken mood of the moment. However, I
must have sensed that something was wrong because the words "Henning racist"

are among my notes from early that evening. Nevertheless, we went along when Henning suggested that we should go to his place and "drink a shitload." Off we drove in Leo's car with a very drunken Leo behind the wheel. We had to take a big detour in order to avoid the police, who often kept the main road under surveillance. It would have been easy for us to take a taxi, as the ride was not long and our employer would undoubtedly have paid for it. This option did not occur to us, however.

It turned out that Henning was living with his parents in a huge house. He had a wing all to himself. It was luxuriously equipped with a refrigerator, minibar, TV, big loudspeakers—and an American Confederate flag covering a wall. I remember standing there gawking at the flag, trying to remember what it signified, and asking Henning about it. Meanwhile, Henning had turned on his computer and put on a scene from the film *American History X*, in which a White supremacist captures a Black burglar and forces him to bite a curb and then stomps the back of his head. The sound of teeth crushing against concrete came blasting out of the loudspeakers. "The nicest sound in movie history," said Henning. Or maybe it was Leo who said it. Regardless, Anna and I had been set up. We had thought that this would be a fun night in good company, but instead we found ourselves being lectured by two neo-Nazis on *Mein Kampf*, the price of bullets, and ways to get rid of immigrants. All the while, the sickening sound of crushing teeth kept echoing because Henning had put the movie scene on repeat.

When doing nightlife ethnography, deep immersion comes at a cost. Heavy drinking is integral to all the scenes that I have studied, yet partaking in such drinking increases the risk of making unethical or unwise decisions, as when Anna and I got into the car with the intoxicated Leo. Heavy drinking also clouds the memory and makes it difficult to write field notes. However, the problems of deep immersion are not solely related to the use of alcohol and other drugs. The sheer energies in nightlife environments can themselves be problematic, especially if one is exposed to them over long periods of time. As Durkheim points out, collective effervescence can be beneficial, but too much of it will lead to physical and mental collapse (1995, 228). Accordingly, many nightlife ethnographers have tried to overdose on effervescence and suffered the consequences, which in my case included sleeping problems, restlessness, and cold-like symptoms that lasted for a couple of months.

My preferred strategy in the field is, therefore, to observe and interview people rather than fully participate in their revelry. I rarely drink more than a beer, and I do not use illegal drugs. This may appear like a boring solution that will generate poor data. However, sustained observation and conversation with other people can provide precious insights into their experiences. For experiences are not isolated, solipsistic events; they are always partly public and rarely more so than in an effervescent crowd of revelers (Tutenges 2013). As Maurice Merleau-Ponty writes, "We must reject the prejudice which makes 'inner realities' out of love, hate, or anger, leaving them accessible to one single witness: the person who feels them. Anger, shame, hate and love are not psychic facts hidden at the bottom of another's consciousness: they are types of behaviour or styles of conduct which are visible from the outside. They exist on this face or in those gestures, not hidden behind them" (1964, 52). Moreover, effervescence is transpersonal in the sense that it is an experience that extends beyond the bounds of singular individuals. The experience is "contagious," and as a researcher, it is possible to feel one's way into it (Durkheim 1995, 221). What this takes is copresence with the effervescent group and sympathetic attention to the flow of emotions that passes from body to body.

Importantly, when I write "observe," I mean a kind of attention that involves all the senses and is directed both at those I study and at myself (Pink 2015). Following Jackson, I think it is a mistake that so much research—including the majority of nightlife research—excludes "the lived experience of the observer from the field of the observed" (1989, 4). A more fruitful procedure, one that inspires this book, is the radically empirical method that "includes the experience of the observer and defines the experimental field as one of interactions and intersubjectivity. Accordingly, we make ourselves experimental subjects and treat our experiences as primary data" (Jackson 1989, 4). This procedure rests on the assumption that we humans are intimately connected and that our species is defined by not only physical but also psychic similarities. There can be moments when experiences are shared.

This book therefore has passages about my own experiences in the field. I present and scrutinize my personal experiences in order to shed light on the experiences of the people I am studying. I thus treat myself as an informant, as someone with embodied knowledge worthy of interpretation. The book also has passages about my friends, since they have played a decisive role in my understanding of collective effervescence. By presenting such data from my private sphere, including embarrassing, confusing, and distressing experiences, I put myself on the line in a way that is unusual in social research, especially research published in the format of scientific journals. Rather than concealing my own emotions and sensations in the field, I present and analyze them. As sociologist Thomas Thurnell-Read points out, the researcher's own reactions in the field are important sources of knowledge that can be used to shed light on the topic under research while bringing some transparency to the way in which the research has been conducted (Thurnell-Read 2011).[10]

A Look Ahead

This book consists of eight chapters. The next one, chapter 2, outlines the basic conditions that produce collective effervescence in nightlife settings. I argue that effervescence in this context is most likely to occur when people come prepared for what they are about to experience, have a sense of security, and are willing to let go of restraints. Moreover, following Collins, I also maintain that people must come physically close to each other, focus their attention on the same thing, and be mutually aware of this common focus. Finally, music, alcohol, or other physiological stimulants are used to facilitate the process.

What follows are chapters dedicated to each of the five experiential building blocks of collective effervescence: unity, intensity, transgression, symbolization, and revitalization. Chapter 3 thus explores the experience of *unity*—that is, of connecting and coalescing with other people—which is the most important aspect of effervescence. The chapter argues that this experience is intrinsically meaningful and not dependent on attaining any goals extrinsic to itself, such as finding a spouse or creating lasting friendships. One of the protagonists in the chapter, the young reveler named Simon, explains this well: "It creates a sense of unity when you are surrounded by a sea of people. [. . .] It's about being together and doing things together."

Chapter 4 explores the *intensity* of what goes on inside and between people in effervescent gatherings. Although different people prefer widely varying levels of intensity, there is widespread agreement that festive occasions should feature an abundance of engrossing conversations, lively movements, strong sensations, and vivid emotions. However, as illustrated throughout the chapter, intensity does not come easily and can be frustratingly hard to find, even in a nightlife resort like Sunny Beach.

Chapter 5 is about the sense of *transgression* that spreads when people enter states of effervescence. This may involve changes in subjective experience, as when a person comes to think, feel, or sense very differently than normal. It may also involve changes in behavior, such as an inclination toward risk taking, deviance, or crime. Drawing on Bataille, the chapter suggests that transgressions may be understood as a form of pursuit and exploration of boundaries and what lies beyond. This can be beneficial or harmful depending on the situation and people involved. A fitting form of transgression in one situation may be completely inappropriate in another. Similarly, while one person may feel pleasantly thrilled by a transgressive act, another person may feel deeply offended by the very same act.

Chapter 6 is about *symbolization*, which is the process of energy transmission that occurs when an effervescent group focuses its attention on a common object and imbues it with their fellow feelings. The object is thereby turned into an emotionally charged symbol with memory traces of the group. Generally speaking, group symbols are emotionally "hottest" during effervescent events, but they keep some of their energy for a period after the effervescent gathering has dissipated. For example, an item associated with a good concert (e.g., an autograph by a music star) can trigger excitement in fans for a long time because it reminds them of the concert feeling, the crowd, and the star at the center of it all. The chapter thus suggests that group symbols—or "effervescent symbols," to be more exact—may be understood as emotionally charged media through which people can tap into past effervescent experiences.

Chapter 7 explores Durkheim's proposition that effervescence is *revitalizing* in the sense that it imbues individuals and groups with new life and vigor. The chapter largely confirms this proposition. Effervescence is an indispensable force in social life, one that accelerates interpersonal exchanges, rouses people to action, boosts self-confidence, and strengthens group cohesion. At the same time, however, effervescence always involves some degree of risk—people may hurt themselves, say things that they later regret, or express their in-group love by doing harm to outsiders. The chapter suggests that the tension between reward and risk, between delight and danger, is at the heart of effervescence and key to its revitalizing effects.

The final chapter takes a look at the COVID-19 crisis, "social distancing," and how revelers have reacted to it. Reactions varied, but one thing was clear: the crisis did not extinguish people's urge for effervescence. Even after the danger of the virus became apparent, reports from around the world described illicit parties with hundreds, even thousands of attendees. This corroborates the Durkheimian view that humans should be conceived as a life-form in need of more than just safety, food, water, sex, and other means of survival. At a fundamental level, we also need effervescent events that can provide us with the vitality and energized symbols required for getting by and pressing through the thicket of everyday life (Collins 2004). The chapter argues that nightlife—along with politics, sports, and religion—forms a key context for the production and experience of effervescence today. The chapter argues, moreover, that the analytical framework developed in this book can be applied to all these realms.

CHAPTER 2

WAYS TO EFFERVESCENCE

The Ringsted Town Festival is one of those rare occasions when the entire Ringsted community comes together for celebration. The young and the old, the rich and the poor, all show up to eat, drink, and see what is going on. This annual event, sponsored by a local branch of the Lions Club, features a wide variety of entertainment, such as beer tents, street parades, concerts, a funfair area, singing in the church, and much more. I attended the festival on a beautiful spring night. The event proved a valuable window into the conditions that lead up to and cause effervescence, and it is with these conditions that this chapter is concerned.[1]

I arrived by train in the early evening but quickly realized that I was late. The streets were already littered with bottles and fast-food wrappers. Yelling and singing resounded from all directions. And people that I had never seen before greeted me cheerfully, which is unusual in buttoned-down Denmark. Clearly, the festivities had already been going on for a while. I walked toward a park that, I had been told, was the center of the fun. Here, I found a range of beer tents with adults and old folks lined up, drinking and people-watching. The kids and young people were livelier, racing about and infusing the scene with restless energy. In the middle of it all, there was a so-called Booster, an amusement ride resembling a gigantic windmill that sends people spinning round and round with tremendous speed.

A crowd had formed in front of a big stage. A man appeared on the stage and announced, "DJ Alligator is coming soon." The man tried to make the crowd jump in sync but was obviously not satisfied with the result. "You look like a sack of potatoes!" he shouted and walked off. Then the bass started thumping in a deep tone that was felt more than heard. In came DJ Alligator. He walked slowly to the center of the stage with a menacing look on his face. By his side were two petite women dressed in military-style clothes that exposed their stomachs and lower backs. They danced frenziedly as DJ Alligator calmly and ceremoniously raised his arms above his head and began clapping. The crowd followed suit. The dancers waved their hands in an upward movement, beckoning us to jump, reach up, take it higher. In a guttural voice, DJ Alligator commanded, "Get physical! Stomp with me!" People started moving. Some people nodded their heads, while others jumped around with their arms up in the air. A group of teenagers was dancing wildly in front of the stage, their eyes wide open and glassy. "Come on!" shouted the dancers. "I like to move it, move it. I like to move it, move it. You like to move it," sang DJ Alligator, although he stood completely still. The sound was so massive that it made my breath quicken and ears ring. It all climaxed at the end of the concert with a big, loud bang as a gigantic party popper exploded onstage. The dancers threw handfuls of plastic whistles into the crowd, and a blast of whistling blared all around. DJ Alligator, a devilish look on his face, shouted something that may have been "Long live tinnitus!"

DJ Alligator and his crew certainly knew how to rev up a crowd. In just an hour or so, they had raised the excitement level at the festival by several degrees, skillfully using techniques that ritual leaders have made use of since time immemorial: loud, repetitive music, synchronized body movements, smoke, lights, and shock effects. These ingredients, in combination with alcohol, create a strong cocktail that can help individuals loosen the grip of self-control and yield to collective emotions. However, this transition does not come easily. As many revelers have told me, it can be difficult to act cheerful, open up to strangers, show sexual interest, laugh passionately, let go on the dance floor, break out in song, get joyfully drunk (but not too drunk), and become fully immersed in the here and now.

In other words, effervescence does not come out of the blue. For most people, it requires determination, effort, and support to get there.

An explanation of the difficulties in reaching effervescence is provided in Norbert Elias's masterpiece *The Civilizing Process* (2000), a historical treatise describing how the affective life of people in the West gradually changed after the Middle Ages. Elias describes how "refined manners" emerged in the courts of the feudal lords and rulers and gradually spread to the rest of society. Strong emotions were withdrawn from public view, bodily fluids hidden, and sexual impulses repressed. People began suppressing everything that they determined to be of an "animalic character." Importantly, Elias argues that such restraint "is enforced less and less by direct physical force. It is cultivated in individuals from an early age as habitual self-restraint by the structure of social life, by the pressure of social institutions in general, and by certain executive organs of society (above all, the family)" (2000, 158). Self-restraint becomes "an automatism, a self-compulsion" that the individual "cannot resist even if he or she consciously wishes to" (2000, 367). Indeed, there is much to suggest that contemporary Western societies like Denmark are marked by a historically high degree of control and self-censorship (Deleuze 1992). I believe that these social circumstances are part of the reason that so many people are drawn to the high-intensity rituals offered by the likes of DJ Alligator.

However, effervescence is never simply a matter of "letting go of restraints," "escapism," or taking a "time out." It is always both an escape *and* an engagement with life, a movement away from limiting conditions and toward moments of heightened intersubjectivity.

Rituals are experienced differently by different people based on their personal preferences and cultural background (Heider and Warner 2010). A tightly orchestrated ritual like the DJ Alligator concert, for example, does not necessarily transport all attendees into states of effervescence. Those who really want to may achieve such a state, whereas others, like myself, will feel less affected due to obstacles such as different musical preferences or annoying ringing in the ears. Six basic conditions are essential for effervescence to take place in the context of nightlife settings. Here I only sketch these conditions but will elaborate and illustrate them throughout this chapter.

First, it is important that the participants in an effervescent ritual come prepared for the turbulent forces that they are about to engage with. If they have been to a similar ritual before—or if they have been informed about, trained in, or otherwise prepared for it—it will be much easier for them to tune into one another and work together according to the ritual protocol, thereby collectively pumping up the energy.

Second, it is important to have a sense of security; otherwise, the body will be tense, the mind will be on guard, and self-censorship will reign. Effervescence, after all, can be frightening and easily goes awry. Intense emotions can lead to confrontations. Drug use can induce "bad trips" full of paranoia and distorted visions. And heavy drinking can end in "blackouts," poor decision-making, and other forms of trouble. The transition from ordinary to extraordinary states of consciousness is thus fraught with difficulties. Many people, therefore, prefer to experiment with their consciousness in a safe environment accompanied by friends who can provide help and support if the experience gets out of hand.

Third, participants have to be willing to let go. One must "resist resisting" and willingly "surrender to body, crowd and sound," as religious studies scholar François Gauthier puts it in a study of rave parties (2004, 76). Even potent drugs might not induce altered states of mind if the user attempts to withstand their effects. Similarly, the effects of large doses of alcohol may be experienced as bodily discomfort more than cheerful drunkenness, such as in situations when drinkers leave a party and struggle to stagger back home. Of course, attempts to sober up or stay calm are not always successful, but resistance can put a serious damper on aroused states of mind.

Fourth, it is crucial that people be close physically. Too much distance will prevent them from being fully able to sense one another and efficiently receive, transmit, and contribute to the affective flows in the group. These flows tend to grow in strength, up to a certain limit, in proportion to the number of people assembled (Wellman, Corcoran, and Stockly-Meyerdirk 2014).

Fifth, those assembled have to focus their attention on the same object or activity and become aware that everyone else is doing likewise (Collins 2004). Focusing on the same thing makes it easier for people to tune into one another and synchronize their bodily and mental rhythms, eventually causing them to move and feel as one—as when dancers move in harmony to the same beat or lovers become so caught up in each other that their breathing and heartbeats sync together. In the words of Collins, rituals are successful when the "nervous systems" of the participants "become mutually attuned in rhythms and anticipations of each other, and the physiological substratum that produces emotions in one individual's body becomes stimulated in feedback loops that run through the other person's body" (2004, xix).

Sixth, physiological stimulants are useful for people to surpass the confines of their habitual ways of behaving and experiencing. In the context of nightlife settings, the stimulants that generate effervescence generally include a whole range of arousing agents that gradually release the body and mind to the affective flows that run through the ritual assembly. As these flows intensify, a growing sense of unity and an attunement of experiences eventually enable everyone to share the same aroused mood. The most popular physiological stimulants in nightlife are alcohol and other drugs, light and laser shows, and rhythmic stimulation by loud music.

Back at the Ringsted Town Festival, the clock had passed midnight, and most people appeared to be in a pleasant state of drunken, compassionate effervescence. The beer tents were still occupied by middle-aged adults and older patrons, but the rest of the park was slowly being drained of life as the young people dispersed toward Crazy Daisy, the only nightclub in town. I tagged along and found the queue a long and chaotic trail of yelling, singing, pushing, and line-cutting. A group of women performed a giggly version of "California Dreaming." A guy randomly screamed "BIF! BIF! BIF!" which makes little sense, even in Danish, and another guy went around with a worried expression, whispering "Hush! Mafia boss! Hush! Mafia boss!"

Eventually, I got inside and was immediately wrapped in a lush carpet of sound. It was soothing after the cacophony outside. One song led to another, the bass line weaving it all together and prompting us to move our bodies. The bartenders also did their part to raise our spirits. They juggled with bottles, turned on the strobe light behind the bar, and shouted "Cheers!" As I would later discover, this was all designed, rehearsed, and performed to entertain the customers and increase sales.

The dance floor was nearly full, giving people an excuse to bump into and touch one another. I watched Ali, a short and energetic eighteen-year-old man with parents from the Middle East. He was generally well liked but also feared because of his taste for brawls and close ties with local drug dealers. He scanned the room with his eyes screwed up and arms extended from his sides at forty-five-degree angles, like a cowboy or gangster ready for a gun-fight. A group of women were doing Madonna's "Vogue" dance with graceful movements and theatrical poses. They played around, experimenting with different personas and bodily poses. The scene recalled Jackson's assertion that role-play is "based upon a bodily awareness of the other in oneself" and that it may assist "in bringing into relief a reciprocity of viewpoints" (1989, 130). From this perspective, the tendency among revelers for role-playing may be understood as a way to explore their own inner diversity and experience the world from new perspectives (see also Grazian 2005). So, for example, when a man moves like a woman, he may get a glimpse of what it feels like to be inside a woman's body or in the body of a feminine man. "Je est un autre" (I is another), wrote Arthur Rimbaud to express a realization that I suspect is common in festive crowds. Alternatively, "I are many others" might be a more apt formulation, since revelers tend to take on multiple personas over the course of a night.

Ali mounted a platform and performed a sexy dance but with ironic distance, exaggerating his movements and putting on funny faces. The staff let him do this, although it was against regulations to climb on things. Perhaps they figured that he was still sober enough to avoid falling down. Perhaps they also appreciated his show and its effect on the crowd. His performance attracted the attention of the crowd and encouraged everyone to focus on the same thing—a vital component for raising the energy of a group and fostering a sense of unity (Collins 2004, 48).

By 5:00 a.m., the party was drawing to a close. The remaining guests were clearly under the influence of more than just dancing, music, and feelings of fel-lowship. Two guys stood swaying silently, face-to-face, looking deeply into each other's eyes with looks that revealed little brain activity. Thoughts and words had evaporated and yielded to reflexes and feelings. The guys fell into each oth-er's arms, clutching each other and swaying for several minutes before letting go and staggering off separately. The drunken, compassionate effervescence was fast approaching the stage of collapse.

THE DESIRE FOR ALTERED STATES

I conducted a series of interviews with Ali in order to better understand the criminal milieu that he was involved with. In particular, I was interested in a hash club called "Klub Imperator," which he and his friends had established to get a place of their own and to "smoke weed," "have fun," and "go crazy." "We

don't have anywhere else to go," Ali would often say, calling himself "a criminal" and arguing that people like him were constantly met with disapproval and
rejection everywhere they went. Good jobs, he said, were unavailable to young
men of Middle Eastern heritage. Parents would not let their daughters date "bad
boys." Teachers were prejudiced. The list went on. He was frustrated by these
circumstances, but at the same time, he obviously took pride in belonging to a
criminal group. I also suspect that he took pride in having me, a member of
a research team, ask him so many questions about crime and deviance.

Klub Imperator was located in the very center of Ringsted. The windows
were shaded, and a sign stating "Members Only" hung by the entrance. Inside,
there was a vivarium that held a snake and a poisonous spider. The space also
contained two decrepit sofas, a PlayStation, a stash of cannabis, and sometimes
weapons. The place reeked of crime, quite literally: the door was often left open
so that the sweet scent of cannabis wafted into the street.

Ali's preferred drugs were cannabis and alcohol, but he often expressed that
drugs were merely one of many ways to get high. He mentioned, for instance,
that the Booster at the town festival had given him a tremendous "kick" that
made him feel almost as if he were on drugs. And then there were the fights,
which also gave him a drug-like rush. When confronting an opponent and spectators encircling them, the adrenaline would start pumping and his head would
spin, he said.

I once witnessed one of Ali's fights. It took place outside of a bar and started
with a long string of insults exchanged between Ali and a muscular man in his
late twenties. Both smiled and laughed as they spewed their abuse, and it seemed
to me that they were interacting with the assembled crowd as much as they were
with each other. Ali had a whole crew of his teenage friends around, whereas his
opponent only had one friend present. I had not seen the opponent or his friend
before and guessed that they were new in town. I pulled the friend aside and
warned him that Ali was no one to mess with. But it was too late. The place was
already flooded with the tension and confusion of violent effervescence, making
reasoning very difficult. Ali said with a grin, "This is my hood. You f-ck off." The
opponent laughingly reciprocated, "You f-ck off, f-cking cousin." (In Denmark,
"cousin" [fætter] is sometimes used to denote males with a Middle Eastern background. In this case, the term was probably used as an insult.)

The exchanges went on for several minutes before Ali pushed his opponent
hard in the chest. In a swift movement that seemed rehearsed, Ali pulled off
his leather belt—which sported a large metallic buckle—to use as a whip. Even
with this weapon, however, Ali was no match for his opponent, who was much
bigger and stronger. The opponent obviously did not want to hurt Ali. He just
grabbed him firmly by the neck and brought him to the ground, holding him
and looking into his eyes with a smile, as if to indicate that this was all just play.

But Ali's friends did not smile. They were fuming with anger and soon jumped in, kicking the opponent all over his body until somebody yelled for someone to call the police.

Did Ali look in my direction as he ran off? I walked away with the feeling that my presence had worsened the situation, since it gave Ali an opportunity to prove what he had so eagerly expressed during all our interviews: that he was a tough guy, a criminal, someone out of the ordinary.

Numerous studies show that individuals may engage in violence because they find it emotionally and socially rewarding. The literature on hooliganism, for instance, is full of testimonies that violence can be "fun," that it creates a "buzz" and an "adrenalin rush," and that it can become "like a drug" (e.g., Spaaij 2006). There are, of course, numerous other reasons behind violent behavior, but one is that it provides experiences that demand such focus that they momentarily divert the mind from its ordinary moods and preoccupations. Depression, angst, sadness, adolescent ennui—such unpleasant states can be temporarily sidelined when stepping into the heat of a fight. This is not to suggest that Ali's life was filled with violent effervescence or that nightlife environments are dangerous. Rather, it is to exemplify that effervescence can be generated in many different ways and can take many different forms.

Ali explained that the best way to stir up effervescence—or "to run amok," as he called it—is to take drugs at a party with a lot of people who are living it up. "It's only possible to run amok when you are on drugs," he told me. "You cannot reach that point in a normal frame of mind. You have to be together with a lot of people to run amok. The attention of the others is necessary. You have to think, 'Hey, I will make the others feel great.' You cannot create that mood on your own."

Ali confessed that he would sometimes get so high that he lost hold of himself. This happened one time at Crazy Daisy after drinking "too much" and doing "some drugs." Everybody was having fun and partying with full force. At some point, Ali was dancing to a song called "Nasty." Without thinking, he jumped onto a table and stripped off all his clothes except for his flashy red underpants. Ali had never done anything like that before. His friends were shocked and tried in vain to bring him back to his senses. They yelled, "What are you doing?" and grabbed him. However, everyone else in the nightclub was cheering and whistling, and even the DJ reacted and made fun of Ali over the microphone. That had been a really good night, Ali concluded.

To come down after a big night out can be difficult, so Ali would often smoke cannabis on his way home. The practice was like a little after-party ritual in his circle of friends. The soothing effects of cannabis helped put a damper on the effervescence. "We sit outside or in our cars and make a mix," Ali related. "It makes you calm down. You can't sleep when your heart is pounding and everything is all wild. That's impossible. Then better smoke some joints. We sit together." He continued with a whisper, "Then everything gets all quiet in the car. It gets totally silent."

My conversations with Ali provided me with many examples of how moods can be changed and consciousness altered. Our conversations also strengthened my conviction that health expert Andrew Weil, MD, is right in his famous statement that "the desire to alter consciousness periodically is an innate, normal drive analogous to hunger or the sexual drive" (1998, 19). There is great cultural variation in how people pursue altered forms of consciousness and what altered states they prefer. In some cultural contexts, like the ones described in this book, alcohol and other drugs play a pivotal role in almost all intoxicating rituals. In other contexts, however, the mechanism might be listening to music, chanting, screaming, dancing, swinging, shaking, overbreathing, overloading the senses, whirling around, or responding to rhythmic stimulation by light (Lindholm 2003).[2] Some techniques for altering consciousness are greatly beneficial while other techniques can do severe harm.

For some months, Ali and his friends were able to meet at Klub Imperator to smoke weed and deepen their sense of being different. "Who wants to be normal?" Ali once asked. To be normal, he said, is "just the same, and the same, and the same." So he sought criminal action and experimented with drugs. However, the police soon became aware of the club and began to search members as they entered and exited. The police were building up a case, and they got the necessary evidence one day, as one of the club members beat a man with an iron pipe and then sought refuge in the club, refusing to come out when the police ordered him to do so. This "mistake," as Ali called it, gave the police an excuse to raid the club. Inside they found guns, knives, and cannabis. Two more police raids followed, and the club was closed down. It did not take long, however, for the members to find a new location where they could meet, smoke, scheme, and relish their outsider status.

DRUGS AND MUSIC

Klub Imperator was a space for the cultivation of laid-back states of mind more than effervescent ones. Club members would sit on the couch and "get stoned" on cannabis while talking, listening to music, and playing video games, often for hours on end. There would be little bodily movement and few transgressive acts. One visit resembled another and rarely left any particular impression. Perhaps someone might get agitated about a game, but otherwise, the atmosphere was relaxed. Nonetheless, there were episodes where the mood intensified, possibly to the level of effervescence—or violent effervescence, to be more exact, since the excited episodes in the club often included elements of tension, fear, and destructive behavior. For example, Ali told me that the club members sometimes had fun fighting and shooting one another with splatter guns. Feeding the snake with mice was also a recurrent thrill. And once, when someone brought a dog to the club, the snake was let out of its cage. This time it was the animals who, as Ali put it, ran "totally amok," an event that really left an impression.

Violent effervescence is not common among the people I have studied, but the combined use of drugs and music certainly is. People generally use alcohol or other drugs to the accompaniment of music. One reason for this is that music helps activate, tune into, and give shape to the effects of drugs. The cannabis high, for example, will be very different for someone sitting on a couch with rap music playing in the background than it will be for the same person listening to loud techno music while a dog and a snake are fighting for their lives just a few yards away. Music can thus serve as a powerful mood modifier. In group settings, it can create a "sonic bond" between people (Vandenberg, Berghman, and Schaap 2020, 2), a sort of "hotline to the collective conscious" (Horsfall 2016).

Indeed, music is one of the most important stimulants affecting the experience of effervescence today. Eighteen-year-old Ditte from Ringsted explained in an interview, "It's impossible to go out without music. There has to be music. Music gives a certain feel to the night." Like those of so many other youths, Ditte's nights out usually followed the same tripartite structure that, I note in passing, corresponds to the three phases in ethnographer and folklorist Arnold van Gennep's (1960) ritual theory: separation, liminality, and incorporation. Ditte would normally meet up in a private home with some friends at dinnertime or a little later. Already at this point, music was played but at a low volume so as to allow for conversations and the gradual buildup of effervescence.

The intake of alcohol at these sessions helped accelerate the interactions and energies. This "warming up," as Danes call it, is about ridding the body and mind of the restraints and rigidity of daily life and gradually working toward a common mood. Later, Ditte and her friends would go to a bar or a nightclub. To a large extent, their choice of destination was based on the style of music being played. If they were in the mood for a cozy atmosphere with a medium level of intensity, they generally opted for a local bar called Løven, whose jukebox featured a selection of pop and rock music. If they sought a higher level of intensity, they headed for Crazy Daisy. There the music was loud and fast, played by a DJ who used the bass line to mix successive songs into one continuous stream. Finally, Ditte and her friends would enter what Gauthier calls the "comedown period." Ideally, this is "a soft, pleasant and safe landing" from the emotional heights of the night out (2005, 250). However, for Ditte and so many others whose preferred intoxicant is alcohol, the comedown is often something of a crash: the arduous journey home, the fitful sleep, and eventually, the day of hangover symptoms and anxiety from not knowing exactly what happened the night before. For Ditte, there was usually little or no music during the comedown period, though other revelers strategically make use of mellow music, such as "chill-out music," to gently decompress and return to normal equilibrium.

Within nightlife venues, one role of music is to unite people and make them move in unison. Cultural geographer Ben Malbon writes about this in a study of clubbing: "Through imposing sonic orderings and spacings upon the social gathering, music can affect emotional responses and can in certain instances effect a coincidence of emotional arousal at the same moment" (1999, 102). When the music reaches a climax, the crowd erupts in jumping, cheering, and whistling. It can all happen so quickly that it seems simultaneous, as if carefully instructed, rehearsed, and triggered by a command. But at large dance events, many people have never met before, and there is rarely anyone giving them (verbal) commands on how to behave. To a large extent, it is the music that synchronizes the bodies and minds. And as Collins points out, only when a crowd focuses on the same thing, such as music or coordinated movements, can the emotional exchanges speed up and create strong feelings of unity. This process, when it succeeds, is a feedback system in which the dancing both cues and is cued by the collective feelings. The experience can be so powerful that it makes the dancers tune into the music, the movements, and the mood to such a degree that they forget all else. After successful music events, audience members as well as musicians frequently comment that they got carried away, that they forgot themselves, that time flew by, that they felt truly alive. Such remarks, and the experiences to which they attest, come from people of every cultural and subcultural background, suggesting that we are here touching upon a universal quality of music. In the words of Malbon, "Participation in producing, reproducing and consuming music can act to re-state our sense of vitality, our thirst and enthusiasm for living, despite other aspects outside of the musical experience being sources of anxiety or uncertainty" (1999, 79). It is no wonder that people so often turn to music in times of personal or social crisis, such as a global pandemic (Vandenberg, Berghman, and Schaap 2020).

Unlike eyes, ears have no lids, so those who are exposed to music have to take it in and adjust to it, whether they like it or not. Music is therefore an intrusive stimulant. It demands attention. And when it is very loud, rhythmic, and uninterrupted, as in nightlife venues, it distracts the mind from its inner dialogue and fills the entire organism with restless energy that almost commands a reaction—whether movement, singing, or shouting—thus contributing to the interactive rhythmic entrainment that is effervescence.

THE PUB CRAWL

Some of the most affectively charged rituals I have participated in were pub crawls, also known as beer crawls, bar tours, and circuit drinking.[3] This type of ritual is popular among students in college towns and tourists at nightlife resorts. It basically consists of a group of people visiting multiple drinking venues over the course of one night and having one or more alcoholic beverages at each of them.

It was during my fieldwork in Sunny Beach that I took an interest in pub crawls. I had attended a few before, but I had found them rather boring and considered them as little more than an excuse to get drunk. However, the pub crawls in Sunny Beach were different. First of all, they were big, with up to six hundred dedicated participants. And they were well organized, with large teams of trained guides who escorted the participants from venue to venue, organized drinking games, and encouraged everyone to dance and sing. Eventually, if someone got hurt, the guides provided consolation, administered first aid, or called an ambulance. I was informed that annual surveys conducted by one of the Danish travel agencies consistently showed that tourists value pub crawls higher than any of the other parties offered at resorts, including the legendary booze cruises, beach parties, barbecue parties, and foam parties. So I decided to pay special attention to pub crawls and started interviewing people about them.

The foundation for pub crawl effervescence is established before the actual event. Often, participants see pictures and hear stories that associate pub crawls with excitement, fun, and danger. The media play an important role in producing such associations through their sensationalist depictions of young tourists going wild. Travel agencies also contribute by presenting advertisements on the internet and in brochures that feature pictures of elated pub crawlers alongside texts full of praise. A sampling taken from the web pages of Danish tour organizers declares that pub crawls are the "climax of the week," "a must," and "highly addictive" and that they "CANNOT BE EXPLAINED, MUST BE EXPERIENCED!!" Travel agencies that specialize in youth tours host "warm-up parties" prior to the vacation, where people can meet some of their future guides and fellow travelers while trying some of the classic pub crawl activities. Consider the following field notes from a "warm-up party" held in Denmark:

> A guide takes the microphone and calls for some of his colleagues to come up to the DJ booth, and for the guests to assemble on the dance floor. . . . "This will make your vacation more fun," a guide says. The guests are divided into competing couples. The men get balloons strapped to their crotches and are instructed to burst the balloons with the help of their female partners and without anyone using their hands. A winning couple quickly emerges when the woman bites their balloon. Bang! That's it. The whole thing was a little

tame, feigned, and awkward. An older, more experienced male guide yells "copulation exercise" and storms up to the DJ booth. He begins to furiously dry hump another male guide who has a balloon strapped to him. It takes a little time before they burst it. That's how it's supposed to be done: in a spectacular and unrestrained manner. (Tutenges 2015, 289)[4]

I find it useful to think of effervescent rituals such as pub crawls as having four stages rather than just the three stages described in van Genneps's classical model (1960). Before the onset of the ritual as such, there tends to be what may be termed a *preparation stage*. During this stage, the participants are introduced to symbols and other collective representations of the activities and energies that lie ahead.[5] Participants might be informed about what will happen, how they are supposed to act, or how they are meant to feel. They might also be invited to events like the "warm-up party," where they can try out some of the activities that will take place at the main event. Importantly, the participants themselves often play a proactive role during the preparation stage by hyping the ritual through shared rumors, encouragement, stories, photos, and videos.

Hospitality and tourism researcher Bharath M. Josiam and his colleagues (1998) observed something similar to the preparation stage in what appears to be the very first empirical study of American college students on "spring break" vacations. They write, "For students going on spring break, there is often a great sense of anticipation of the vacation" (1998, 502). This anticipation is expressed on many platforms, including chat forums on the internet. The following messages are two decades old and written by university students from the United States, but they are almost identical to messages being shared today among far-flung international tourists who are preparing for vacations at nightlife destinations:

All goin' down to Panama City Beach between March 8–17 beware!! We will drink all your beer!!! The parties WILL be the best ever. The Ramada Inn/ Days Inn will never be the same. And they thought the hurricane made a mess. Where is everyone stay'n?? Let me know. You'll probably want to party with us. If your not in Panama, watch for us on MTV.

Joe, Canisius College

As of approximately 8am on Saturday March 2nd, Penn State University will descend upon South Padre! We're looking for warm skies and warmer women with little regard for morals. It's −30 degree in State College, and our brains are fried! Look out Texas, here comes the number one party school in the nation!

Patrick, Pennsylvania State University[6]

Indeed, messages like these convey a great deal of anticipation. They are an important part of the preparations that will eventually enable the tourists to succeed in the difficult task of overcoming their habits of self-control and indulging in states of effervescence.

For some years, I have been following exchanges on chat forums hosted by two of the leading Danish youth tour operators. Both tourists and guides contribute to these forums. The guides often take on the role of nightlife experts. They give advice about nightclubs, suitable clothing, hotel facilities, and beer costs while reminding everyone to buy tickets for the pub crawl. The tone is almost unanimously enthusiastic (e.g., "BEST PARTY EVER"). Critical messages are not tolerated. When one tourist made disparaging remarks about a nightclub, his message was swiftly removed. "Party poopers" should "get their shit together," a guide replied, or use another tour organizer. Negative attitudes are not welcome because they are bad for business and disturb the sense of solidarity among like-minded peers seeking an unforgettable blast of a vacation.

In the context of nightlife, effervescence is generally the culmination of a long process that involves collaboration, an alignment of expectations, and finally, a physical merging at a ritual event where physiological stimulants will be used to pump up the energies.[7]

The following field notes from Sunny Beach convey some of my impressions at a pub crawl:

A flyer informs me that the pub crawl will start out at the Sunset Bar. I am late and the place is already swarming with people as I arrive. I count ten guides in the crowd. Two are carrying a banner saying [name of tour operator] and there is also one with a megaphone. . . . The megaphone guy tells us to get going and to follow the banner. I estimate that we are at least 500 people. The mood is still relatively calm, but there are drunken shouts and occasional outbreaks of song. We snake our way up Flower Street and cross the main road, forcing the cars and pedestrians to stop and wait. Other tourists look at us, point their fingers, and take photos. We arrive at a nightclub called Inferno. A group of guides greets us and hands out free shots to everyone. We are ushered inside and onto the dance floor. A tall, suntanned guide [whom I will later refer to as "Oliver"] is standing on a podium with a microphone in his hand. "Get in quick," he says. Everyone is standing really close. The music starts pumping. "Yeah, that's the way I like it," says the guide with the microphone: "I think this is going to be the wildest night of our entire lives." Now he speaks louder: "GET THOSE HANDS UP IN THE AIR. WE ARE GOING TO DESTROY THIS CITY. THAT'S IT. UP WITH THOSE HANDS!" He continues shouting commands at us, but pauses as the music reaches a climax. He is in control now and looks at us triumphantly. He then yells aggressively, imperiously, in time with the beat: "JUMP. SWEAT FOR ME." People all around start jumping up and down. It's an inferno of noise, stroboscopic lights, artificial smoke, and dancing bodies. (Tutenges 2015, 288)

It is difficult to find the right words to describe what it feels like to be in the middle of a tightly packed dance floor with everybody doing their best to pump up the energy. I personally like metaphors that connote heated fluids, such as to foam, bubble, boil, steam, sizzle, and of course, effervesce. At the pub crawl described above, the participants were bubbling with enthusiasm just minutes after entering the second venue of the night. Many were still relatively sober, but other ritual mechanisms—including the preparations that had taken place before the pub crawl—ensured that the party was in full swing right from the start.

After leaving the Inferno nightclub, the level of effervescence dropped a few notches as the participants walked to the next venue. Of course, there was still some singing, shouting, and jumping around, much to the entertainment of other tourists in the vicinity. Many stopped to watch, wave, take photos, film, and so on. Nevertheless, the effervescence had definitely mellowed into a kind of low-key, drunken, compassionate effervescence. People were able to carry on conversations, and I was able to jot down a few field notes.

There are many reasons why the effervescence tends to abate when pub crawl crowds are in transit between venues. One reason is that collective effervescence is a peak experience that most people prefer in short time intervals. Though some individuals like long spells of effervescence—"party animals" who are often praised for their debaucherous stamina—most people need pauses to tone down their activities, especially after bursts like our forty-five intense minutes at Inferno. Leaving the venue, the pub crawl participants and guides were less invested in raising the collective energies, and their attentions scattered. The rhythmic entrainment ended once we left the club and was replaced by leisurely walks outside, conversations within separate groups, and occasional shouting and singing by the liveliest of the participants.

This dissolution of physical and psychic unity—or "group mind," as Durkheim sometimes calls it—also has to do with the physical environment. The streets of Sunny Beach do not have the same destabilizing technologies as nightclubs. There are no smoke machines, sound systems, or stroboscopic lights. Moreover, in the streets, the participants were no longer forced to be as close to one another as they were inside the nightclub. This distance makes a huge difference. For as Collins makes clear, something exceptional can happen when multitudes are thronged together in the same place: there is mutual bodily awareness, strong emotions arise, and the boundaries between self and other become blurred (2004, 34).

Some have argued that individuals can turn into an excited crowd without being in physical contact with one another (see, e.g., Le Bon 2001). A contemporary example of this could be an internet-based group that never meets face-to-face but nevertheless fervently unites in a common political struggle. But will the group that never meets be able to reach the same emotional heights as the group that gets physically together? I think not. Consider the difference between watching a football match on television and at a stadium. Or think of the difference between studying a course over the internet versus in a classroom. When humans gather in the same place, they can sense and affect one another with their entire bodies—not only through sight and hearing but also through touch, smell, and taste (as when people kiss). At present, digital technologies cannot replace or compete with this kind of corporeal interaction. Copresence is crucial for fueling high levels of effervescence (Collins 2004).[8]

THE ENERGY STAR

I asked Oliver for an interview in order to hear about his job as a tour guide and his experience with organizing parties. We met for lunch at a place called Viking Bar, one of the venues on the itinerary for his weekly pub crawls. The waiters nearly stumbled over themselves to serve us, and the manager came several times to ask if everything was to our satisfaction. Oliver explained that six hundred excited pub crawlers shell out huge amounts of money at each of the venues they visit, so he often ate for free and got good service in Sunny Beach.

Oliver lived up to his reputation of being charming and bright. He also had a certain aristocratic air about him, though it disappeared completely when he broke out in tirades of swearing or hoarse laughter. Oliver was a true twenty-first-century libertine. He was thirty-seven years old at the time of the interview and had been working with tourists since he was a teenager: "Back in the day, this business was completely unstructured, which was perfect for someone like me: a young, completely egoistic boy. I could just have this summer job, party full on, and do all the things that today are considered mortal sins in this line of work. But because there was no structure, I was able to develop, and as the years went by I found my feet. I worked like that for six years, six seasons. Like a summer job, alongside my studies."

Oliver liked the job so much that one day he teamed up with some friends to start their own travel agency. They changed the concept. Their agency catered exclusively to young tourists and tried to avoid "cheap hotels" with minuscule rooms that "look like shitholes"—the kinds of establishments where people were piled up in bunk beds and forced to lie there with no air conditioning, "sweating like pigs," as he put it.

"That doesn't fly today," he went on. "These days, goddamn, if you promise them thirty-two TV channels and it turns out there are only thirty-one, they'll start a riot. They are so focused on these things. [...] As long as things are nicely packaged, then they don't give a f-ck about the contents. [...] The hotels down here are made of cardboard but look nice, so people are happy."

"The kinds of parties that people like, has that changed too?" I probed.

"Yeah, for sure. I can tell how they are influenced by the mass media. It's like MTV all over. What they see in the music videos, that's what they want for themselves. When you have these musicians or R & B artists sitting there on a big leather sofa with sexy ladies all around them and the champagne flowing, that's what they want. They want to be high rollers [. . .] throwing around money even though they don't have any. Of course, everyone wants a cheap vacation. Like here [in Bulgaria] where things don't cost anything. Here they can be high rollers, right? It's like a fantasy, right? Here they can live the dream."

Oliver's company offered cheap but nicely packaged vacations. They were for "the beautiful people" who wanted a week or two of sunshine, sea, sand, sex, and lots of partying. Six days a week, Oliver's company hosted a party that the tourists could buy into, and many went for the whole shebang. At the time I interviewed Oliver, the weekly activity program was as follows: On Sundays, planes arrived with a new crowd of tourists, so there was a welcome meeting followed by a welcome party. Mondays started early with mingling and drinking at a bar on the beach followed by a pub crawl in the evening. Tuesdays heralded the booze cruise, which Oliver described in these words: "You hang out on the deck with a cold beer in your hand, right there in the middle of the Black Sea, and the sun is shining and everything is perfect." Wednesdays featured a barbecue party with lots of food served at long tables and a show performed by the guides with lots of dirty dance moves and naked skin. Thursdays were for the beach party, where people "choose whether they would prefer to just relax and soak up the sun or dance in front of the loudspeakers." Fridays ushered in a foam party at one of the biggest nightclubs in town. And Saturdays were dedicated to nursing the hangovers and sending home some of the tourists.

Indeed, as one tourist put it, you do not go to Sunny Beach to "play with Lego." Some party away most of their waking hours throughout the week. The level of alcohol consumption among the tourists was made clear by some surveys my colleagues and I conducted at the local airport. Before boarding their plane back to Denmark, the tourists (1011 in total) filled out a questionnaire. The results revealed that 41 percent reported drinking twelve or more units of alcohol per day, six or seven days per week. Moreover, the results showed that 5 percent reported drug use and 9 percent reported that they had been involved in a fight during their stay (Tutenges and Hesse 2008). The most alcohol was consumed by tourists traveling with "party package companies" like Oliver's. Of this group, 59 percent reported consuming twelve or more units per day six or seven days per week (Hesse et al. 2008). We defined a "unit," according to the Danish standards, to be twelve grams of alcohol. Expressed in more common terms, most of the tourists traveling with party-package companies consumed at least twelve beers (of 4.6 percent alcohol) per day of their vacation. The mean age of the tourists we surveyed was twenty years old, but a substantial proportion was no more than sixteen to seventeen years old. (In Bulgaria and Denmark, the minimum legal age to buy alcohol is eighteen.)

Obviously, with all the drinking—plus the heat, junk food, lack of sleep, crowds, and so on—the tourists and guides became increasingly disconnected as the days passed. Many reported feeling "dizzy" and as if they were "in a haze," "in a bubble," or like "a different person." These reactions corroborate Durkheim's observation that sustained celebrations can significantly destabilize people. He writes that "a very intense social life always does a sort of violence to the individual's body and mind and disrupts their normal functioning. This is why it can last for only a limited time" (1995, 228). In Sunny Beach, many people accepted the strong reactions they were having as part of the package, but for some they became unbearable. For example, I talked with a tourist who woke up one morning with a massive panic attack, something she had never experienced before. And I observed at least two tourists who, it seemed, were suffering from psychotic fits. One of them claimed that he had wrecked his hotel room, which led to the confiscation of his passport. He believed that the police and the mafia were after him, so he had gone underground and was sleeping on the beach. He asked me if I, by any chance, knew of an apartment he could buy.

Effervescence is a state of psychophysical disequilibrium that many people find pleasurable, but only as long as they retain a certain degree of control and are able to avoid a complete collapse.

The vacations offered by Oliver's company were much the same as those offered by the larger, better-known companies such as the British "Club 18–30" and the American "Sun Splash Tours." Typically, these vacations take place over several days in an affectively charged environment full of youths who are far away from the restraints of school, work, and family life. These factors all contribute to the production of collective effervescence. As Oliver pointed out, many of the tourists have hardly ever been away from their parents before, so the vacations have a strong effect on them. Some "go nuts," wreck their hotel rooms, or even jump off their balconies. Oliver therefore emphasized the importance of having a team of skilled guides capable of everything from receiving tourists at the airport to creating good parties: "Some think that you can do the job without using your brain, but [being a guide] is a highly responsible task involving a multitude of roles and situations in a constant flux. You have to be a parent, a best friend, a teacher, a psychologist, and a medic—all at the same time."

I asked Oliver what he did to create good parties. He mentioned the case of pub crawls and said that he always prepared the tourists mentally before this "party marathon" of their lives:

"We make them understand that this is different from an average night out where you dance for twenty minutes and then go take a break," he explained.

"The point is to build up the mood from place to place to place to place. Maybe they think that they really lived it up at the first nightclub, but they have to take it higher. They have to sweat. We tell them that they're not supposed to wear high heels. They're told that in their hotels so that they have a chance to go to their rooms and change. They're also not supposed to cover their faces with makeup, because they're going to sweat. We want the venues covered in sweat. You know, this is a marathon! We have this goal we have to reach. No one can quit. [. . .] The other companies, they just walk with people to different bars and say, 'Welcome. Here you can buy this and that in the bar. Have fun.' That's it. Then they go to the next place after an hour. We don't do that. We actively kick things off, right? Get people out on the dance floor, just using a few tricks. You know, full speed."

"What kinds of buttons do you push to kick things off like that?" I asked.

"We tell them how it's all structured so that they feel they are with people who have things under control. Then they think, 'Hey, if these guys say so, then that's how it is.' They come into a club with six hundred people, and you get them going with just a few manipulative words. You tell them some story. You invent a story about how the manager [in the nightclub] has said that Danes don't know how to party. Then this sense of competitiveness wells up in them. They want to prove that they know how to do this shit. [. . .] You know, it has to be wilder than anything they have ever experienced before. So here we are, six hundred people, and then it's got to be wild, right? Controlled, but wild. And then we kick it off and people start jumping all around. Maybe some will start climbing up on tables and chairs. They shouldn't do that, so our night guards [guides in charge of the security] go and take them down and grab the microphone [to inform them of the rules]. We have things under control, and at the same time we are constantly building it up."

Oliver and his team made an effort to give their customers the impression that they were in good hands. If someone fell, there would be a night guard to catch them, eliminating any need to hold back. Parties that are safe, or appear safe, make it easier for people to alter their minds.

I attended several parties in Sunny Beach that were marked by a sense of insecurity, primarily due to the presence of intimidating men who appeared to be members of the Bulgarian mafia. Almost uniformly, they had muscular bodies, black clothes, golden jewelry, shaved heads, and cold eyes. Their presence put a serious damper on things. The Bulgarian mafia more or less controls the venues in Sunny Beach, and Oliver had several thug stories to relate. One time he was at the Inferno nightclub dancing when, suddenly, the music was turned off. This happened several times, so he finally asked the manager for an explanation. The manager pointed with a sigh toward an older man who was flanked by what seemed to be a team of bodyguards. When the old man's cell phone rang, he would signal to the DJ with a lackadaisical wave, and the music in the club would go silent until the phone call was over. Talk about party poopers.

I pressed Oliver to tell me more about how he made people live it up during his pub crawls.

"People need to be encouraged, right? [We get them] to dance around and do the same dances and things together. They have to concentrate on initiating something. It's really simple. These are things kids do in kindergarten, things like 'Let's touch our knees,' 'touch our shoulders,' 'touch our feet.' Stuff like that. And they do it all together. It's really fun when six hundred people are doing the same thing at once."

Of course, such simple exercises hardly produce high levels of effervescence, but they help people loosen up. They encourage physical interaction and make deep conversations difficult. Bodies tune into one another, which may eventually lead to the large-scale rhythmic entrainment of collective effervescence. The silly-looking movements also serve as icebreakers that puncture any reserved attitudes. It is hard to remain serious when surrounded by six hundred young adults moving like children at their first gym class. At times, however, the guides instructed the tourists to move in more demanding ways. The following field notes were taken at a beach party:

> The beer relay race begins after dinner. Three teams are formed, and each participant is supposed to run sixteen yards to a waiting guide who is holding a large draft beer. The participant must down the beer, run around the guide five times, do a summersault, run back, and give way to the next in line. Everyone must take two turns and drink two beers. The participants are overwhelmingly male. The guide says into the microphone: "Now we're gonna play a game we learned in Spain. We're gonna dig holes, so grab a shovel." He laughs into the microphone. There are four teams, each with three players. They are told to dig for 10 minutes. The guide with the microphone tells those not participating to come close and cheer. Some of the other guides encourage others nearby to "Come watch. This is cool as hell." The diggers are given small shovels, and they really get to work. Some discuss tactics while digging. Others just give it their all. A female guide runs up to the bar: "Beer, beer, lots of beer." She walks around with a tray and serves the diggers, who are laboring under the relentless sun.

Oliver and his team of guides always opted for the road of excess to generate effervescence. They did not employ ascetic body techniques such as silent group meditation or respiratory exercises, which can arguably also generate experiences akin to effervescence (Pagis 2015). The tourists were instructed to move and shout, to wiggle and roar. "The sweat has to flow!" Oliver often shouted into his microphone. Also, the chosen activities generally had strong elements of what Mikhail Bakhtin calls "degradation," meaning "the lowering of all that is high, spiritual, ideal, abstract; it is a transfer to the material level, to the sphere of earth and body in their indissoluble unity" (1984, 19–20). When people dig holes on the beach and compete in drinking games, they inevitably become soiled with sand, sweat, and beer. This has the effect of pulling them down to the same earthy or subearthy level, regardless of their everyday status. The distinguishing signs that normally separate them are washed away. The beautiful and the ugly, the rich and the poor, females and males—everyone is urged to lower himself or herself and partake in collective acts of cheerful indecency. The following notes describe another classic pub crawl game, which also illustrates how acts of degradation can bring people closer:

> When we are about to leave, the guide tells us to stand in line. We are supposed to reach one of our arms through our legs and lock hands with the person behind us, so that we're all standing together, with our arms more or less in each other's laps. We get to know each other well during these group games! The guy in front of me smiles and tells me that he's in a great spot. His partner in front of him is a woman wearing a miniskirt and his head is only a few centimeters from her ass, and his arm is between her legs. I suggest to the guy that if I pull my arm as hard as I can, he will do a somersault. He declines the offer. Then we begin to walk. We move away from [the bar] and out onto the crowded beach promenade.

People certainly make fools of themselves by waddling along in a human chain like the one described above or by doing "nasty body tequilas," a drinking activity in which pairs lick salt from each other's feet or buttocks, down a shot of tequila, and suck on a piece of lemon. But the laughter that erupts in situations like these is generally inclusive and directed at the entirety of ritual participants. The degradation is collective. The guides also readily put themselves in awkward situations, performing in strip shows, participating in drinking contests, or dressing up in silly costumes. They thus expose themselves to laughter and show with their bodies that there are myriad forms of degradation—many of them fun. This willingness may help others win their inner battles against self-censorship.

The degradation performed by revelers tends to be a deeply social mechanism that undermines hierarchies and brings people close by revealing some of the basic traits that we humans share—most notably, our endless capacity to make fools of ourselves.

However, in some cases, attempts at joyous degradation become perverted or harmful. For example, one of the travel agencies once hosted a party that, according to the official announcement, would feature a world-famous band to be flown in by helicopter. The band turned out to be two unknown, tone-deaf individuals with dwarfism. The concert did generate a lot of laughter, but it was the two people on stage who were being laughed at, not the ritual gathering as a whole.

The "Buffalo Rule" is another example of how degradation can lead to divisions. This game is named after the alleged Wild West practice of drinking with one's left hand so that the right hand is always ready to grab one's gun. Tourists as well as guides who are caught drinking with their right hand have to chug all the alcohol still in their glasses. Offenders are quickly surrounded by a pack of people who unremittingly yell, "Buffalo, Buffalo, Buffalo!" until the glass is empty. Sometimes the rule is used strategically and repeatedly against weak, unpopular, or drunken individuals to deepen their state of inebriation and, eventually, cause them to vomit. The targeted individuals might not necessarily have broken the rule by drinking with their right hand, but it can be difficult to explain this when surrounded by a group of people yelling "Buffalo!" at the top of their lungs.

I asked Oliver about when and how he would speak to the pub crawlers, and how he timed this with the music.

"It has to peak," he said. "This, oh, this is an art form! I discovered this when training my staff how to do it. We do training sessions for those who want to learn. We talk about how to find the flow. You should know what you want to say before you begin talking. Then people will listen. You need to control people. You need to make sure that the volume on the microphone is loud enough and the music turned down. You have to indicate with your tone of voice what is coming: when they are supposed to respond and when they have to listen. You activate them by talking in a voice that goes up and peaks; that will make them respond. Then you make a pause; move the microphone away from your face and give them a few seconds to get attentive again. If they don't listen, you tell them, 'Hey, listen up.' It's simple. And then you should talk in a consistent tone of voice, and they'll listen. And then talk in a relatively slow tempo after that. Firm and determined. You don't need to yell and scream. You should be clear and precise. When you are there and you want them to respond again, then full power. You pull it, you pull the bow back, all the way, you pull it with all you've got, and when you can't hold it anymore, that's when you let go. The DJ will know that now is the time to set in. He can feel it too. He punches the play button to start the music, right then."

Oliver's words, indeed his whole personality, bring to mind Elias Canetti's description of how to spellbind a crowd: "The art of a speaker consists in compressing all his aims into slogans. By hammering them home he then engenders a crowd and helps to keep it in existence. He creates the crowd and keeps it alive by a comprehensive command from above" (1978, 311). Oliver was a charismatic speaker who had perfected his art through many years of practice. Importantly, however, the masses of people he spoke to were very keen on coalescing into a crowd—that primeval creature with multiple limbs and heads—and the youths actively contributed to the metamorphosis by cheering one another on, shouting out commands, and initiating drinking games.

Effervescence may be orchestrated by a single individual, but it always comes to fruition through collaborative efforts. A person who addresses an energized crowd—whether a guide at a pub crawl, a DJ in a nightclub, or a musician at a concert—should be understood as a social medium and conductor rather than the actual genesis of affective flows. Crowd members may have the impression that it is a lone individual or a sacred object that possesses the energies and passes them on, but this is not the case. From this Durkheimian perspective, God is not a singular being or an illusory construction. Rather, God is a force—a very real force—that emanates from a communion of humans. God and society are one (Durkheim 1995, 208).

I find it useful to think of Oliver and his kin as *energy stars*, a term coined by Collins (2004) to designate individuals with high levels of emotional energy (EE) who are able to draw attention to themselves and boost the emotional energies in other people. Collins writes that "energy stars" have "an EE-halo that makes them easy to admire" (2004, 132). Correspondingly, I have often heard guides being referred to as "rock stars," "superstars," and "Gods." Some of them even have groupie-like followers who do their best to be as close as possible to their preferred "star." Again, it is not that the energy star has effervescence and transmits it to other people. Rather, the energy star is a magnetic person who is good at attracting attention and helping other people go beyond themselves so as to "form an interdependent system in which all parts are linked and vibrate sympathetically" (Durkheim 1995; quoted in Duffett 2015, 187).

The leaders of effervescent rituals are expected to generate high energy. When they do not, disappointment often follows. This was made crystal clear to me in Sunny Beach by a team of guides who remained calm and reserved throughout most of the week. A tourist complained that the guides had bored her from day one. On the thirty-minute bus ride from the airport to her hotel, for example, the guides had not sung any songs or shouted, "Let's drink!" even once, she lamented. The guides made only one comment en route: "Now we are in Sunny Beach."

Another female tourist made the following comments about the same group of guides: "They're supposed to make sure that people are in a good mood and stay with us. They're supposed to kick things off and yell 'Cheers!' and make us do the same. But they're not doing it this year, not at all. These are the worst guides I have ever seen. They just walk around and do nothing. These guides have no training whatsoever and don't know the place at all."

"Why is it so important for them to lead the party?" I wanted to know.

"Because that's what they are here for. That's why we pay them. They're supposed to make sure that people have a great time. I mean, if they're only interested in practical things, then I don't think they should be guides."

A male tourist echoed these opinions, emphasizing that guides should be festive and help others become festive as well. He said the guides from his previous vacations were great because they "went totally crazy, just didn't give a damn. We had one last year [who . . .] just went crazy: painted himself and yelled and was really fun and just didn't care what he looked like. He actually appeared on the front page [of a newspaper] when we came home because he had sold Viagra to the guests. He didn't sell any to us. But he just didn't care, and he showed so much energy. [. . . He] stripped off his clothes up at the bar all the time, showed people the path they could follow and act just as dumb as he was. He was totally full of energy."

"And what was so fun about that? Another dumb question."

"It's just that he shows that there are no limits for what you can do down here—how dumb you can act. Just be as crazy as you want and totally ignore what people think about you. And it worked. People really let down their guard when they see a guide stand up there and do that. If you have guides who take the lead, then that's the way it is. They are the ones who have to kick off the party."

CHAPTER 3

UNITY

Some of the most revealing experiences during my fieldwork occurred during my downtime: having a break, walking home, carousing with friends, and so forth. One such experience played a major role in my understanding of effervescence. It took place one late summer night in the hippie settlement Freetown Christiania in Copenhagen. A friend of mine, Suresh, was working there, selling colorful clothes that he had brought back from Nepal. His stall was just next to Pusher Street, which has a constant flow of people who come to watch the scene or buy cannabis from the pushers who have given the street its name. Cannabis is an illegal drug under Danish law, but it has nevertheless been traded openly in Christiania since the 1970s. Suresh had heard rumors on Pusher Street that an underground rave party was coming up. To avoid police interference, however, the time and place of the event were only to be announced at the last minute to an in-group of trusted friends. I was eager to go to this party, so Suresh promised to let me know whenever he got news about it.

It turned out that the rave would take place on Rabbit Island, which is located in the middle of a canal that runs through Christiania. The island is no more than a couple of hundred yards wide and covered with trees and greenery. Suresh called just a few hours before the party; I raced on my bike to meet him at his stall. He is not a big drinker, so we only had one beer before we walked down to the canal. A wobbly boat brought us across to the island and we jumped on shore. The ground under us was soft and the air damp with the smell of earth, rotting leaves, and cannabis smoke. The sound system was facing a small dance area. No one was there yet besides a DJ and a group of men who looked like the biker types who sell cannabis on Pusher Street: muscular bodies, tattoos up their necks, big cannabis joints, and the occasional flash of a shark's smile. We had paid no admission fees. Perhaps it was the pushers who were financing the event. The Christiania pushers sometimes do "charity work"—donating money for parties, strip shows, and smaller building operations—presumably to improve their reputation and recruit new customers.

It was a dog that got things started on the dance floor, racing after a laser dot that whirled across the ground. A woman in hippie clothes joined the chase. We drew closer and started dancing. Suresh put his sunglasses on, formed his hands into pistols, and mock-fired all around. I was jumping on the spot, trying to loosen up. There was an underlying simmering of anxiety in my body, so I turned my back to the pushers and the lights and sought release in the music. The hippie continued her hunt for the dog and the laser dot. Her laughter helped me relax. Everyone was focused on her and the dog, not me. My face was probably covered in darkness, anyway. A warm sensation filled me: I was dancing at a rave party, surrounded by smiling faces. Suresh seemed to be having the time of his life.

We went down to the water to rest and sat down in silence, all smiles. Here we were, at a secret rave right in the middle of Copenhagen. There was no way the police were going to shut down this party. We were close to the rest of the city and yet far away. The anxiety had left my body, and I felt happy and in harmony—with myself and everything else. This feeling grew as we went back to dance, and it stayed with me all through the night before slowly waning over the following days. Was I just having "fun" or feeling "excited" that night on Rabbit Island? I think the term *effervescence*—or more exactly, *compassionate effervescence*—better captures what I experienced.

I consider my experience on Rabbit Island to be an instance of effervescence because it meets the five criteria that define this altered state. First and foremost, the experience involved a sense of *unity*. I felt united on a deep level not only with my friend Suresh and the other people I danced with but also with something else: nature, humanity, or life, perhaps. Second, what I experienced was *intense*. I felt elevated, taken out of myself, and more alive in a way that has only happened a few times in my life. Third, the experience was *transgressive*. It made me relate to myself, others, and the world in a fundamentally different manner from what I am used to. The experience was thus unusual but, at the same time, strangely familiar. It all made perfect sense. Moreover, the rave party had elements of secrecy, criminality, and subversion, and these added to the transgressive quality of my experience. Fourth, the experience was so powerful that some of its energy was transfused into *symbols*—namely, the rave's location and music. Today, when I look at Rabbit Island or listen to certain types of electronic dance music, I sometimes feel reconnected with my experience at the rave. Finally, the experience was *revitalizing*. It made me feel very good, and it changed something inside of me.

Unity, intensity, transgression, symbolization, and revitalization: These are the experiential building blocks of effervescence. Each will be explored in turn in separate chapters, beginning with this chapter on unity.

"Being Together and Doing Things Together"

Durkheim emphasizes that the crux of effervescence is that people are united, that sentiments are felt in common and expressed by common acts. There is, he argues, something inherently gratifying in being physically close to others, meeting new people, moving to the same beat, and engaging in the same activity. To feel and act in common involves a mutual awareness that diminishes the distance between self and other. There is a sense of being enlarged and of merging with something bigger and more powerful than oneself. Durkheim writes, "When men are all gathered together, when they live a communal life, the very fact of their coming together causes exceptionally intense forces to arise which dominate them, exalt them, give them a quality of life to a degree unknown to them as individuals" (1994, 183). People at effervescent gatherings are elevated above themselves and freed from their "temporal and mundane interests" (1994, 185). What Durkheim has in mind is much more than just "fun," which does not imply that people attend such gatherings for networking purposes or to seek a partner, long-term friendships, or some other lasting gain. Rather, people come together precisely in order to be together. Unity is its own reward.

Many people describe their nightlife experiences in similar terms. Of course, some go out with the express goal of building networks or for some other practical purpose, but such goals rarely exist alone. The general desires to meet up, hang out, and be close, for no specific reason, are what really make things move in nightlife.

Consider the case of nightlife tourists. Most of them prefer not to spend their time unwinding, contemplating, reading books, visiting monuments, learning languages, or hiking in nature. Rather, most of their waking hours are spent in intimate verbal and nonverbal exchanges with each other—in swimming pools, at restaurants, at drinking venues, in hotel rooms, or on beaches. Even sleeping often has a social element to it, as most nightlife tourists share rooms with fellow travelers.

Søren Kierkegaard's expression "human bath" has often come to my mind when contemplating tourists (1983, 170). He used the expression to describe his daily walks in the crowded streets of Copenhagen, an experience that filled him with the energy he needed to pursue his predominantly solitary work as a writer. Vacations at nightlife destinations may also be thought of as human baths. These baths, however, last for several days and pump up the tourists with so much energy that they become overloaded by it. Yet far from being unexpected or unimportant, the overload is one of the key mechanisms that destabilize the tourists and push them toward the effervescent states that they have come to find. Popular nightlife destinations attract swarming masses, and the masses are part of what makes the destinations popular.

I had long discussions about these themes of masses, energy, and exhaustion with Simon and John, two big guys in their early twenties whom I followed during their one-week vacation in Sunny Beach. One afternoon, I interviewed them with my audio recorder as we were sitting on the balcony adjacent to their hotel room. The room, so small that it could barely fit the beds, reeked of alcohol-infused sweat and male deodorant. Their friend and travel companion Kim was lying on one of the beds. He said that Simon and John could speak for him because he was too tired, and anyway, he agreed with whatever they had to say.

"Yeah, man, you just do what you do best: go to sleep!" Simon roared at Kim.

Then turning to me, he summarized matter-of-factly that their aspiration for the vacation was to load up on alcohol, sun, and parties, as well as to meet lots of new people. The alcohol was important, he explained, because it helped him overcome inhibitions.[1]

"When I'm sober, I don't have the courage to go over and talk with a girl," he confessed. "But when I'm drunk, there ain't nothing holding me back."

The three friends usually began their evenings by tanking up on food and liquid courage. Then they typically went to a bar to continue drinking and start their search for women. They always stuck together, because this was more "fun," and also because it made them feel safer. Sunny Beach is marred by crime, so being drunk alone can be a real hazard, they said. Their nights in Sunny Beach lasted till around sunrise, when they would stumble their way back to the hotel and get a few hours of sleep before the hangovers started setting in. The first one to wake up would soon wake up the others. Only during toilet visits would they have some time for themselves, although some of these visits were made with the door left open. Indeed, as Simon pointed out, they were in it together.

I asked them how they would define a good party, and they agreed that good parties are wild parties. People have to get drunk and cheerful and dance on the tables, they explained. Cozy parties were obviously not their thing—especially not in Sunny Beach, where one is supposed to "go nuts." Simon estimated that on every single day of their vacation, each of them drank the equivalent of eight or nine liters of pilsner beer with an alcohol content of 4.6 percent.

John confirmed, "We drink lots and lots, so much that it seems impossible."

"If we told people about all the shit we have done, they wouldn't believe us," Simon said. "Really. Parents can't understand that it's possible to drink this much. They just can't."

"And the crazy thing is that it's only Kim who has vomited. We have been drunk as pigs all the time, but almost no puking. And seriously, with the loads we've taken, wild."

Drunkenness was certainly important for them, but they did not see it as a goal in and of itself. Rather, alcohol was, for them, more like a remedy to remove inhibitions and enter a happy and extroverted state of mind so they could talk with women and do lots of "wild things," like going to a strip club.

Everybody at the party has to get drunk, John explained, but not "completely gone." One has to retain some degree of control; otherwise, people will get hurt. John preferred it when everyone at a party was cheerful and "the good mood gradually builds up from the ground." You get excited by the other people's excitement, Simon explained, drawing a parallel between the crowds at a party and those at a sporting event.

"It creates a sense of unity when you are surrounded by a sea of people," he said. "When we all yell and scream to a Danish song at a bar here at the resort, it's the same emotion that I get when I'm at a sports stadium. It's about being together and doing things together."

This simple motivation of "being together and doing things together" is a cornerstone of most rituals, whether religious or secular. It has the effect of allowing people to tune in to one another and, as Durkheim puts it, reach "agreement" on a moral and experiential plane: "It is by shouting the same cry, saying the same words, and performing the same action in regard to the same object that they arrive at and experience agreement. . . . The individual minds can meet and commune only if they come outside themselves, but they do this only by means of movement. It is the homogeneity of these movements that makes the group aware of itself and that, in consequence, makes it be" (Durkheim 1995, 232).

The collective attunement during rituals can give rise to strong feelings of freedom, power, and solidarity. Some people even get the sense, however brief, that they are connected with the wider universe as well as to their fellow humans. This is a deeply meaningful experience, which provides a glimpse into the connectedness and interdependence of all things. In the words of John, "There has to be a nice group feeling. You have to feel united with the people you drink with."

As mentioned, the effervescent recognition of unity is an end in itself and does not necessarily point beyond its own immediacy toward lasting friendships or any other future reward. This argument is central to the work of Maffesoli, who uses the expression of an "undirected being together" to emphasize that, in general, people come together for the sake of being together, period (1996, 81). Rational reasons may be advanced to explain why people assemble—political reasons, for example—but such reasons should not blind us to the affective drives and rewards that also, and always, play a major role when people get together. Maffesoli therefore warns against the tendency to interpret the human impulse to unite as a mere *project* (pro-jectum), meaning an activity that is aimed ahead of itself toward some well-defined goal in the future (1996, 16). The unitive drive is an anthropological constant that is fueled by and centered on the instant gratifications of people taking part in the same activities, the same movements, and the same states of mind.

However, it may happen that the connections made in nightlife lead to something durable. John and Simon met a woman in Sunny Beach who they were very fond of and saw as a potential friend. She had so much energy and had even asked if they wanted to go to a strip club.

"She got a lap dance!" yelled John, his eyes wide open with astonished admiration. "That's so f-cking classy. . . . She was the one who wanted it, and she asked if we wanted one too."

Simon laughed and added, "When she goes home and tells that story, nobody will ever believe that it happened."

John pointed out, however, that this woman was special. Most of the other people they had met were just "vacation pals. [. . .] You won't ever meet them once you are back home."

The bonds forged in nightlife are often fleeting, but this does not necessarily make them shallow, illusory, or meaningless, as some scholars would have it (see, e.g., Melechi 1993; Briggs 2013). Fleeting relationships have certain advantages over long-lasting ones. Most importantly, since they are not weighed down by future obligations, they facilitate an engagement with the pleasures at hand. Of course, fleeting contacts can sometimes be hollow, pointless, heartbreaking, and so forth. But they can also be liberating. To embrace the fleeting is to seize the moment and make the most of opportunities that are available in the here and now instead of cultivating something that may or may not provide joy or comfort in some uncertain future (Maffesoli 1985). Many also find it easier to engage in play when they are in an anonymous setting and surrounded by people they will never meet again. Indeed, as the performance researcher Alice O'Grady points out, "The party offers a play zone that protects its players from the outside world" (2012, 94). Here individuals may choose to adopt a "party persona" and behave in ways that would be difficult to get away with in other contexts. This allows the imagination to operate more freely and facilitates play and flirtation as well as risk taking and crime.

According to Durkheim, humans have a recurrent need to connect with the turbulent energies that come from being close to others. These energies can be just as powerful in an assembly of strangers as in an assembly of friends (see also Canetti 1978). Accordingly, Maffesoli argues that the fact of assembling—no matter why, where, when, and with whom—generally has the effect of raising the social temperature. It allows people to rub shoulders—"keeping warm together"—and temporarily set aside their personal problems and concerns (Maffesoli 1996b).[2] An expression of this in nightlife is the widespread practice of sharing. People buy rounds of drinks for their friends—and sometimes for strangers. They give away cigarettes for free. They pass around cannabis joints rather than smoke them alone. They ask someone to come join them when they go to the toilets to sniff cocaine. And they generously exchange compliments, hugs, and kisses. These practices are both causes and effects of unity among the revelers. They illustrate that in nightlife, group needs have precedence over personal needs. The collective "WE" is more important than the individual "I" (Maffesoli 1985).

Simon and John were eager to meet new people, especially female people who would like to have sex with them. They did not want sex with men but were otherwise open to various constellations: couple sex, group sex, oral sex, drunken sex, sober sex, sex in front of a camera, and much more. Sexual experiences and experimentation were at the very top of their list of priorities in Sunny Beach—and pretty much everywhere else. From a Durkheimian perspective, sexual intercourse in its various manifestations may be understood as an essentially effervescent mode of being (Collins 2004, 223–257; Mellor and Shilling 1997). Intercourse usually assembles very few people, typically two, but it nevertheless has the capacity of producing a form of effervescence: symbolically significant moments of intersubjective union, intensity, transgression, and revitalization. Sexual experiences tend to be so effervescently powerful not only from genital friction but also from the whole bodily proximity of the sexual partners, their coordinated actions, and the way that they almost inevitably come to focus on each other's movements, touch, breathing, and state of mind. This proximity and mutual awareness may trigger what Collins calls "rhythmic entrainment," meaning that the partners intensify their rhythmic movements and become caught up in each other's bodily rhythms (2004, 233). There is a synchronization of movements, including movements of the breath and, sometimes, synchronized advancement toward sexual climax. Collins writes that in heterosexual sex, the synchronization is "not necessarily perfect," in part because "female orgasms may go on longer or more repetitively and involve many more spasms than male ejaculation" (Collins 2004, 234). Collins observes, however, that even moderate levels of synchronization during intercourse may generate "considerable pleasure and solidarity" (2004, 234). And if the partners meet repeatedly to have sex, they may develop relatively stable sexual practices and a strong sense of moral obligation and solidarity (Mellor and Shilling 1997).

John and Simon did not go into much detail about their sexual practices, but they made it clear that sex sometimes involves little pleasure and commitment. As John put it, sex may be nothing more than the physical act of "letting off pressure," adding, "There is nothing in it." This type of sex is common in places like Sunny Beach, especially when it is performed under the influence of large doses of alcohol. Simon admitted that he once had to interrupt sex with a woman because he had to vomit, and I have heard several sex stories from others that involved one of the partners being so drunk that he or she fell asleep or had a blackout during the act. This type of very drunken sex may not induce much pleasure while being performed; it can even be traumatizing if one of the partners feels taken advantage of or abused. However, when there is mutual respect and consent, drunken sex is generally considered rewarding in the long run because of the symbolic value associated with having had many sexual partners and experiences (Pedersen, Tutenges, and Sandberg 2017). In many Western countries, young men—and, to a lesser extent, young women—may use stories of their sexual encounters to entertain friends and project themselves as being sexually successful and attractive. Here, the sexual intercourse does not primarily produce pleasure and solidarity between the sexual partners but rather between those who share stories about past acts (Collins 2004, 238).

Simon and John spent a lot of time, money, and effort trying to seduce women, but they found it depressingly difficult to reach their goal of "getting laid." This is the situation of countless male revelers around the world. As sociologist David Grazian points out, "It is statistically uncommon for men to successfully pick up women in bars and nightclubs" (2008, 140). So why bother searching for casual sex in nightlife venues? Why not focus on other platforms that give better chances, such as dating sites on the internet? Grazian explores these questions and finds that in nightlife, "males do not necessarily engage in girl hunting as a means of generating sexual relationships, even on a drunken short-term basis" (2008, 138). It may be that men portray their "girl hunting" as a pursuit of sex and nothing else. But Grazian convincingly argues that these missions also serve homosocial purposes by bringing together two or more men who collaborate in spotting attractive women. These friends typically encourage, assist, accompany, or watch as one of them performs his seductive moves toward the chosen "prey." Male-to-male bonding is key to this practice, as the huntsmen work together toward a common goal while boosting their sense of being real men on a manly mission. And as he makes his moves, the hunter can demonstrate and sharpen his seductive skills in the presence of a woman, perhaps under the lustful gazes of his male friends. Grazian therefore describes girl hunting as an "activity for which one's male peers serve as the intended audience for competitive games of sexual reputation and peer status, public displays of situational dominance and rule transgression, and in-group rituals of solidarity and loyalty" (2008, 138).

These observations illustrate that collective effervescence can be discriminatory—and sometimes viciously so—with a division between an in-group of fellows who nurture their own interests and an out-group of others who, whether they like it or not, serve as opponents, rivals, or mere playthings. The sense of solidarity may be high within the group but low or absent toward individuals deemed outside of the group. As Durkheim was well aware, collective effervescence does not only manifest itself as cosmic feelings of love toward everyone and everything; it sometimes involves a strong sense of in-group solidarity combined with fierce out-group hostility.

The practice of girl hunting, as described by Grazian, is an important reminder that effervescence is a volatile force. It can bring people together but also rip them apart. Another more extreme example is the violent effervescence caused by war. A war can lead to the most atrocious acts but can also inspire deeds of incredible bravery, as when a soldier dives on a grenade to save lives or runs into a rain of bullets to drag out a wounded comrade (Blake 1978).

Acts of self-sacrifice are also common among revelers. Examples are legion, but for now, I will only mention one: that of the *wingman*. In a military context, this term signifies a fighter pilot whose aircraft is positioned near a leading aircraft to engage in enemy fire if need be. As Grazian points out, the term has another sense in the context of nightlife, where it refers to "an accomplice who assists a designated leading man in meeting eligible single women, often at costs to his own ability to do the same" (Grazian 2007, 233). The wingman may, for instance, act rudely toward a woman in order to position the leading man as the good guy who steps up to defend her. The wingman hereby sacrifices his own reputation in an effort to secure the sexual success of his friend.

Though effervescence is conducive to selflessness, selflessness is not always a good thing. Simon and John always hunted for women together or with trusted friends, never alone. Yet they rarely employed advanced wingman tactics, such as those featured in Grazian's work. Rather, they preferred the simpler, well-established model of going to a place frequented by women, getting drunk, and hoping for the best. This model paid off one night—sort of. Simon managed to seduce a Swedish woman, but they "only" got to the stage of kissing. John was there and described what happened: "Nothing came out of it because we suddenly staggered on to the next bar. [Simon and the woman] began making out right there in the middle of the bar, and then I don't know what the hell we were thinking, but we left. So nothing came out of it."

"It went down the drain," Simon confirmed.

John and Simon blamed themselves and their drinking for having abandoned a woman who appeared genuinely interested in more than just kissing. One of them was finally close to having sex, and then drunken stupidity made them walk away. That is how they reasoned. Without alcohol, they were incapable of approaching women, but too much alcohol made them "dumb" and "disgusting."

However, there are alternative explanations for the seemingly paradoxical procedure of collaborating in chatting up and seducing a woman and then collaborating in walking away from the woman soon after she has been seduced. One explanation is that Simon was so drunk that his sexual desire and potency were diminished—or gone altogether. He derived pleasure from the masculine game of drinking and hunting for women, but perhaps he had reached a stage of drunkenness that would hinder him from having pleasurable sex with the allegedly very attractive Swedish woman.[3] Instead of attempting to have sex with her, he returned to John and their game of drinking and hunting for women. Another possible explanation is that Simon and John preferred to stick together and cultivate their male-to-male bond rather than split up so that one of them could have a drunken one-night stand with a woman. They placed enormous value on casual sex but even higher value on their friendship. And by turning his back to a willing woman, Simon rendered proof of his loyalty and love: he would give up almost anything, even sex, before he would give up his friend.

BAND OF SISTERS

I met Sarah, Tine, Natasha, Signe, and Denice at a pool party in Sunny Beach. There were several hundred revelers, but these five women stood out because of the many drunken stunts they performed and the inflated Lolita doll they carried around all night. I asked them for an interview, and we agreed to meet at their hotel the day after.

I found them in their hotel room, with the Lolita doll sitting in the sun on the balcony and almost looking more alive than the rest of the group. We all went outside by the pool to talk.

The doll was named "Linda," they said, and when I asked about her age, Sarah assured me that "she is old enough."

"We wanted to win this competition on who had the best rubber [pool] toy," Tine explained, "and we thought that we would need the world's coolest rubber toy, and we were walking by a sex shop and figure that, 'Hey, we can win this thing with a Lolita doll.' So we dressed her up, put her in some nice underwear and a T-shirt. Because we found the clothes she was wearing a bit too daring."

"Was this before the pool party?" I asked.

"Yes it was. It was—" Sarah began.

Tine cut in: "It was actually in the afternoon, so we brought her out to eat, and we got free champagne, and she got her own chair and plate and everything."

They won the rubber pool toy competition.

After this introduction to Linda, I asked some standard questions from my interview guide: "Could you explain what kind of place this is? What kind of vacation is it?"

"I would say that it's about partying and having fun with your friends," Sarah said.

Denice added, "Perhaps also getting to know other people."

But Sarah was not so sure. "Yeah, well, but not getting to know people and later making contact with them and stuff," she said. She continued with a question to me: "But this is a binge vacation, if that's what you're getting at? I mean that [binge drinking] is what it's all about, and all the parties here are built around that."

"But also just being with your friends," Nathalie said. "We get to know each other in a whole new way. . . . We see sides of each other that we didn't know before. . . . Because we are, like, together round the clock for an entire week. You're never alone."

"Also, we have to protect each other," Denice confirmed. "You have a responsibility. At home, we have our parents and all that, but here we only have each other."

The five of them had been friends for most of their approximately eighteen-year lives. However, they had never been on a "binge vacation" before. They had been drunk together on numerous occasions, but not for as long as an entire week. They had seen one another naked, but not on stage during a beach party.

"Here in Sunny Beach, you do all kinds of crazy stunts that you would never do at home," Denice explained.

One of the best stunts they had performed, she recounted, took place at a karaoke night organized by their tour operator.

"We had put on dresses, each in a different color . . . and we thought, 'Ah, why not do a song?' and, you know, Tine was in a yellow dress and yellow shoes and yellow all over and Nathalie was completely in turquoise. So we get up on a table and sing 'See My Dress' [a children's song] in front of everybody. We also won that contest."

Nathalie added, "The guides have also told us many times that they think we're cool. We're just game for anything. . . . So you could say that we want a bit of attention . . . at least come up with one funny idea per day."

"That's right. We make our own fun," Denice confirmed.

The five friends had lots of fun talking about their stunts—both done and yet to be done—and they perpetually threw themselves into new challenging situations, which sometimes put their health and reputations at stake. When Nathalie performed one of her strip shows in a bar, there were probably some in the crowd who thought badly about her.

"I mean, sure there were these two hundred people, but the only ones I will ever meet again are these girls who are sitting right here," she reasoned.

I had seen one of Nathalie's strip shows. She was battling with a man over who dared to throw off most clothes. She won, as always. I interpreted her expression during the show as one of determination and defiance—or perhaps it was disdain. She showed no sign of amusement whatsoever. I should have asked about that experience during the interview, but I did not. So I am not sure what to make of it.

I did ask, however, whether they were concerned about all the photos and videos that were being recorded whenever they performed their stunts.

Nathalie answered, "I don't give it any thought."

Denice said that, since they were in Sunny Beach, she did not mind much either. It was different than being at home, where pictures and videos easily "start circulating" and people get "shocked" and gossip. This had already happened to them once, she said. They shot a video of themselves as they were having fun in a swimming pool, drunk and almost naked.

"Somebody got a hold of that video and sent it out to everybody," she recalled. "That wasn't cool."

Studies from many parts of the world show that, compared with men, women risk greater harm to their reputations when experimenting publicly with their sexuality, gendered behaviors, or altered states of consciousness (Armstrong et al. 2014; Bogle 2008). Writing about the Norwegian context, which is very similar to the Danish context, Eivind Grip Fjær and colleagues observe, "Even within modern 'hookup cultures,' heterosexual men are expected to be sexually active while women who are equally active risk stigmatization through 'bad reputations' and 'slut-shaming'" (Fjær, Pedersen, and Sandberg 2015, 961).

The five friends knew that their behavior in Sunny Beach could damage their reputations, but they emphasized that these were minor risks and that they would stand up for one another if anyone dared to question their behavior. They systematically violated traditional codes of gender and sexuality—sometimes for fun, sometimes simply because they could, and sometimes perhaps to express and exhibit their newly won autonomy as young adults. In Sunny Beach, they said, everybody was acting crazy anyway, so why hold back? They were primarily concerned with their emotional bonds of friendship, not with what outsiders might think of them.

Few things can unite people more powerfully than acts of collective transgression. When individuals join forces to transgress boundaries—whether boundaries of etiquette, morality, law, or religion—they tend to become acutely aware of one another and what they are doing as a group. There is, almost by necessity, a high level of mutual attention, a coordination of actions, and a fusion of individual wills. The senses are sharpened by the social or physical risks posed by the transgression, and the transgressors may become so caught up by the collective action that they set aside their own needs to focus completely on those of the group. Afterward, when the transgression has been accomplished, the group will have an exciting experience that they can think back on and relate to others, something that may help define them as a group and further solidify their group unity. Probably no one has expressed this mechanism more famously and forcefully than Shakespeare. As Shakespeare's Henry V declares to his men on the day before a grand battle,

> From this day to the ending of the world,
> But we in it shall be remembered—
> We few, we happy few, we band of brothers;
> For he to-day that sheds his blood with me
> Shall be my brother; be he ne'er so vile,

This day shall gentle his condition;
And gentlemen in England now-a-bed
Shall think themselves accurst they were not here;
And hold their manhoods cheap while any speaks
That fought with us. (2014, 508)

The five women were not engaged in the transgression of war, but they were in a battle nonetheless. Their adversaries were oppressive social forces, such as conventions, stereotypes, and gendered expectations. They were not a band of brothers but a band of sisters. Their common battle consolidated their group unity. They did not shed blood together on the battlefield but rather lots of sweat, tears, vomit, and clothing. The women said that they would always remember their vacation and all the crazy things they had been through together. They emphasized, however, that the reason behind their stunts was not to boast and build a reputation. Their war stories from Sunny Beach were first and foremost theirs to keep and not designed for others to hear.

"We just want to have fun without anyone interfering or criticizing us," Nathalie explained. "What happens here is between us, between close friends. . . . And right from the beginning we agreed: what happens in Bulgaria, stays in Bulgaria. It's best if people back home don't know what we have been doing here."

"There is another kind of moral down here," Signe added.

"For sure," Nathalie confirmed.

"Can you tell me more about that moral?" I asked.

Signe replied, "Here it is less acceptable to abstain from drinking. When I see someone who doesn't want to party, I kind of think that they are boring."

"People should go out and have fun while they can," someone chimed in.

"People are generally more tolerant down here, more open," another voice added.

The women were indeed tolerant when it came to wild behavior, but not so when it came to restraint and self-discipline. Their tolerance did not, for example, extend to the practices of staying sober, saving money, doing sports, eating healthy food, reading books, and going early to bed. They were fervently in favor of excess—in the context of Sunny Beach, that is. At home, they were allegedly much more moderate and "boring."

Tine explained that they drew inspiration from a group of their male friends who had visited the resort earlier that summer. Back in Denmark, the men had told all sorts of crazy stories about what they had done at the resort.

"They were here just two weeks before us," she said. "We want to do it better than them."

"We have something to live up to," Nathalie said.

"You wanted to beat them? What did they do?" I asked.

"They decided to drag all the furniture out of their hotel room and dump it into the swimming pool. They were just constantly drunk," Nathalie recalled. Then she asked the group, "What else did they do?"

Everyone became animated and spoke fast (I am not sure who said what):

"I don't know. A lot of crazy shit. They wouldn't even tell us."

"They shouldn't come and tell us that we can't party!"

"Yeah, that's it. The guides and bartenders all remember those boys."

"It's also because [the boys] told us before we came, 'Bah, you can't cope' and like, 'It's too wild for you.' So I thought, 'Hell, I'll show you that we can do this.'"

These comments made me ask about the differences between male and female partygoers.

"I can't cope with as much [alcohol as men], let me put it like that," Tine said. "Also, [men], how to put it, they exaggerate more, right?"

"Yeah, but still," Nathalie objected. "All those times a boy has challenged me to a drinking contest. . . . I have beaten them all. They are not that tough."

Historically speaking, men used to be the "intoxicated gender" (Pedersen 2006, 81–84). They traditionally began using alcohol and illegal drugs at an earlier age than women and consumed larger quantities of both. They were the big smokers of tobacco, and they had a near monopoly on public displays of intoxication. These gender differences are no longer as accentuated as they used to be, especially when it comes to alcohol consumption. The last half-century has seen a gradual decrease in, but not complete disappearance of, the differences between young men and women.

The level and frequency of drinking among young men and young women have thus converged in recent times, but their intoxicated performances less so. Generally speaking, I would say that the intoxicated performances of women are comparatively more eroticized, whereas those of men are comparatively more risk oriented. For example, I have seen more women than men engage in erotic bar-top dancing, pole dancing, strip teases, seducing drinks out of strangers, and playful kissing with friends. On the other hand, I have seen more men than women engage in violent confrontations, vandalism, stealing, drunken driving, paying for sex, drug use, and drug dealing. Importantly, these observations should not be read as support of the old-fashioned understanding of gender as biologically determined and locked into the familiar binaries: women and men, passive and active, oppressed and oppressor, risk averse and risk prone, and so forth. Gender is a flexible, cultural construct, and in nightlife environments, people are expected to exhibit and experiment with their gender roles. This may involve adopting and exaggerating various stereotypical roles, like the "macho" man and the "slutty" woman. Part of the reason that such stereotypes persist is because they are so simple, striking, and widely known. This makes them easily imitated and conformed to (Hall 1997). Moreover, men from an early age are taught to be independent and navigate risks, whereas the socialization of women tends to place more emphasis on caretaking and looks.[4]

Denice brought up an episode that illustrates another gender difference.

"There was one night where we wanted to go back home together, but two of us wanted to go to this place and eat," she recalled. "You goddamn can't do anything, even when you walk around [with] two people. If you meet some locals or something. Not that something really bad happened. We weren't like raped or anything, but still. People come over and grope you and push you and yell and stuff."

"You know, we were just walking on our own," Tine continued. "It was not some back alley or something, but quite dark. Then come these three Bulgarian men and stand there and touch us and say 'Do you wanna f-ck?' and like that. So we hurry on. I wouldn't say they were, like, offensive. They didn't follow us. But they were really, like, pushed her and stuff."

Across the world, female revelers are at greater risk of being sexually harassed than male revelers (Fileborn 2016). Indeed, this problem is so pervasive that some young women take it for granted that going out involves unwanted sexual attention and abuse (Tutenges, Sandberg, and Pedersen 2020). Note that Tine said that the Bulgarian men were not offensive, even though they had committed the clear-cut crimes of pushing and sexually touching the women without permission. Tine and her friends downplayed the whole incident, perhaps because they were used to this kind of offense, were confused by it, or were unaware that it represented a crime. They insisted that they were having a good time, that nothing had gone wrong, and that they were safe from harm—as long as they kept together.[5]

As if to demonstrate how much fun they were having, Nathalie suddenly leaped onto an air mattress in the pool and managed to stand upright for a brief moment before she splashed into the water. That was part of her daily routine in Sunny Beach: trying to find her balance on the wobbly air mattress.

"You have to give her that. She has really sacrificed herself for the team," Denice commented. I never asked what Denice meant by this—another blunder in my interview—but I suppose she employed the expression "sacrifice" because Nathalie's performances involved giving something of herself to her friends as well as other spectators. She risked her neck and personal reputation while elevating her group of friends by drawing attention to it. She also delivered entertaining performances for everyone to enjoy and remember. What she did was not simply for her own personal kicks.

I asked them how they got the ideas for their stunts, and Denice swiftly replied, "hangover humor." They explained that when they woke up, it usually took several hours before they really got out of bed. Perhaps they would go to the pool and have one beer to fight the hangover symptoms, but otherwise, they would just lie down, moan, talk, and as Tine put it, "have these far-out laughing fits over weird things." They also planned the upcoming night, sometimes spending several hours discussing what to wear and how to create some new, spectacular scene. They thus gave advice and (im)moral support to one another so that they, individually and as a group, could push still farther down the road of excess. When night fell and one of them performed a stunt, the others would always applaud. No criticism would come from the group, only approval, and none of them had done anything they regretted—or so they said.

I think that the performances of Nathalie and her friends are best understood as a collective form of behavior. They would not have taken place were it not for the group, and they had the effect of strengthening the group's cohesion. Moreover, when one person in the group performed a solo stunt, it was, in a sense, done on behalf of the entire group. Both the individual performer and group were praised for the effort by other tourists and tour guides, and I suspect that it was the performer who derived least (immediate) pleasure from it. This is a general trend among the people I have studied in Sunny Beach and elsewhere. They prefer to venture down the road of excess together with friends. Their exploits are collective; they are performed with, for, and because of the group.

CHAPTER 4

INTENSITY

Durkheim argues that something fundamentally destabilizing can happen when people come together for celebration. Collective presence stimulates intersubjective exchanges, and this can sometimes create a whirlwind of emotions that transports people beyond self-centered existence into states of collective effervescence. He writes, "In the midst of an assembly that becomes worked up, we become capable of feelings and conduct of which we are incapable when left to our individual resources. When it is dissolved and we are again on our own, we fall back to our ordinary level and can then take the full measure of how far above ourselves we were" (Durkheim 1995, 211–212).

There are varying degrees of intensity in different nightlife settings. Consider the quiet buzz of a small pub, the animated atmosphere of a nightclub, and the explosion of energy when superstars go onstage at a densely packed music festival. The varying intensity is produced by a complex combination of human and nonhuman factors, including smells, temperature, lighting, music, decor, performative practices, substance use, and most importantly, crowd dynamics (Duff 2008).

Most people prefer venues that facilitate medium- to high-intensity experiences—experiences that involve a strong emotional involvement in the perception of or participation in events. They therefore shun empty venues because these are "dead" and "bring you down." What they want is to indulge in effervescence of one type or another. These nightlife aspirations need to be seen in relation to people's everyday lives. Many spend their weekdays working for money or studying for an education. They follow strict professional and academic schedules, and their bodies and minds are regimented to move through a specific, controlled set of tasks. Their immediate desires have to be put on hold. High-intensity experiences are rare. Thus, not unlike the Aborigines Durkheim writes about, many people today alternate between periods focused on accumulation and restraint and periods where the focus is on expenditure and abandon. This is the cultural lifestyle of "work hard, play hard," where "play hard," for many, signifies celebrating with friends and enjoying the intensity of group intoxication.

IN SEARCH OF INTENSITY

Moments of high intensity do not come easily, however. They can be few and far between, even in affectively charged places such as nightlife resorts. This was one of the themes I explored together with Thomas, who lived next door to me during my first days in Sunny Beach, Bulgaria. He was a tall, blond eighteen-year-old with radiant eyes who described himself as "one of the party people." He loved to party and went by the motto "always bottoms up," suggesting that as soon as someone put a drink in front of him, he would inevitably empty it. Sunny Beach was paradise, he said, full of "party people" like himself and bursting with an abundance of "super cheap" counterfeits of the best brands of clothes, belts, sunglasses, and all else one could wish for. However, he had traveled to Sunny Beach with Karen, a woman who he hardly knew, and he was frustrated not to have any of his friends to go out with.

Karen's parents owned a vacation apartment in Sunny Beach, and on a whim, she had asked if he would come join her for a short trip to the resort. She was also eighteen years old, just as blonde and good looking as Thomas, and shared his interests in partying and shopping. When I first saw them, I thought of Barbie and Ken. They were the kind of people who make heads turn and jaws drop. However, their relationship was far from romantic. They actually found it difficult to get along, and they spent less and less time together as their vacation progressed, which meant that Thomas often sought my company.

On the first night of their stay, I was invited to their little preparty in an apartment belonging to Finn, a guy in his thirties who worked in Bulgaria as a real estate agent for low-cost vacation apartments. Finn had done business with Karen's dad and had promised to look after her during her stay.

I climbed the stairs to Finn's place at 10 p.m. and found him together with Karen and Thomas sitting in front of the television with a row of colorful bottles on the TV table. I opted for rum and Coke, and Finn generously poured me a big glass while remarking that the rum was of excellent quality, unlike what the Bulgarians and average tourists drink. The TV was tuned into a music channel featuring pop songs, but Finn said we needed something more spicy and switched to a channel showing hardcore porn. Thomas commented on the action on the screen, but Karen looked to the side with an uncomfortable smile. Finn grinned and switched back to the music channel. He continued to tease Karen by asking about an episode earlier in the day when she had accidentally walked into the wrong apartment and yelled in alarm, "Hey! Somebody has been in here!" Finn laughed and called her "Blondie."

Thomas turned the conversation to drugs, sounding like a real expert—I later found out that he had never used any. He said that the professional dancers outside the strip club across the street were all on speed, cocaine, or something else. They danced and danced with no sign of exhaustion. Certainly they had something in their noses, Finn replied, and took on a shrilly woman's voice: "Excuse me, could I have some more of the Colombian washing powder worth a million bucks?"

Karen was texting on her cell phone with her father, who wanted to know if everything was OK. Finn suggested that she write, "Congratulations! You are now a granddad and I am a single mother."

"Hey! I could also text him to ask if he has heard anything from you lately," he joked. "Ha-ha. No. That would be cruel. All we need to do is find a big, nice, hairy Bulgarian to look after you."

We all laughed robotically.

"But I tell you what, sex is highly overrated," he continued. "I mean, it's just some movements in sticky fluids."

And so the conversations went for a couple of hours, with Finn cracking jokes, telling stories, and teasing Karen while positioning himself as a man with lots of money and life experience. He kept turning back to his role as Karen's protector, reminding her of the many dangers in Sunny Beach and how to avoid them. She should not take a taxi without him, he said. She should never walk around alone. She should not go to the beach after dark. She should stay away from drugs. And so on.

I have often wondered why we silently accepted Finn's patronizing attitude. The situation was unpleasant, at least for me, yet I sat through it without objecting. Part of the problem was that Finn was hosting the party and gave us free drinks. I was on the receiving end of the relationship. To criticize him would have been unusual and rude, and it would have impeded the interactional flow of the situation. The whole point of preparties, which also go under the name of "warm-up sessions," is to have fun, get drunk, and raise the level of effervescence before going out. Who was I to criticize the host and puncture the mood? I already felt that my presence was putting a damper on the intensity of our interactions because I was low on energy, listened more than talked, and drank more slowly than the others. So I just sat there and tried to keep up appearances instead of breaking the ritual protocol by confronting the host. This was the easy path to follow, of course, because as Collins explains, all sorts of unforeseen trouble may arise when we step outside the routine rituals that all social life is based on (2004, 20).

What further complicated the situation was that Finn was actually trying hard to cheer us up and make us laugh. I really think he meant us well, and his manners were not out of the ordinary. Rather, he drew on a very common, rough style of speech, which playfully uses puns, wordplay, and teasing to exhibit situational dominance and verbal skill while having a laugh. The cultural critic Antony Easthope calls this style of speech "banter," which is practiced mainly, but not exclusively, between men. He writes, "Outwardly, banter is aggressive, a form in which the masculine ego asserts itself. Inwardly, however, banter depends on a close, intimate and personal understanding of the person who is the butt of the attack. It thus works as a way of affirming the bond between men while appearing to deny it" (Easthope 1992, 88). Paradoxically, therefore, bantering can be a way to acknowledge and show affection toward another person. It can be a friendly gesture masked as hostility, which has the effect of creating a concentrated mood of transgressive intimacy. Those involved creatively and wittily exchange insults and thereby test each other's limits and capacity to endure humiliation (Gardaphé 2014). In so doing, they also test whether their friendship ties are strong enough to withstand the stings of verbal combat. When bantering works well, it can really intensify the interaction in a group by making the group members focus on the same thing—namely, the fierce words and body language of the banterers. However, Finn was nearly twice as old as Karen, and his way of bantering did not give her much of a chance to answer back. She was pushed into the role of the "good girl" who is demure, polite, and accommodating (Armstrong et al. 2014). That night, Finn's banter was creating divisions rather than breaking them down, and Thomas and I supported his show with our presence and laughter.

Nearly all the topics discussed at Finn's place were part of what Bataille (1979) calls the "heterogeneous," meaning phenomena that have an aura of excess and taboo. We talked about pornography, illegal drugs, drinking, and erotic dancers—not about our studies, workday lives, or future careers. This is typical of preparty situations, where the focus is on intensifying the interactions and facilitating the transition away from an ordinary state of consciousness and toward states of effervescence. To talk about the heterogeneous facilitates this transition because it is antithetical to mundane life—which, to a large extent, is centered on the principles of propriety and productivity. As Bataille puts it, "Heterogeneous reality is that of a force or shock. It presents itself as a charge" (1979, 70). The heterogeneous is thus disturbing and titillating and can quickly stir the emotions of a person or a group.

Of course, it sometimes happens that participants at a preparty bring up mundane, workaday themes, which have no force or shock effect. However, such themes are usually only discussed briefly and early in the evening, when the participants are still entangled with their ordinary consciousness. Later in the evening, such themes tend to be avoided completely—or if they are brought up, it is usually with an air of humor, confession, or rebellion. For instance, at Finn's place, we briefly talked about the investment in Bulgarian apartments, but this talk quickly switched to the issues of having money and the fun of spending it in a poor country like Bulgaria, where "the booze is dirt cheap," as Thomas put it. Similarly, I was asked about my research project and did talk about it, but only for a couple of minutes and without going into details about my methods, theory, or life as a researcher. It would have been culturally inappropriate of me to speak elaborately about my project. That would most certainly have deintensified our interactions and brought our awareness back to the realm of productivity and propriety. As observed by theologian Harvey Cox, "Celebration is . . . a time when we are not working, planning, or recording. Hence the wise custom that outlaws talking business at parties. People who exploit festivals for purposes other than festivity endanger the festive air" (1969, 46). A nightlife ethnographer, therefore, must tread carefully so as not to disrupt or destroy the phenomena that are being researched.[1]

In spite of our efforts, we did not succeed in building up the mood at Finn's place. The preparty had all the characteristics of a failed ritual, as described by Collins. Failed rituals are marked by "a low level of collective effervescence, the lack of momentary buzz, no shared entrainment at all or disappointingly little . . . either a flat feeling unaffected by the ritual, or worse yet, a sense of drag, the feeling of boredom and constraint, even depression, interaction fatigue, a desire to escape" (2004, 51).

Karen said that it was time for us to go, but Finn was getting tired.

"Come on," she said, "just drink some more."

"Bottoms up," said Thomas, and emptied a large glass of rum.

Finn and I also emptied our glasses, but Karen pushed away hers and said it tasted awful. We then walked a few hundred yards to a nightclub called Orange. The entrance area was teeming with Swedish teenagers who were in a state of very drunken effervescence. Several bouncers were standing around and staring at the crowd. Some bouncers are smiling, polite, and welcoming. Not this crew. Their eyes were dead cold. As we stood waiting in the line, I was wondering whether I would actually prefer to take a beating from one of the Swedish teenagers than to receive help from these bouncers. A woman lurched past and fell headlong, losing one of her high-heeled shoes. A man tried repeatedly to make her stand up, but her legs were like jelly. Another woman was sitting by herself at the edge of the crowd, head between her knees and throwing up, adding to the nauseating atmosphere of the whole scene. I felt apprehensive and repulsed, probably because of the drunken effervescence I was witnessing combined with the aftereffects of the failed warm-up session we had just been through. Failed rituals leave memory traces in the body that can be long lasting and difficult to get rid of.

I was told that the crowd of Swedes had arrived at the club in multiple buses earlier in the night. They had apparently come from an outdoor foam party featuring foam canons and several feet of bubbles on the dance floor, allowing the revelers to dance in their swimwear and to move without restraint under the anonymity of the froth. No wonder that the crowd was so sunburned and chaotic. They had been partying for most of the day and some of them were experiencing a sort of meltdown from the prolonged intensity. Indeed, more is not always better, even when it comes to partying. Revelers, too, need pauses: moments away from the crowd in which to digest their experiences, engage in low-intensity interactions, and perhaps regain a bit of mental and physical balance before going back to the destabilizing intensity of the crowd.

We finally got inside the nightclub. Professional female dancers were performing on elevated platforms to fast-paced electronic dance music. Two of them danced erotically together, but the others danced alone and allowed no one to get close to them. I estimated the professional dancers to be around twenty years old. The combination of smoke, darkness, and the sweeping laser lights made my eyes water. A group of women danced on one of the bar tops, but these were definitely not professionals. They were almost crying with laughter and had difficulty keeping their balance.

Karen was out on the dance floor making new friends. Thomas suggested that I buy drinks since I had an income. I ordered two White Russians. He wanted to know more details about my project and quickly concluded that I had the best job in the world.

"Do you have a notebook?" He took it and wrote in big letters, "THOMAS IS EXTREMELY HORNY."

Finn saw this and grabbed the book to show it to some Swedish women. Somebody tore out the page with Thomas's message and pinned it to his chest. The rest of the clubbers also had messages on them in the form of little stickers. Those with a green sticker were interested in hooking up. Those with a yellow sticker were semi-interested. And those with a red sticker were not on the market.

Thomas downed his drink and declared, "If you want to interview someone who drinks a lot, then just talk with me."

Karen came over to us and said that a Bulgarian man had just kissed her all over. She laughed and ran back to the dance floor. Thomas and I stayed at the bar. I took notes as we talked and had a warm feeling of excitement from all the nice data spreading on my notepad. However, the excitement appeared to be on my side only. Thomas was looking with yearning at the dance floor and, at one point, said that he missed his friends. It was easy to understand why. We did not have the same plans for the night and, in a sense, did not focus on the same activity. I was doing research while he was trying to party. As a result, we did not experience what Collins calls "feedback intensification," which is an arousing interactional process between two or more persons who emotionally feed off each other and synchronize their behaviors (2004, 48). Thomas and I were inter-acting at cross purposes, and the effervescence between us was low.

After a few hours, we all went outside. There was a strip club on the first floor, just below Orange. Finn suggested we should all go in there, but Karen objected. She preferred to go dancing. Finn was not happy about this and started patron-izing her again. Thomas suddenly and abruptly turned on his heels and marched into the strip club. I suggested that I could walk Karen home later, if she wanted to stay and dance. She seemed happy with this plan, but Finn went on and on about her safety and said that he felt responsible for her. The discussion was turning into a quarrel, and I gave up on getting their attention.

I went after Thomas and got in without paying a fee. The music and general atmosphere were remarkably subdued. Thomas sat at a table and spoke with two Turkish men in their thirties or forties. A waiter was standing at their table, try-ing to get Thomas's attention and demanding that he place an order. But Thomas would hear nothing of it and waved his hand with an annoyed gesture. The waiter walked off and solemnly talked with some people behind the bar. He came back to repeat his demand, but Thomas did not change his mind. They started arguing. Other guests looked in our direction. I pulled Thomas up to his feet and shoved him in front of me toward the exit.

"There is mafia behind this," he pronounced loudly. "I swear, there is mafia behind this."

I kept pushing and shushing, and just as we reached the exit, two women in biki-nis materialized in front of us, smiling at us invitingly. We stopped wrestling and walked past them in silence.

Outside we found Karen in tears and Finn still rambling on about her safety and saying that he felt obliged to walk her home immediately. Thomas mumbled words to Karen, perhaps trying to console her. A few meters away, a group of men vented their frustrations on a punching bag machine. They fed money into it and took turns throwing punches. I felt like joining them and concluded it was time for me to go home. Thomas raised his voice and said that he would go and get us all a round of beers, as if that would sort things out. I yelled a "goodnight" at his back, as he pushed his way toward the nightclub.

I woke up at 9:00 the next morning, my mind swarming with thoughts and my ears hissing like leaking steam pipes. I gave up on falling asleep again and instead made breakfast and went out on the balcony to eat and write up field notes. At half-past one, I headed out for lunch and met Thomas by the pool. I asked if he was hungry. He indicated that he had just finished his breakfast, pointing at two empty bags of chips on the ground. We went to the beach and walked down the esplanade. A smell of burned meat was in the air. It came from the restaurants, some of which displayed big grills with whole pigs on spear-like skewers that turned round and round over a fire. The pigs seemed so naked, with no hair and the skin greasy and brown.

"This is goddamn awesome," Thomas exclaimed and spread his arm as if gesturing to all of Sunny Beach.

We walked by a booth with sunglasses, sex toys, and crossbows on sale. He bought a pair of fake Gucci sunglasses and said that his plan was to get a job as a tourist guide so he could spend entire summers in places like this. Later, he wanted to become a police officer, but he was in no hurry. First, he wanted to live life to the fullest. Sudden screaming interrupted us. It came from above. Two persons were being dragged in a parachute after a speedboat that zigzagged its way through the bathers. The parachute plopped into the water, and sea gulls broke out in laughter from all around. I thought of journalist Hunter S. Thompson and his description of Las Vegas as a place so twisted that it is comparable to the experience of psychedelic drugs (2005).

One of the appeals of tourist destinations like Las Vegas and Sunny Beach is their twistedness. These are places that constantly confront visitors with the heterogeneous, which typically comes in the form of intoxication, nakedness, madness, violence, and gluttony. This overload of heterogeneity puts constant pressure on cultural assumptions about life and humanity, and it may create a sense of being in a parallel world governed by its own obscure logic. In Sunny Beach, heterogeneous is the norm, even during a lazy midday stroll. You do not have to actively seek it out; it will come to you, imposing itself and confusing the lines between right and wrong, real and surreal. Nightlife resorts provide ready-made heterogeneity. Some hate it; others love it.

Consumer culture researcher Russell W. Belk writes that Las Vegas is "instructing us through its farcical architecture and spectacles to adopt a playful mood of irreverent disregard for our normal behaviors and sensibilities" (2000, 111). This playful mood is good for business because it increases the willingness to gamble and consume, but it also serves more honorable purposes: "The childishness and playful spirit that can be found among tourists to the fantasy worlds of Las Vegas is the same frame of mind that nourishes imagination, hope, and unapologetic fun. We need play . . . and not just as release, ritual, refreshing re-creation, or rule-governed activity. We need play because it is a joyful, self-transcendent part of life. Las Vegas is not the only possible play venue, but it is largely elitist and ethnocentric to condemn it in favor of 'higher' forms of play in music, literature, poetry, art, or other personal favorites" (2000, 118).

Thomas said that he liked Sunny Beach because it was "cheap," "crazy," and "far-out." He expected that, with age, his life would become ever more routinized and predictable. He would limit himself to one sexual partner (his future wife), one job (as a police officer), and mainly stay in one part of the world (his hometown). There would be little room for traveling and adventures, which is why he so urgently wanted to "party hard," "live life to the max," and come back to Sunny Beach. Tonight, Thomas had hesitantly agreed to go with Karen and Finn to a nearby town, Bourgas. They had rented a room, and he was worried that the trip would involve sightseeing.

"I'm not into all that local stuff," he said. "I like Orange better."

The next evening, I met Karen by the pool. She said that she had been quite drunk the other night at Orange and that, after I left, she had asked a bouncer to hold her purse, cell phone, and camera in order to dance more freely. However, she forgot about her things and went home without them. Now she would never see them again. She smiled and shook her head, which I interpreted as an indication that she disapproved of her own drunken forgetfulness but was not deeply distressed about the loss. We agreed to meet later so that I could interview her and afterward go out to eat.

Thomas joined us for the interview. We went outside to sit on my balcony, and he said again how much he liked Sunny Beach because there were so many young people who all wanted to party to the max. However, he did not like the Playboy strip club.

"It was kind of corrupt," he said, noting that it advertised free entrance. "But once you get inside, there comes some kind of bartender flying over even before you get a chance to sit down, and [the bartender says], 'Buy stuff or go!'"

Thomas concluded that the strip club "just wants to make money and nothing else." He had never before been to a strip club, but during these vacations, he was set on seeing lots of different places and trying lots of new things. Karen sometimes nodded and smiled at my questions, but otherwise, she just sat with her hands in her lap, looking out from the balcony or down at her hands. When she spoke, it was in monosyllables. I thought it might be the interview situation that was making her feel uncomfortable, so I turned off the audio recorder after fifteen minutes.

The three of us went to have dinner at a restaurant called Mamacita. Karen and Finn ordered nachos and beer, nothing else. This was the kind of diet they lived on throughout their vacation. I said I was amazed that they were able to survive, to which Thomas replied that after a recent earthquake in Turkey, "a woman was buried alive. She laid in there fourteen days but survived by licking up dew."

"Good, though, that you are not here for fourteen days," I said.

He assured me that he could survive in Sunny Beach for a very long time because "it rains a lot here." We continued for a while with this kind of nonsense conversation, but Karen was not taking part in it. I tried to change the topic. What were her plans for the rest of the summer? Had she made friends in Sunny Beach? My hackneyed questions did nothing to change her mood. She politely answered but looked as if she would rather be anywhere else than here with us. Whenever Thomas addressed her, she frowned and her replies were dismissive.

Thomas grabbed my notebook and wrote, "Karen is bored."

Karen finally said that she would go meet a Bulgarian friend called Stefan. I later met Stefan and saw them together. It was clear why she would rather be with him—their interactions sparkled with compassionate effervescence. He talked with her and listened to her. They laughed together, and their body language was mutually supportive. There was, in other words, lots of feedback intensification between them. It was completely different when Karen was in the company of Finn, Thomas, and me. With us, there were no rhythmic exchanges of words, sounds, smiles, and gestures, which are the hallmark of uplifting interactions. Especially at Finn's place, Karen had not been given much opportunity to express herself. She was talked to, rather than with, and she was exposed to sexist humor, pornography, and offensive remarks that left her objectified, belittled, and silenced. Later, at the nightclub, she was asked to go to a strip club and after declining was nagged that it would be safest for her to go home.

What might further have complicated Karen's position was that Sunny Beach, like so many other nightlife scenes around the world, predominantly caters to heterosexual men and their presumed desires. It is almost exclusively young women who act as go-go dancers, strippers, lap dancers, and street prostitutes. The alcohol advertisements and billboards abound with seminude women. Even some of the family restaurants have female staff in skimpy outfits who perform erotic dance shows and staged flirtation with the male customers. Young women are thus widely presented as mere sources of entertainment and sexual satisfaction.[2]

However, as shown by Qian Hui Tan (2013) in her study of nightclubbing in Singapore, the heteropatriarchal organization of nightlife may be strategically exploited or subverted by women. Some women take pleasure in mimicking and mocking the blatant stereotypes that circulate in nightlife, while others enjoy that the female body is being so widely worshiped through imagery and masculinist rituals such as nightclubs' "Ladies' Night" promotions, during which "'appropriate-looking girls' gain complimentary entry because they are perceived as already paying with their presence" (Tan 2013, 718). Some women may find it satisfying to be watched and pursued, and they may enjoy the game of attracting, dodging, and refusing sexual attention. Tan therefore concludes,

> The club need not always be a masculine space that empowers only men, as Ladies' Night can be (re)read as a celebration of femininity—a femininity recognized as having the ability to wield soft sexual power over men. For this reason, the seemingly compliant, docile, female body may be an agentic choice, rather than a subservient subject. Girls who do not make the first move may be outwardly passive, but this does not imply that they have a diminished capacity

to act and affect. They are able to tease flirtatiously, in order to ensnare men into the seemingly irresistible trap of lust. (Tan 2013, 726)

That said and acknowledged, Karen seemed anything but amused or empowered by the patriarchal aspects of her vacation. She liked Bulgarian culture and "all the nice people" in Sunny Beach, but she did not like having to watch her back to avoid being stolen from or harassed when she went dancing. She had no problem with flirtatious men, as long as they looked good, were charming, and were her age. But she hated the disrespectful ones.

Thomas and I strolled down the esplanade toward a bar called H. C. Andersen, one of the favorite spots among Danish tourists. A man stopped us outside a strip joint to ask, "Do you want women?" Thomas inquired with feigned earnestness whether the women were Danish. The man changed tactics and offered us cannabis or cocaine for a "cheap price." Thomas continued making fun until the man left us alone. Thomas did not like "criminals" and was not afraid of telling them so to their face—a procedure that had gotten him into quite a few ugly fights.

We heard the bar before we saw it. An old Danish pop song was playing to the accompaniment of drunken chatter and attempts to sing along. Two women and two men stood around a table by the entrance. They had shots lined up in front of them, and within a few seconds, the men each downed five or six shots, and the women took three. They all appeared sober but were obviously bent on quickly changing just that. We bought beers and found a table.

"You got to hear this story," Thomas said, leaning over. "My big brother was in this small town and went to a local bar. There sits this guy from Greenland just pouring down beers. My brother walks over to sit next to him. The Greenlander says, 'For me it's always bottoms up.' So the guy gets a beer and gulps it down. He gets another one and gulps it down. Seven beers he empties, just like that. This started at 10 a.m. and lasted till around 12. That's goddamn cool! He will not live past his thirties."

I deduced that this was the episode that had given Thomas his motto, "always bottoms up." He laughed and nodded in confirmation.

We sat in silence for a while, looking at the other guests. Before I could protest, Thomas went to the bar to buy shots of sambuca, which is an anise-flavored liquor so sweet that it makes your teeth hurt. He placed the shots on the table and explained how to drink them. First, pour the liquid into the mouth but without swallowing. Next, put a lighter to the mouth and ignite the liquid. Finally, suck in air through the mouth.

"The alcohol vapor will go straight to your brain," he said and went on to demonstrate. The flame that came from his mouth was blue. He sat dead still, watching me closely, eyes wide open, mouth open—and his teeth on fire! Was he waiting for a reaction? He continued to stare while slowly sucking in air until the flame finally went out. He said that he had done this trick numerous times during a vacation in Turkey. People just loved it. They gave him Sambuca shots all the time so he could entertain them.

"But you have to be careful. One of my friends got nasty burn wounds from it," he cautioned.

The friend had made the mistake of taking too much Sambuca in the mouth. Some was on his lips, and some trickled down his chin. When he put the lighter to his mouth, the lower part of his face caught fire and left wounds that made it look as if he had brown slobber down his chin. The friend looked like that for several weeks before the skin returned to normal. We laughed. I took a sip of my shot glass and looked around for reactions. No one seemed to have noticed Thomas's show.

He said that he was "goddamn happy" to have met me. None of his friends were around, so without me he would have been all alone. But I knew that I was a poor substitute for his friends. I enjoyed being in his company and talking with him, but I did not have the motivation to help build up the mood to the effervescent heights that he was longing for. Accordingly, we did not enter the self-reinforcing feedback loop of "mutual rhythmic intensification" (Collins 2004, 243).

He must have sensed my lack of energy because he took on a serious look and said, "I don't know why, but I have lately begun to throw up when I go drinking." Not during this vacation, but back home when going out with friends. He added that a friend of his, "like this clever dude," had told him that if you become drunk often, the risk of Alzheimer's increases tremendously. I began on a little discourse about what I knew of alcohol's negative effects, but then Finn arrived with two lively looking men. I quickly retreated to my hotel room, hoping that Thomas would get a good night out after all.

I continued my conversation with Thomas the next day, this time with my audio recorder turned on. He explained that the previous night had been "cozy" and "sort of nice and easygoing" because the people he had been with (i.e., Karen and me) had not taken part in his drinking. He laughed and added that after I left, he had shared a bottle of booze followed by Sambuca shots with some people he met. He admitted, however, that besides getting "very drunk," nothing really memorable happened.

"Had I been with some of my old pals, things would probably have been a bit easier, like meeting people and getting in contact with girls. . . . Because you couldn't drink with me and Karen had a hangover, so she also took it easy. Then you sit there by yourself and it's not like jumping around and dancing, more like talk and take it easy. I tell you, had I been at that bar with five of my boys, there would have been some real guzzling. After two seconds, we would have bought a bottle of booze and the situation would have been completely different. . . . I am 100 percent sure that the bungee jump device outside of the bar, the one you can jump in two persons at a time, sure thing, me and my friends would have done it. We would have done that straightaway and taken photos of it to bring home and tell about it. And I am sure that, before long, we would have found a girl that we could do a body tequila on, preferably with the girl lying on the bar top. I am 100 percent sure. . . . That's the way that we do it at home. You need to start things, action, you can't just sit down and drink. . . . Also because it's fun for yourself, you get that kick, and also you can tell people, 'It's so cool. We just flew up in the air and did backward saltos,' I can really imagine that happening." Thomas was beaming with excitement as he put together this script for a perfect night out in Sunny Beach, which I note in passing, contained all five components of effervescence: group unity between Thomas and his imagined friends; an intensity of emotion, movement, and expression; various acts of (minor) transgression, such as an on-top-of-the-bar "body tequila"; the generation of symbols, including photos and stories of tandem bungee jumping; and a sense of revitalization from having had a "complete blowout" with "the boys."

I returned to the issue of his hangovers and new tendency to vomit after episodes of heavy drinking.

He explained that he woke up today around 3 p.m. and that his main symptom was tremors. "It feels like the whole body is shaking and it feels really awful," he said. "No feeling of having to vomit, just, yuck—you don't want to do anything. Go down to the pool, perhaps, lie down and sleep. But the damage had been done, and I really couldn't get up. I had to open my phone because I received a message, but I think it took me fifteen seconds to open it because my fingers just didn't want to move like I wanted them to."

"Because your whole body was shaking?"

"Yes. You are beside yourself. You can't do dick shit."

"Did you have other symptoms? Did you have nausea?"

"Not at all. But I felt like I was two persons, because the brain functions all right, like, 'Get up!' But the body wouldn't listen. It's a real struggle."

"And what about your consciousness? Were you still drunk?"

"Yes. But not 'party people' anymore. Just drunk."

"Not lively drunk?"

"No. When you wake up, you are not up for anything wild. But then again, had other people been with me in the apartment, like true party people who were up for it, then sure, I would have gone out on the balcony and had another beer or something. If other people had pushed, 'Come on,' I would maybe have pulled myself together and gotten out there, sat some minutes, and then started on that first beer. Then we would get it all started again . . . because it's like this, you have to get started on those beers. Right now, I have had about two liters of beer, right, and I can feel it. I can speak better. Everything is better. I feel good."

Thomas said that in his hometown, he was renowned for being a "big drinker" and an "all-out-party dude." Many people knew that he lived by the motto "always bottoms up," and they knew that his doctor had been cautioning him. He said this laughing, but I pressed him for information about what his doctor had said. The doctor had given him a thorough examination, and the results indicated a number of problems, including elevations in liver enzymes and cholesterol. The doctor concluded that Thomas should stop getting drunk so often, or his internal organs would become seriously damaged.

"Did you follow the advice?" I asked.

He shrugged and said that, perhaps, he had begun to drink a little less. But he was sick and tired of health advice and of being told what to do and what not to do.

"You are not allowed to smoke," he groused. "You are not allowed to drink. You are not allowed to stay outside in the sun. You can't do anything anymore. I think that you should live while you dare, live while you live, live life to the fullest. I don't want to end up being the richest man in the cemetery."

Thomas's words illustrate what may be a universal feature of youth experience: the tendency to engage in activities designed to court danger and controversy. These activities come in many forms, depending on the cultural context, but they all have the potential to generate an intensity of emotion and a depth of experience (Lyng 1990). They range from health-threatening drinking and illegal drug use at youth parties to various forms of sexual risk taking and to violent acts like bar fights, armed robbery, and terrorist attacks. Many researchers interpret these activities rather one-sidedly as the result of some underlying problem such as socioeconomic disadvantage or psychological deficiencies. However, people sometimes do "deviant" things not primarily because they have a problem but because they like it. Indeed, as sociologist Jack Katz puts it, "Deviance is not merely a reaction against something negative in a person's background but a reaching for exquisite possibilities" (1988, 73).

In Thomas's case, his preferred form of "deviance" was clearly heavy drinking. He was one of the "party people," which for him entailed seizing any opportunity for a good party and taking that party "to the max" by drinking heavily and being "crazy as a bat." I do think that his drinking was related to, and partly driven by, personal problems and anxieties. Yet it was also simultaneously a means of reaching for effervescent moments that would make him feel wonderfully alive, appreciated, and connected with other people. His pursuit of intoxication was thus multiply motivated by a desire to have fun and forget it all, to bond and reduce fear, and to create memories for a lifetime. This is one of the key attributes of effervescence: it can momentarily focus one's attention on the potentialities of the present moment—sometimes to the exclusion of all else. Thomas was well aware that his drinking habits were bad for his health, but this did not worry him as much as the menace of being bored and boring. Like so many other young people across the world, Thomas was concerned about social risks, peer approval, and having fun more than health risks, parental approval, and survival.

CHAPTER 5

TRANSGRESSION

When people reach states of effervescence, they become empowered, embold-ened, and volatile in a manner that makes them more likely to engage in acts of transgression, ranging from the playful to the dead serious. This has to do with the sense of anonymity that comes from being in effervescent groups, espe-cially large ones (Le Bon 2001). Individual group members easily come under the impression that they are hidden by the group and that they can do what they want without being identified or held accountable (Borch 2012). Moreover, effervescence is an enticing social force that can push its members to do what they would not have been able, willing, or bold enough to do on their own, such as going beyond boundaries set by the law. Durkheim writes, "The effervescence often becomes so intense that it leads to outlandish behaviour; the passions unleashed are so torrential that nothing can hold them. People are so far outside the ordinary conditions of life, and so conscious of the fact, that they feel a cer-tain need to set themselves above and beyond ordinary morality" (1995, 218).

Durkheim gives several examples of where this may lead, including acts of sacrilege, fights, incest, war, sexual experimentation, self-mutilation, bloody bar-barism, self-sacrificial heroism, and physical and mental burnout. Effervescence is an unpredictable and potentially explosive condition. Yet Durkheim insists on its value and necessity in society. Life without effervescence would be simply unthinkable. There would be no creativity, no innovation, and no vitality.

The work of Bataille (1986) extensively treats this theme. He argues that by transgressing boundaries (e.g., restraints, rules, and regulations), we put ourselves and our boundaries to the test. So besides causing trouble—and sometimes fatal trouble—transgressions can provide new insight into the hold that boundaries have on us. They can show us who we are in the face of uncertainty and fear. They can also clarify what boundaries are made of and why they matter (Jenks 2003). A short, Bataillan answer to the question "Why transgression?" would therefore be because boundaries are there, beckoning to be explored and pushed. A supplementary answer comes from the cultural criminologists who argue that in contemporary consumer culture, all sorts of transgressions are packaged and marketed "as cool, fashionable cultural symbols, with transgression thus emerging as a desirable consumer decision" (Ferrell, Hayward, and Young 2015, 166).[1] This marketing is done today on an unprecedented scale, adding to the allure of heavy drinking, street fights, "thug life," and other shady business.

The transgressions among revelers tend to be minor and are generally undertaken in the spirit of "Why not?" Lines are crossed out of curiosity, for the thrill of it, and for the esteem that comes from peers for having the nerve and capacity to go against rules. People dance on tables, expose their buttocks, and yell things they would normally keep to themselves. Nightlife settings can encourage such unruliness by contributing to cultural notions that minor transgressions are cool, and indeed expected, for instance through advertisements saying, "To me, 'Drink responsibly' means don't spill it" and wall paintings of drunken celebrities having fun.[2] Transgression-enabling cues like these—combined with assembled masses, music, dancing, alcohol, and drugs—create a powerful cocktail that disturbs the ordinary functioning of body and mind, weakens the ingrown habits of self-control, and strengthens the capacity for abandonment. The negative consequences are typically limited to hangovers on the day after, but the effervescence sometimes spirals out of control and creates lasting harm.

HEDONISTIC IMMEDIACY

My fieldwork in Sunny Beach made it clear to me how dangerous effervescence can be when it takes hold of people in places with poor security standards. My wife and our friend Tine had come to the resort to help me conduct a survey. One night, as we were winding down after a long day's work, a man drank himself to death during a pub crawl. It happened just a few blocks away from us. The pub crawl had just arrived at the bar Sunny Dreams when he threw up and choked on his own vomit. The guides who led the pub crawl rushed to give him first aid, but it was too late. The man was only seventeen years old. Three days later, a twenty-five-year-old Swedish man was killed by three bouncers at a nightclub. Witnesses reported that the man had threatened the bouncers with a knife. They took him outside and punched and stomped him. A police officer was caught on camera watching idly as the murder took place—something that says a lot about the security forces in Bulgaria. Soon after, a young tourist from Holland was found dead in a swimming pool, followed by a series of reports of young tourists who had been robbed, kidnapped, and raped at the resort (Tutenges 2009).

A group of eight female friends flew to Sunny Beach as these tragedies were taking place. The women were all well aware of what was happening. They had heard about several incidents in the media, and they had discussed them with their worried parents. However, the trip was already paid for and planned. They were determined to go and enjoy themselves as much as possible.

"We take it to the max," the one called Yvonne told me. "You don't pay for a vacation like this and then come down here to be boring."

I interviewed six members of the group the day after they had celebrated the eighteenth birthday of their friend Helle. The celebration had been thorough, and now they were lying around, three of them on beach towels and the others on inflatable, pink Chesterfield couches. It was early in the day, but some of them had already downed "repair drinks" to fight the hangovers. I asked them what they thought about the safety situation at the resort.

"Very good," Helle replied. "The media have written all sorts of bad stuff about the guides—that they don't look after us. But they actually do. They take care of us, and they are nice people. They walk around and talk with all their guests. Not just some guests, but with everybody. One or two of them stay sober [i.e., to serve as 'night guards,' who watch out for the tourists' safety], and then the rest drink with us. Yesterday, there was security staff all over the place."

I tried to get the group to talk more about the safety conditions.

"It's fine," Yvonne simply answered.

Birgitte snapped, "I haven't paid attention to any damn problems."

Helle's answer was similarly brief. "The safety in Sunny Dreams is not that good," she said. "That's where all that happened; where the guy died. But it's a nice club. They play a lot of Danish music."

I met resistance in the group every time I asked questions about safety and crime, but they answered enthusiastically when I switched to lighter topics, such as what they had done on Helle's birthday. They did not exactly deny that Sunny Beach was unsafe, but they avoided the issue. They emphasized that they had fun and were safe from harm as long as they kept together and avoided ice cubes, which they believed were sometimes spiked with drugs. Also, several in the group pointed out that their vacation lasted for one week only. They were young and had to make the most of it before they had to go home, grow old, raise kids, and live out their lives.

This sense of hedonistic immediacy is typical in festive contexts (Maffesoli 1985). It is an attitude toward life, a variant of the Nietzschean amor fati, which seeks to derive a maximum amount of enjoyment from whatever comes to hand (Nietzsche 2006). Existence is accepted for what it is and destiny embraced in spite of its capriciousness. The focus is on cherishing this present moment rather than pushing toward some future award or transcendent reality. This is what true joy looks like, according to Nietzsche: to be content with what comes and want nothing more than what is. As Nietzsche's Zarathustra expresses it in what is sometimes referred to as the "Drunken song," "Pain says: 'Refrain! Away, you pain!' But everything that suffers wants to live, to become ripe and joyful and longing,—longing for what is farther, higher, brighter. 'I want heirs,' thus speaks all that suffers, 'I want children, I do not want *myself*'—But joy does not want heirs, not children—joy wants itself, wants eternity, wants recurrence, wants everything eternally the same" (2006, 262).

The sense of hedonistic immediacy is often coupled with a taste for the forbidden. Limits are crossed out of curiosity, for fun, and also quite simply because the limits are there. For as Bataille points out, we humans are simultaneously repelled by and drawn to limits, whether they are defined by God, parents, convention, or any other authority. We cannot lead our lives in passive submission but are compelled to assert ourselves by questioning, violating, and redefining the limits that we meet. And when a limit is crossed, the effect is often a heightening of our senses that makes us fully present in what we are doing. To transgress can, therefore, be a way to seize the moment (Presdee 2004).

"We try to push each other to get some fun," Yvonne said. "We have this little game where we give each other dares, and if you don't do your dare, you have to pay a round of drinks to the others."

Helle elaborated, "For example, yesterday, Caroline had to strip from her waist up, and I had to slap a stripper on his butt cheeks. It was like this man stripper in a discotheque."

"And I had to do a body tequila. Somebody had to go up on a stage and yell 'Cheers!' into a microphone. And Yvonne had to dance on a table," Birgitte said.

Everyone began to talk at once, visibly excited by these memories and the telling of them.

"It's hilarious. We don't normally do that at home."

"Also, back home I don't just wake up at some random place."

"Hey girl, I've done that!"

"But down here, nothing is planned for. We just do random things."

I asked them if there were dares that they had refrained from doing.

Birgitte answered, "I didn't do mine. I had to do a bull shake on some random person, but I didn't do it."

I asked what a "bull shake" is.

"You just shake everything," Birgitte explained. "I didn't do it, so have to get that one done tonight."

"Louise failed to do her dare too. She was supposed to tell Tom that we have a sex room. That we have this extra room for f-cking."

"Hey, Katja also skipped hers. She was supposed to dance with the ugliest dude we could find for her."

"See, that's the kind of stuff we do down here."

"Yeah. It's totally fun. We do it to get some action, to get something to laugh about."

During their entire vacation, the group of women constantly encouraged each other to engage in activities that they found challenging, awkward, embarrassing, taxing, or outright frightening. They said that what they did was "just random stuff," "spontaneous," and "nuts"; however, there was a certain logic to their activities, an antinomian logic that takes its bearings in relation and opposition to established truths, prevailing rules, and mechanistic routines. According to this logic, the bourgeois ideals of self-control and decency are profoundly boring and, therefore, to be avoided, at least in festive contexts.

Bataille was a fervent advocate of the antinomian, and he captures some of its essence in the following declaration: "It is time to abandon the world of the civilized and its light. It is too late to be reasonable and educated—which has led to a life without appeal. Secretly or not, it is necessary to become completely different, or to cease being. . . . Life has always taken place in a tumult without apparent cohesion, but it only finds its grandeur and its reality in ecstasy and ecstatic love. He who tries to ignore or misunderstand ecstasy is an incomplete being whose thought is reduced to analysis" (Bataille 1985, 179).

The group of eight women toyed with the antinomian throughout their stay in Sunny Beach. They drank copiously, slept very little, challenged each other with dares, and thus purposively and persistently pushed each other beyond the "world of the civilized and its light" (Bataille 1985, 179). This behavior may be interpreted as a pursuit of the sensual immediacy that comes from transgressing boundaries and venturing into new psychosocial terrains. But not only this; as Bataille (1993) makes clear, transgressions should also be understood as an *exploration* of the boundaries that are being crossed, for it is often when we cross a line that its purpose and meaning become clear to us, just as we may come to understand the value of something (e.g., an object or relationship) only after we have broken it.

The exploratory dimension of transgressions is probably most evident and extensive among children and youth. Jackson writes, "Children typically test the boundaries of what their parents decide and define for them. In this way, they experiment with their individual capacities to define the world for themselves" (2015, 8). Consider the example of toddlers seated at the dinner table who yell, throw their food, and run off if they get the chance. This behavior appears illogical when considered from a survival perspective. The child needs food; the parents need food. Indeed, all parts, including their digestive systems, would probably benefit from a relaxed eating atmosphere. However, humans are not, as some biologists would have it, "survival machines—robot vehicles blindly programmed to preserve the selfish molecules known as genes" (Dawkins 1989, xxi). Rather, any one human being is a bundle of contradictions, a sublime complexity, with much more on the agenda than self-preservation. So when children turn the eating situation into chaos, it may be in an attempt to test their parents' patience and love for them while exploring the boundaries of the etiquette rules that their parents are trying to transmit. Is it really that important to close the mouth when chewing one's food? Can the cup survive a fall to the floor? What are the consequences of throwing food on the wall or at a parent? Such questions may be clarified by way of transgression.

In order to understand transgressive tendencies among children and youth, we must bear in mind that they inhabit a social world composed of myriad norms and rules that have been established by their parents and previous generations—not by themselves. Young individuals have to familiarize them-selves with these norms and rules, and they also have to grow accustomed to their own bodies and minds, which, day by day, develop new features, new abilities, and new desires. In addition, as they go through these developments, they have to deal with changes in their social statuses and in what other people expect and require of them. The teenage years are especially associated with overwhelming, metamorphic transformations. New boundaries have to be discovered and redis-covered, defined and redefined, crossed and recrossed (Tutenges and Rod 2009).

Boundaries can be explored through actual acts of transgression but also through the telling, planning, and observation of transgressions. Writing from a Norwegian context, sociologist Eivind Grip Fjær (2012) observes that the sometimes hangover-ridden and remorseful day after a celebration is an important occasion for young people to talk about their transgressions and, perhaps, come to terms with them. He writes that a party can "stir things up" and that it may involve transgressions that "generate a chaos of gestures, feel-ings and relations," which need to be dealt with on the following day: "Maybe one got drunk too fast, flirted in an awkward way, or simply does not remem-ber what happened. Interacting with the other party participants the next day involves agreeing on a definition of what happened and getting confirmations from others that the transgression was not seen as serious, or excusing them if they were" (2012, 1007).

Norwegians describe the psychological aspect of hangovers with the expres-sion *fylleangst*, which may be translated into "binge-angst" (Fjær 2012, 999). This typically involves a sense of regret and anxiety coming from not knowing exactly what one has done, what other people have done, and what will be the conse-quences of whatever happened. The youth in Fjær's study regard the psychologi-cal hangover symptoms as worse than the physical ones—namely, fatigue, nausea, and a crushing pain in the skull. This is because the psychological symptoms may evolve into long-lasting embarrassment, as when a person has committed trans-gressions that peers consider sincerely shameful or abhorrent. Fjær mentions the example of fights, and he also mentions an incident with a young woman who "had spent a party whining and bothering strangers with questions about the whereabouts of her friends" (2012, 1007). The woman was subsequently sanctioned for her behavior with threats that she would be excluded from future parties. Being stigmatized as a brute or whiner can be more painful than breaking a leg, especially when you are young and yearning for inclusion in peer groups (Jørgensen et al. 2007).

One way to deal with binge-angst is to collectively revisit the transgressions of the night before by telling stories of what happened either face-to-face—for instance, when a party is followed by a "sleepover"—or by means of communication technologies such as cell phones and WhatsApp. Indeed, numerous studies show that the day after celebrations tend to be marked by intense peer-to-peer interaction about who did what, when, where, why, with whom, and to what effect (e.g., Cullen 2011; Brown 2013). This interaction can help fill in the memory gaps for those who had a blackout during the celebration, and it can also serve to collectively scrutinize, assess, redefine, or come to terms with the transgressions that took place.

The group of eight women certainly spent a lot of time talking about their transgressions. Their morning routine was to wake one another up with talk and mutual teasing, often relating to deeds done the night before. Those capable of motion would then walk down to the hotel buffet to talk some more, poke at the food, and perhaps have a few drinks. Afterward, they would head out to find a good spot on the beach or by the nearest swimming pool to watch the crowd, soak up sun, doze off, have another drink, take a dip, and talk.

"It's goddamn cozy," Helle said. "It's like this group relaxation."

Laughing, Louise added that what they talk about is "so far-out, totally hallucinating."

"You chill, relax. You are more relaxed in your body somehow. Everything is in a fog. But that's probably because you're still a bit drunk."

"The funny part is when you are told about all the crap you did on the night before."

"There is always a lot to laugh about [. . .] because we are usually several who are hungover together."

I asked what they had been talking about today.

"Louise's shit face!" Birgitte shouted.

"No, listen," Helle said. "We were sitting outside of Club Magnum. Some guy came over. He babbled about something that we didn't get. Like, he was talking with Yvonne, right? But she said to the rest of us, 'Make this guy go away! He's playing. He's nasty.' So Caroline walks over and talks with the guy, telling him that we girls are having fun, that we don't think he is particularly charming, that we don't like him, and that he should go 'f-cky-f-cky' himself. But then all of a sudden the dude says, 'I understand what you are saying, Danes.' Turns out he's Danish! So he had just babbled in Dutch to fool us. That was really funny."

"Yeah. So we became good friends and talked with him for an hour or so."

"But this is just one of the things that happened. Thousands of other hilarious things happened!"

"Yeah. Katja thought she could jump over a two-meter-high billboard. She crashed into it and messed around."

"Gertrud and Lilly disappeared in the middle of the night. They only came home, like, what time was it? Three in the afternoon?"

"We woke up at some hotel room," Gertrud explained. "We had no idea where we were. That was also kind of fun. And hey, also, some of the girls ran around on the street and whipped the boys."

"With a long whip! They went around and whipped people," Birgitte said.

"I think they whipped themselves more than they whipped other people."

"Yes," Helle admitted. "I whipped myself on the thigh."

I asked where they had acquired the whip.

"Stolen."

"We took it when the vendor looked away."

"You can say we borrowed it because we gave it back later."

"We were forced to give it back."

The women gave many more examples of the stunts they had done, smiling and laughing as they did so. This type of transgression talk is much more than mere entertainment. It is also a way for people to convey who they are or wish to be, as individuals and as a group. Typically, young people engaged in transgression talk present themselves as wild (but not completely out of control) and immoral (but not to the extent of harming other people). To borrow Nietzsche's terms, the self-images that emerge usually have clear Dionysian traits but also a few more-subtle Apollonian tinges. Helle, for example, said that she was acting raving mad in Sunny Beach, drinking and flirting all the time and sometimes vomiting and making a fool of herself, whereas back home in Denmark, she took it much easier. The overall impression I got was that the women were normally well behaved and functional but that they had the capacity to switch into a misbehaved and rather dysfunctional mode. They were capable of going wild at will, which is a highly valued skill among contemporary youth.

Those who talk about transgression often express with words, sounds, and body language how far one may, can, and should go in the heat of effervescent moments. For example, Louise mentioned that one night they all invaded a random hotel to dance and fool around in front of three hotel guests, and as she told this, she was backed up by others in the group with affirmative smiles and the evaluative remark, "That was quite fun." This little story and the reactions to it established that their hotel stunt was daring and yet completely acceptable. By contrast, when Helle said that Katja had disappeared one night and that this was "really funny," Yvonne objected and called the disappearance a "downer" that had made her deeply worried. Louise sided with Yvonne and reminded her that mobile phones sometimes do not function properly in Sunny Beach due to weak signals, making it absolutely necessary that no one walks off on their own. Katja's disappearance was hereby established as unacceptable, and Helle also ended by agreeing that sticking together is "the most important thing" and that "down here, you have to take more care of each other than in Denmark."

Transgressions and their stories can, somewhat paradoxically, help draw the line between acceptable and unacceptable behavior. Therefore, young people's tendency for actual and storied transgression should not be interpreted as mere naughtiness or nihilistic negation; it is also an expression of curiosity and vitality. As Bataille famously puts it, "The transgression does not deny the taboo but transcends it and completes it" (1986, 63). In other words, when revelers violate a taboo, they also confirm its existence. When they cause havoc, they demonstrate the importance of order. And when they laughingly celebrate madness, they point to the necessity of sanity. This is not to deny that transgressions and their stories can be harmful. Rather, it is to emphasize that the human tendency for transgression is universal, unavoidable, and potentially beneficial.

Nocturnal Role-Play

Transgressions are often inspired or enabled by role-play.[3] People assume the bodily, mental, and stylistic dispositions of another human or nonhuman being, which assists them in doing things that they would not normally do. Role-playing in effervescent environments typically comes in small-scale variants, such as when a group of friends at a music festival decides to behave as a band of dogs and starts crabbing around on all fours, barking at suspicious strangers, and peeing on tents. However, role-play may also be organized on a larger scale around a particular social event, such as the carnival parade of the city of Port of Spain in Trinidad and Tobago. Here, thousands of people dance bawdily through the streets in the anonymity of costumes, colorful headdresses, body paint, and the swarming masses. The parade also features tradition-bound carnival figures, such as the black-and-white-clad "Midnight Robber," who makes bombastic speeches about his own deeds; the massive-bosomed "Dame Lorraine," who playfully flirts with "fans" that she picks out from the crowd; and groups of sex-crazed monkeys who gyrate and grind against everyone they can get near to (King 2011; Mason 1998; see also Fine 2002).

Effervescent moments call for role-playing just as they call for rhythmic movement and sound making. Whenever and wherever collective energies start to rise, there is an almost compulsory tendency for people to open up to others and to imitate how they move, sound, dress, and behave—a tendency that is only logical, given that states of effervescence are characterized by a heightened mutual awareness and engagement. Why confine yourself to a single persona when you feel intimately connected with and emboldened by a multitude of others? Why be your own all-too-familiar self when you can be someone else who has prodigious skills, exotic manners, and a fascinating story to tell?

The theme of role-playing came up in a late-night conversation I had in Copenhagen with a thirty-five-year-old shopkeeper, Allan, and a thirty-five-year-old chef, Janus. We were sitting over beers in a bar, swapping local gossip and watching the crowd. They mentioned that they had recently spent the better part of a night pretending that they were working in the film industry. That was "fun" they said, without going into details. I phoned them some time later for more information.

Janus said that he had a vivid memory of his night as a moviemaker. "I smoke and drink like a madman, but oddly enough, my memory is intact," he said and rasped out a coughing laugh as if to emphasize that, indeed, he was a man of excess. "Allan was my assistant, and I was the famous Italian moviemaker Brunelli." He repeated this name, "Brunelli," with a strong Italian accent and laughed again. "I think we had planned this setup beforehand. We went to Blaster Bar and started talking with this girl. To begin with, I thought that I would not be able to go through with it. I was just this arrogant sleazebag. Nasty on purpose. It was hilarious to permit myself to be so full of disdain."

I asked how she reacted.

"She was repulsed. I behaved like a swine. But you know, there is this stardust effect. I was a famous movie star. So she became interested in me, and that, in a way, was what the experiment was all about. To see if wealth and stardust can outweigh sleaziness. The experiment was a success. She didn't see through me, and she even became interested in me. I didn't get any p-ssy, but that was not the point. Not at all. See, that would have been just plain wrong and in so many ways. I mean, a guy like Brunelli doesn't live in Copenhagen in a tiny flat like mine, right? Had I scored her, I would have been forced to continue my act and pay for a very expensive hotel room, and I would have been obliged to have sex with her as Brunelli. Man, that would have been so wrong."

"She didn't see through your act?" I asked.

"I don't think so. I guess that I am perfect for that role."

I asked what he meant.

"I can sometimes have an arrogant take on things. There is something of it in my personality. I have a flair for arrogance, you could say. But I obviously don't want to be an arrogant swine on a daily basis. I normally try to restrain myself."

I called Allan to get his version of the story.

"Sure, I can tell you what happened," he said, although he was abroad on holiday. "Janus pretended that he was an Italian filmmaker, a sleazy one, and socially awkward as hell. I was the guy who took care of him. The guy who prevented the maestro from getting himself into trouble. I clearly remember that night because it was fun. But it was definitely not a fun period in my life. It was a low point, actually. I was stuck. When I went out, it was always to the same bars. So I guess that me and Janus just wanted something different to happen. Because we went to the same f-cking round of bars every time we went out. [. . .] That night, we went to one of the usual joints and it was, you know, like a ringside. We sat in the bar, away from the action, watching people dance. How the hell do you get in contact with people if you don't want to dance? So that's when we started on the Brunelli act."

Allan interrupted his own account with a sudden laugh.

"I just remembered, hey, before we hang up I have to tell you about my night as an artist!" he said, laughing so much that his sentences came out in bursts. "It was totally hilarious. I was on vacation in Skagen [a popular vacation spot for the very rich, situated in Northern Denmark]. I pretended that I was a sand artist. That's, like, impossible to pull off! It's like giving yourself a really tough challenge. It was really difficult for me to keep it going because I know next to nothing about sand art."

I asked why he did it.

"For kicks." He paused and then added, "You pretend that you are somebody else because it's no fun to be yourself."

Janus's and Allan's stories illustrate a common form of nocturnal role-play—namely, the occupational role reversal that involves one or several persons pretending that they have another type of work and work history than what they actually have. Certain themed parties are all about occupational reversals. Take for example the "hospital party," where participants are dressed up in blood-stained coats, surgery caps, masks, latex gloves, stethoscopes, and so on. Or consider the "school teacher party," where people wear geeky spectacles, ugly sweaters, carry around big books, and have stern looks on their faces. However, Allan and Janus did not buy props or dress up for their acts. What they did was more spontaneous and more obscured. They tried their best to perform their roles convincingly and to conceal their usual identities.

Anthropologist Gregory Bateson (2000) writes that play is laden with meta-messages that signal, "This is play." He gives the example of a group of monkeys who is engaged in something that appears to be a fight but in fact is a playful exchange of harmless nips. The exchanges remain harmless because the monkeys are able to transmit and receive signals that frame the activity as playfulness rather than serious-ness (Bateson 2000, 179–180). Nocturnal role-play also comes with metamessages that indicate playfulness, but these messages are sometimes encrypted so that only certain people can decipher what is going on. In the episodes described by Allan and Janus, only a select few received clear signals about their occupa-tional reversals. All others were kept in the dark. This covertness infuses the act with suspense because there is a constant threat of being exposed and, perhaps, criticized or punished. For if the performance is weak, if it is flawed by self-contradictions or interrupted by a laughing fit, then the reactions could be anything from a smile to a shrug to a slap in the face.

Part of the excitement of role-playing comes from its unpredictability and the risk of receiving negative feedback.

Nocturnal role-play can be conceived as a mild form of what sociologist Stephen Lyng calls "edgework," meaning an activity of voluntary risk-taking that requires vigilant attention, engagement, and skill on the part of the risk-taker (2004). One wrong step, or one wrong grimace, can cause damage to those involved, either physically, mentally, or socially. The attraction of such behavior is related to the immediate rush of confronting danger and the sense of mastery if the performance is done well. Lyng argues that the draw of risk-taking lies in the contrast it offers to everyday life, which many young people experience as disenchanted. He writes that "edgework serves as a vehicle of escape from social conditions that produce stunted identities and offer few opportunities for personal transformation and character development. . . . Risk-taking generates qualities, such as group cohesion or personal character development, missing from people in certain social positions" (Lyng 2004, 6).[4]

These words aptly capture Allan's situation at the time when he performed the roles of Brunelli's assistant and the sand artist. He had just been through a divorce, was unsatisfied with his job, and felt caught up in the same routines day in and day out. He was always going to the same bars, meeting the same people, having the same conversations, and not knowing where to go in his life. Role-playing was, for him, a way to have a little fun while getting respite from the frustrations of being himself. These two effects, entertainment and self-escape, are typical outcomes of role-playing. To pretend to be somebody else, whether this is done histrionically or covertly, can quickly raise the emotional energies in a social situation and create memorable scenes of confusion, retribution, and amusement. Role-players have to be alert and creative in order to adjust their performances to their audience. Theirs is an act of improvisation, which cues and is cued by a specific situation and its emotional flows. Little room is left for thoughts about anything but the challenges at hand.

So when Allan pretended to be a sand artist, he could no longer rely on his habitual bodily language and had to constantly and mindfully modify his way of reasoning, choice of words, tone of voice, facial expressions, and movements. He also had to invent answers to the difficult questions he was asked, such as "How do you earn money?" and "What do you do to keep the sand sculptures from collapsing?" The role-play complicated his interactions with the people he met, compelling him to be in the moment rather than preoccupied with thoughts about mistakes of the past or uncertainties of the future.

From a learning perspective, covert role-playing can be a way to test, rehearse, and improve dubious yet important social skills such as those of manipulation, trickery, and deception. These skills are useful in many social situations beyond nightlife environments. In a job interview, for instance, it can be advantageous to downplay or conceal discrediting personality traits while exaggerating or inventing appealing ones. Indeed, as Erving Goffman (1990) has shown, we all work on our self-image and present certain fronts according to where, when, and with whom we find ourselves. However, this type of impression management has to be done convincingly; otherwise, the result may be negative appraisal and condemnation (Johnson 2013).

The role-play that Janus and Allan engaged in could potentially have resulted in unpleasant feedback in the form of anger and so forth. However, such negative feedback was most likely to come only from the strangers they were deceiving rather than from more significant others such as their close friends. Their acts, therefore, did not seriously jeopardize their social reputation, and this is the case with nearly all forms of nocturnal role-play. Moreover, as Allan said when asked whether he considered his behavior unethical, "Not really. It's part of the game when you go out, isn't it? You fool around. You mess with yourself. You mess with other people. They mess with you. And it's not like I go around and trick people all the time. It's just something that has happened a few times. And what do you think people would have said if they found out that I was no sand artist? It's not that I was hurting anybody's feelings."

Indeed, role-play is widely, though not unanimously, accepted in nightlife environments, especially among young revelers. This permissiveness facilitates social experimentations that people can use for their own entertainment and also for their personal development. For the lessons learned through nocturnal play may bear fruit well after the party has ended. As O'Grady explains, nightlife environments are like social laboratories in which life can be rehearsed, skills sharpened, and new insights gained: "What has been felt, experienced and tried out in the safety of the play zone might inform and shape how we act and take action in the world of the everyday" (2012, 101). People very rarely engage in nocturnal role-playing because they want to learn something. Nevertheless, learning may be an outcome of the experience (Katz 1988, 76–78).

The type of role-playing that I have seen most frequently during my fieldwork is doubtlessly gender reversals: men who act like women, women who act like men, heterosexual men who act like homosexual men, heterosexual women who act like homosexual women, and so on. Following Jackson, I consider such reversals as expressions of embodied potentialities that tend to be moderated, repressed, or hidden in an everyday context (2013, 64). In the process of growing up, various genders become "inscribed in the body" (Bourdieu 2001, 103) in the sense that individuals gradually—through observation, imitation, and practice—acquire an intimate embodied knowledge of how different genders speak, move, gesticulate, and dress. This embodied knowledge makes it possible to perform different genders, but in day-to-day life, most adults perform one gender only because this is seen as "natural" and "in the order of things." Moments of effervescence are different, however, because these are marked by a general disorder of things. Here, role-playing, including gender reversals, is widely accepted as a welcome contribution to the mutual entertainment and entrainment.[5]

DARK PLAY

O'Grady distinguishes between what she calls "light" and "dark" forms of play. Light play is "theatrical, spectacular, fun and socially engaging," whereas dark play is "subversive, disturbing, disorientating and potentially fatal" (2012, 90). She notes, however, that it is difficult to draw a clear line between light and dark because "play does not sit comfortably in neat binaries. [It] slides between categories and has no difficulty adopting dual positions. For example, play can be both fun and dangerous simultaneously. Indeed, the fun is often in the danger.... Play recognizes and revels in the inbetweenness of things" (2012, 90). In spite of this fundamental ambiguity, it is possible to place instances of play somewhere on a spectrum between light and dark. "Fun" can be found on both ends of the spectrum, but the fun in dark play tends to be one-sided and have harmful effects. What follows is a description of a group of three men who, during a seven-day stay in Sunny Beach, immersed themselves in what I interpret as a predominantly dark form of play. From what I gathered, the men had no criminal record, and there was seemingly nothing unusual or deviant about how they normally led their lives.

I first met them as I was finishing my lunch in a bar on Flower Street. They languidly walked in, wearing only shorts and shoes, and what first struck me was how skinny and red they all were. It looked as if the sun had burned away all their body fat and energy. They sat down at a table and started surveying the menu and the waitresses. I guessed they were from Denmark and went over to ask them for an interview. After a long, awkward moment, I was gestured to sit down. Two of them, Michael and Carsten, avoided eye contact. But the third guy, Lars, had his watery eyes fixed on me and kept them there during most of the interview.

After interrogating me about my project, they hesitantly began to answer my questions. They let me know that they had come to the resort for the beer and women.

"Beer first, then women," Michael explained.

"I got a blow job from a prostitute," Lars said, somewhat out of the blue.

I pretended that this information left me indifferent and asked whether they had gone to a strip club. They confirmed that they had. I asked what had made them go in there.

"I actually don't know," Michael answered. "It was just, got to try it. Now we can say that we have done it."

"So you had not planned it from home?" I asked.

Lars answered, "We hadn't planned it, but it was in the air. 'F-ck, man, we have to try to get a blow job from a prostitute.' Like that. Just for fun. To say we did it."

I asked whether the others had the same resolution for the vacation.

"No, not specifically," said Carsten.

Michael said, "I had agreed with a friend that we wanted to f-ck a whore, but then I found out that they rob you. So now I don't dare."

I asked Lars, "What about the blow job you got, how did that happen? Did you find her here on the esplanade?"

"Actually, I got the blow job from one of the hookers who robbed me. I got blown in a back alley. That was fun. My friend also got one. We stood there laughing. It was so unserious."

"She had robbed you?"

"Yeah, first day I was here. She stole from my pockets; a pickpocket. That has happened twice." He laughed as he said this.

"Did she rob you twice?"

"No, two different ones robbed me. But the first one who robbed me is the one who gave me a blow job." He laughed again.

"Did you hang out with them or talk with them or how did it happen?"

"F-ck no, man. We don't talk with her. She can't talk. She's not a real human. [Me and my buddy, we] just walked over there [with two prostitutes], and then mine takes off my pants and takes my dick in her mouth. Condom on first of course. She tries to give me a hard-on, but it doesn't work. I can't get a hard-on. I look at my buddy and he's standing like this [with his right arm stretched out as if cruising in a car]. Then the whores left. They thought it was too unserious. Hilarious, man."

Lars laughed and added, "I punched a hooker too. She slapped me."

"The hooker slapped you?"

"I don't know why. Kind of a fun thing. I just thought, I'll punch her back."

Lars had a fresh tattoo on his shoulder that said "F-cky F-cky."[6] I asked him about it.

He explained that "hookers" say that all the time. "Everybody here has had a hooker come over to ask, 'F-cky f-cky?' Lovely. It's just lovely. [. . .] You can buy anything down here. Look at it this way. It's a win-win situation: she gets money; I get a blow job. She gets happy. She gets food on the table. Her kids get food on the table. F-cking lovely."

Lars made other remarks along these lines, and my initial interpretation was that he wanted to test me. I have experienced this many times during fieldwork. When I first meet them, some present themselves in a negative light, presumably because they want to see how I, a sober adult and scientist, will react and judge them. However, as I learned more about Lars, I got the feeling that his negativity had deeper roots. His eyes, speech, and whole demeanor gave me an impression of deep-felt hatred. He mainly took out this hate on local prostitutes but also on other individuals whom he referred to as "not a real human," "miserable," and so on.

As mentioned, effervescent environments can function as laboratories or playgrounds where teenagers and adults toy with different roles and project different images. The most common types of role-play involve shifts in occupation, gender, sexuality, age, nationality, and style. Lars exemplifies another type of role-play: the moral reversal that involves taking on an immoral role such as that of the hater, the thief, the fighter, the pervert, and the woman molester. I may be wrong, of course, but I think that Lars metamorphosed when he set foot in Sunny Beach. He transformed into a perverted version of himself and did things that he had never done before and that he would not do at home. His group of friends also used the vacation to experiment with perverted, hypermasculine behavior. But no one went as far as Lars.

Much can be learned from Fyodor Dostoevsky and his writings on individuals who take on an evil persona, momentarily or permanently. I am thinking in particular here about the character Rodion Raskolnikov in the book *Crime and Punishment* (Dostoevsky 2003). Raskolnikov is a poor and miserable man living in the slums of St. Petersburg who decides to kill a woman. But the woman is not a real human, according to Raskolnikov. She is just "a loathsome, useless, harmful louse" (2003, 497). To kill her, therefore, is not a crime. Raskolnikov thus proceeds by dehumanizing his victim, and at the same time, he fantasizes himself to be a latter-day Napoleon for whom everything is permitted and who has the capacity to decide who lives and who dies. He reflects that "power is given only to those who dare to lower themselves and pick it up. Only one thing matters, one thing: to be able to dare!" (2003, 499). Through murder, Raskolnikov tries to prove his own superiority. It is not the woman's money he is after but a moment of omnipotence: "What I needed to know, and know quickly, was whether I was a louse, like everyone else, or a man. Whether I could take the step across, or whether I couldn't. Whether I could dare to lower myself and pick up what was lying there, or not. Whether I was a quivering knave, or whether I had a *right*" (2003, 500; see also Avramenko 2013).

Lars was also a crosser of barriers who built himself up by dehumanizing other people. There is great freedom in this attitude: freedom from the rules of order and decency that, from a certain perspective, subdue us in our everyday lives. Indeed, society may be viewed and experienced as a "regulative force" that imposes limits on us humans and our insatiable desire for stimulation, enjoyment, and power (Durkheim 1979, 248). But Lars did not accept the limits laid down by society. He wanted to be his own master. If he felt like insulting someone, he would do so without hesitation. When a prostitute slapped him, he punched her back. I think Lars was cultivating hate in his system and that this hate enabled him to commit the transgressions of mocking, humiliating, and punching other people.

Of course, one need not go to the extremes of Lars in order to experience the joys of transgression. The empowering sensation of being beyond rules can also come from nonaggressive acts, such as the performance of a strip show, or the observation of transgressions undertaken by professional artists. Indeed, there is a whole business around the production of transgressions to be consumed by the masses. Extreme metal music, for example, is an art form that uses anger, violence, and brutality to excite the performers as well as the fans. Merely listening to this aggressive music can reportedly make fans experience moments of cathartic release (Kahn-Harris 2007). And during concerts, fans can collectively fantasize about forbidden acts and express negative feelings but without inflicting any harm whatsoever. What this type of music offers is transgression by proxy, the vicarious thrill of witnessing others go against oppressive rules.

However, Lars preferred to commit his own transgressions, and he took great pride in them. He presented them as "for real" because he allegedly committed them spontaneously and instinctively. It was different with Jonathan, a travel companion that Lars referred to as an "idiot." Jonathan was fake, Lars said, because he did "crazy things" just to impress people. For example, one night Jonathan suddenly drew a fake gun at a strip club and stuck it into the face of a bouncer. There are lots of real guns circulating in Bulgarian nightlife, so the bouncer probably felt seriously threatened, until Jonathan exposed his hoax and ran off. Three furious bouncers tried to pursue him, but their large bodies could not keep up with the light-legged, giggling tourist.

"That morning we couldn't find him," Lars recounted. "He was gone. Because, this is probably going to interest you, this guy had no friends before he went to high school. He did some sports, but really his parents were his only friends. Then in gymnasium, he suddenly got some friends, and he is all happy and he always wants to prove something. He always wants to show that he is the funny guy. That's so obvious. You can see it. A lot of the things he does when he is wasted are completely on purpose. He wants us to laugh at him."

"What kind of things?" I asked.

"All kinds of things. Like falling asleep in Pete's room with the keys in his hand. I know he does these things on purpose. I am 100 percent sure of it."

"It's not something that just happens? It's strategic?"

"Well, he is drunk," Michael started, but Lars interrupted, "Sure, he is drunk, but a lot of what he does is just because he wants us to laugh at him."

"Do you sometimes do that yourselves?" I asked. "Do things just to . . . ?"

"Hell no!" Lars said angrily. "Not to make people laugh at me. F-ck, man, I do things because it's fun for me."

"What kind of things?"

"Whatever. Put on women's clothes and walk around town for fun. It's for the f-cking fun of it."

"What about Jonathan?"

Lars answered with another example.

"Jonathan came into my room this morning and said that he had messed up again," he said. "That he had stolen a jar of marmalade. He steals with arms and legs. He steals plants from the nightclubs and stuff like that. So he had stolen marmalade because he was angry at the shopkeeper. She didn't want him. So he takes this jar and starts pouring it out on the sidewalk. I don't know why. And the other day, the idiot, a pusher asks him if he wants pills. He asks how much and it's two hundred of these monkey money [Bulgarian lev currency]. Then he steals the pills and runs off. He found out later that the pills were made of glucose, but still. What a dumb thing to do. The pusher will beat him up if he sees him."

"Jonathan does these things to gain recognition?"

"Most definitely," Michael answered and Lars added, "Also when he is by himself, he does stuff so he can tell the story afterward. And when he tells the story, he sits there trying to get attention, trying to catch your eyes."

"But what he is doing doesn't sound much different from what you are doing. What's the difference?"

"What we do just comes to us," Michael said. "It just happens."

"We do mindless stuff," Lars added. "We do it without thinking about it."

Some observers associate nightlife with freedom of expression, respect for diversity, and liberation from patriarchal structures (McRobbie 1994; Pini 1997). However, the discussions regarding Jonathan illustrate that there are limits to the freedoms provided in nightlife settings (see also Vaadal 2019). Even at the best of dance parties, the freedoms on offer are circumscribed by rules about how to break rules—and not everyone is welcome at the party (Saldanha 2007). Revelers cannot do as they please but rather are compelled to act out their freedom in a way that peers will find convincing and aesthetically satisfying. Sociologist Peter Johnson has explored this in a British context, and he notes that young drinkers can be ruthlessly critical of peers who present themselves as something that they are not, such as those who embellish their drinking exploits: "Teenagers who 'pretend' or 'fake' are likely to be stigmatised by their peers, while those who behave in an authentic manner will be rewarded with acceptance" (2013, 753). Jonathan was harshly condemned by his travel companions because they believed that he got himself into trouble, not out of drunkenness or out of destructive instincts, but because he desperately wanted attention. They deemed him inauthentic. Even Jonathan's falling asleep on the floor with keys in hand was suspected to be a strategic act meant to generate laughter. By contrast, Lars insisted that his own transgressions were genuine because they were impulsive and based on who he was rather than who he wanted to be.

Lars was trying hard to convince me and his friends that his transgressions were "for real," as if they were emanating from some inner, hideous True Self. He took pride in being bad, to the extent that he got the words "F-cky F-cky" tattooed on his skin. This raises the following questions: Why are so many people, especially young people, proud of their transgressions? Why is it so common to see people parading their transgressions? Why would anyone like to be seen as evil? Theologian John Milbank sheds light on these questions in a passage that deserves to be quoted at length:

> Evil can be "banal" . . . but it can also be attractive and seductive, not least when dressed in the alluring garbs of the transgressive. It can seem to offer us excitement, to break the shackles of the routine of our everyday lives and to afford us the opportunity to be different, to stand out from the crowd and make a distinctive mark in the world. Evil on a grand enough scale has a fair chance of being remembered, for, as Mark Antony sagely remarks [in a tragedy by Shakespeare], "the evil that men do lives after them; the good is oft interred with their bones." A life of merely average goodness or unremarkable rectitude, by contrast, may appear, especially to those with imagination and ambition, second rate and more than a tad dull and unadventurous. The norms and rules that govern our lives can be experienced as constraints on our desire to assert ourselves or to secure a place in posterity. (2011, 173–174)

I am aware that many transgressions are uncalculated and nonstrategic. A verbal argument turns into a physical fight because the opponents work each other up into a rushing rage that makes them snap and commit violence. A flirtatious interaction suddenly shifts into violent abuse because one side is overcome by lust and feels entitled to take control and advantage of the other. However, if my interpretation of Lars is correct, the transgressions he perpetrated were strategically designed to create an image of being bad to the bone.

CHAPTER 6

SYMBOLIZATION

Durkheim writes that people get pumped up with energy when they are gathered for celebration. Most of this energy is channeled back into the event through intensified movements and interactions, but some of it is saved up for later through a process of symbolization. One of the principal ways that this happens is through an object, such as a totem symbol, that becomes the focus of attention and is imbued with collective energies (Durkheim 1995, 232–233). Collins explains, "What is mutually focused upon becomes a symbol of the group. In actuality, the group is focusing on its own feeling of intersubjectivity, its own shared emotion; but it has no way of representing this fleeting feeling, except by representing it as embodied in an object. It reifies its experience, makes it thing-like, and thus an emblem, treated as having noun-like permanence" (2004, 37).

The emotionally charged symbol functions somewhat like a battery: after being charged or recharged, it can supply energy for a certain period before going flat. Similarly, after the end of an effervescent event, individuals may remember and reexperience some of the effervescence by turning their attention toward an energized object that reminds them of the event. Symbols can thus help keep collective emotions "perpetually alive and fresh" (Durkheim 1995, 222).[1]

What I here refer to as an "effervescent symbol" is a special type of group symbol: an affectively charged medium through which group members can access and tap into a past effervescent experience. Not all group symbols are effervescent, however. Some are emotionally flat and insignificant. The effervescent symbol represents the group of people who filled it with their collective energies, and reverence for the symbol is, in this sense, a form of group love. This is why effervescent symbols can become so existentially important to people. Durkheim mentions the example of the soldier who risks everything to protect a flag—a mere piece of cloth with some drawings on it but also a potent symbol of the soldier's country and compatriots: "The soldier who dies for his flag dies for his country, but the idea of the flag is actually in the foreground of his consciousness. Indeed, the flag sometimes causes action directly. Although the country will not be lost if a solitary flag remains in the hands of the enemy or won if it is regained, the soldier is killed retaking it. He forgets that the flag is only a symbol that has no value in itself but only brings to mind the reality it represents. The flag itself is treated as if it was that reality" (1995, 222).

Anything can potentially be transformed into an effervescent symbol, including physical objects (e.g., flags and commercial logos), living beings (e.g., totem animals and rock stars), words (e.g., stories and slogans), and bodily movements (e.g., ritualistic hand gestures and dance steps). The essential component, according to Durkheim, is that people infuse the symbol with collective energy, again and again. Eventually, it may become so powerful that it can drive people to make extreme sacrifices in its pursuit or defense.

COLLECTING SYMBOLS

The process of symbolization is a largely understudied but vital aspect of nightlife. Revelers place a high value on retaining stories, photos, video clips, and other symbols that can connect them with past effervescent experiences. The desire for energized symbols is so strong that many go to great lengths to obtain them. For example, in Sunny Beach, a group of women told me that they kept records of all the "stupid things" they were doing. They had a "stupid list" with descriptions of "stupid things and who did them," and they also had a "stupid hat" to be worn by the person who had done the stupidest act within the last twenty-four hours.

One of them, Fie, explained, "We want something to laugh about when we get home and when we hang out in our hotel room."

Her friend Merete added, "So for example [last night] Berit was so drunk that she forgot that I had brought bottles of water to our room. She went around in the hotel, knocking on every door [presumably to get water] and waking up the entire hotel. She can't even remember it."

"She was sleepwalking, that's what she was doing."

"I was thinking to myself, 'Oh no, she will wake up everyone,' and I could just hear her bumping around upstairs."

Berit subsequently received many comments and friendly teasing for her drunken "sleepwalking." She was forced to wear the "stupid hat" for the duration of a day, and the episode was jotted down on the "stupid list." The group hereby made concrete symbols out of the effervescent episode, something that in all probability strengthened and prolonged the memory of it. For as Durkheim points out, "Without symbols . . . social feelings could have only an unstable existence. Those feelings are very strong so long as men are assembled, mutually influencing one another, but when the gathering is over, they survive only in the form of memories that gradually dim and fade away if left to themselves" (1995,

232). The group of friends certainly did not let their effervescent memories die away but instead repeatedly infused new life into them through storytelling and meticulously attending to their list and hat. And on later occasions, when they brought out these stories and objects, they could vividly reconnect with the effervescent moments they had shared in Sunny Beach. They would laugh at the stupid acts they had committed and, probably, they could feel some of the same excitement involved in these acts.

They also made extensive use of cameras to record their excesses both when they partied in their home towns and during vacations abroad.

"The best thing that happened last year [during a vacation in Spain] was probably that video we made," recalled another member of the group, Felicia, with a laugh. "We have watched it over and over and over again. That's the best thing, to watch all those stupid things I did. Then I know what *not* to do this year."

"What did you do in that video?" I asked.

"I fell and made some really stupid comments," Felicia answered. "I had gone home to wash my feet, because, I tell you, you get some pretty dirty feet when you walk around without your shoes on. But we only had this bathtub with a curtain around it, and I accidentally tore down the curtain. I tried to put it up again because I didn't want to ruin it. Then Kirsten came in with the video camera. They filmed me as I was standing there totally wasted and nearly falling into the bathtub, and I also smashed the curtain rod into the mirror."

"Yeah, you nearly shattered that mirror," someone said.

"And I was *so* drunk, you know," Felicia said. "When I got the curtain back up, it fell down right on top of me. That's the kind of thing you can laugh about afterward, right? Thank God we have no curtain in our bathroom this year."

These stories support Durkheim's argument that effervescent moments can have effects that last long after the actual ritual gathering. Revelers are often quite conscious of this and actively try to create and accumulate symbols that can help transport the collective energies into the future. Some make "stupid lists," while others go autograph hunting, take "selfies" on the dance floor, write dirty diaries, and hold cell phones overhead during concerts to film the show. In other words, people indulge in moments of effervescence not only for immediate pleasure but also to collect energized symbols that they can enjoy later in life. Effervescent situations are thus much more than short-lived outbursts of transient joy—embodied in terms like *carpe diem, no future,* and *flow.* This is not to deny that many revelers long for, and actively seek, the experiential intensity of being fully in the moment. However, such experiences do not come easily and tend to be brief, even for people who are under the influence of potent drugs, loud music, repetitive dance movements, and stroboscopic lighting. In other words, people partaking in nightlife are frequently aware of, mindful of, or downright preoccupied with the enduring symbolic potentialities of their effervescent situations.

Lyng (1990) observes that extreme experiences can be difficult to translate into language and that some people, including many skydivers, prefer to keep their extreme experiences to themselves. He writes that "if people typically find it difficult to describe edgework, it is very likely because the reflective self is simply not present at the height of the experience" (1990, 880). This is very probably so, but again, people are rarely at experiential heights for long spates of time. Experiences change, even when we do not want them to: Moments of full absorption in a complicated task suddenly shift into scatterbrained rumination. Intense joy becomes melancholic longing. Inner stillness is disrupted by inner cacophony (Jackson 1998, 10). The constant oscillations between states of experience partly explain why extreme situations may be punctuated by flashes of awareness of the moment's symbolic potentials.

Even the most heated moments can thus give way suddenly to an awareness of symbols and efforts to collect or create them. During violent confrontations, for example, fighters sometimes perform in a stylized manner to make the situation more memorable, pausing to attract more spectators, moving gracefully despite the imminent danger, or saying something funny before throwing a punch. Folklorist James P. Leary thus writes in a study of male fights in rural American bars that although fighters may be primarily concerned with victory, they are often also filled with a "concomitant desire to have their own struggles commemorated positively in narratives told by themselves and others" (1976, 36). In another study from the United States, sociologist Curtis Jackson-Jacobs (2009) observes that the young men he studied sometimes strategically provoked fights and risked spectacular beatings because they wanted memorable action that they could later tell others about. Many of these fights were group fights, and they were almost always followed by "excited group storytelling" (Jackson-Jacobs 2009, 179). Jackson-Jacobs explains, "Much of the thrill of fighting was to establish solidarity and membership in the local violent elite and to reveal one's strong character. A further motivation was narrative: to make good stories" (viii). This is yet another illustration of how far people will go to obtain energized symbols that signify who they are, what they can do, and which group they belong to.

Particularly good stories about effervescent events may have the attributes of effervescent symbols. That is, they are highly valued and told regularly within friend groups, and when they are told well, they generate effervescence among those who are sharing them. Moreover, much like national flags, they can become important group-identity markers that incite group members to undertake certain actions. Those who know and respect the stories are likely to be insiders, whereas those who do not know the stories are likely to be outsiders. As for those who show disrespect for the stories, they may be deemed enemies of the group (Collins 2008, 118).

CREATING SYMBOLS

The most treasured symbols of nightlife effervescence are the ones that are self-made, exclusive, and difficult to obtain. Consider the practice of "balconing," which has been observed among tourists—typically young male tourists—at seaside resorts across the world. This practice involves various acrobatic, high-risk maneuvers on balconies, such as climbing from one balcony to another (vertically or horizontally), trying to keep one's balance while standing on the railing, and jumping from a balcony into (or at least in the direction of) a swimming pool.

Most acts of balconing that I have heard about and seen were premediated, staged, and marked by clear efforts to generate symbols. Typically, the performer or performers first discuss the stunt with friends, then announce the impending event, and then finally carry out their antics in front of their attentive comrades. Talking up the acts before doing them has multiple purposes: to assess the benefits and dangers of the stunt; to obtain practical advice on executing it; to gather moral and emotional support from a group (i.e., build courage); to elicit maximum dramatic effect; and, perhaps most importantly, to ensure that there will be people to witness the performance and communicate it to other people via storytelling, photography, or video recordings.[2] Needless to say, social media such as YouTube abound with nerve-wracking stories, photos, and videos of tourists engaged in balconing. Acts of balconing tend to have a long and impassioned life on social media as well as among the people who directly witnessed or performed them.

Balconing is rarely a solitary pursuit of excitement. It is generally a social ritual meant to generate effervescence in a group while creating emotionally charged symbols that can help the group remain cohesive long into the future. These symbols of youthful death defiance may thus strengthen ties within a group, but they may also, simultaneously, boost the reputation of a single group member. Indeed, certain acts of balconing are so spectacularly outrageous—and the stories, photos, or videos of them so impressive—that their performers become internationally known.

A team of Spanish researchers has studied the phenomenon of balconing, which has claimed numerous young lives in recent years (Pérez-Bovet et al. 2015). They observe that balconing in Spain is most prevalent among young tourists at certain coastal resorts in the Girona province and on the Balearic Islands. They write, moreover, that the activity of balconing "generates a small but constant flow of patients with fall-related severe brain and systemic injuries. . . . Several cases have confronted us with young and healthy individuals in their late teens or early twenties, with promising careers in their countries of origin, sustaining devastating brain injuries" (2015, 41). There has even been talk in the media of a balconing "craze" and "epidemic" among young, predominantly British tourists in Spain, although no one knows how prevalent the activity actually is.

What is it about hotel balconies that make them so tempting to climb between, balance on, and jump from? The work of narrative criminologists Lois Presser and Sveinung Sandberg can help illuminate the seductions of balconing and the related phenomena of "buildering," "roofing," "night climbing," and "place hacking," which are the high-risk activities of climbing on buildings and artificial constructs, with or without protection, during the day or at night (Garrett 2013).[3] Presser and Sandberg (2015) argue that stories are a fundamental component of the human condition. They are necessary for our social existence and instrumental in shaping how we understand ourselves, other people, and the wider world. Stories are thus constitutive rather than merely representative of reality. They provide us with meaning, form our experiences, and guide our behavior. Presser explains that a "narrative serves as a sort of script for action, although a highly dynamic one insofar as our narratives are ever-changing. Our narratives communicate who we think we are and who we hope to be" (2013, 25). So a young man's jump from a balcony into a swimming pool may be interpreted as a scripted performance that takes inspiration from existing stories that circulate in his cultural milieu. Perhaps the man has seen photos and videos of people jumping from balconies, and perhaps he would like to have photos and videos of himself jumping from a balcony. The very manner in which the man performs and experiences his jump may also be narratively cued. Perhaps he says a funny line from a movie just before he takes the leap, and perhaps his descent toward the swimming pool is marred by sensations, images, and snippets that stem from tragic balconing stories about people who missed the target.

The enthusiastic circulation of hotel balconing stories, photos, and videos is arguably one of the main reasons that so many young people choose hotel balconies as stages for their high-risk performances. We humans are mimetic creatures who follow the example of other people, speaking in borrowed words, enacting familiar narratives, and reproducing cultural codes (Frank 2010). However, balconing symbols are not all bad and inherently dangerous. They will only motivate the odd few to undertake actual acts of balconing; most people will be demotivated or scandalized by those very same symbols. This is why the authorities and travel agencies in certain countries have engaged proactively in creating and disseminating tragic balconing stories, videos, and images in order to make people think and take better care of themselves. The British authorities, for instance, have led an information campaign based on a harrowing balconing story of a nineteen-year-old from Liverpool, Jake Evans, who fell down seven floors from a balcony in Magaluf, Spain, and miraculously survived. This campaign included a leaflet called "Booze and Balconies Don't Mix," which states in big letters, "Your hotel balcony is there for relaxing on. It's not a shortcut to your mate's room or a diving board to the pool. So please enjoy the views and don't let them be the last ones you see." The leaflet also includes testimony from Evans and a photo of his mangled, near-dead body:

> I hit every balcony on the way down, as they jutted out like steps. I landed on a sun lounger which broke my fall and probably saved my life. . . . I fractured my skull, broke front teeth which pierced through my upper lip, snapped my right wrist and broke all the fingers on my right hand. I hurt my back which was excruciating and cut a considerable hole in my leg. . . . Looking at the height I fell and my injuries I know I am lucky to be alive. But, the accident has changed my life—a year on and I have recurring problems with my back and right wrist and doctors have told me I probably always will. (ABTA 2012)

Prevention campaigns often make use of tragic symbols, like Jake Evans's story, to make people "think balcony safety," "drink responsibly," "say no to drugs," "drive safely," and so forth. It is uncertain, however, whether such campaigns appeal to the target group and change their opinions and behaviors.[4] Part of the problem with such campaigns is that symbols may lose some of their potency when they are recontextualized into reasonable or moralizing projects that tell people how to think or behave. The "tamed," unambiguous symbol (e.g., a preventive leaflet) delivers a clear message that calls for acceptance and conformity, whereas the "wild," ambiguous symbol (e.g., an amateur video of balconing) calls for interpretation and effervescent discussion.

SHARING SYMBOLS

The traditional Danish "brown bar" is a typical location for sharing effervescent symbols such as drinking stories and party pictures. These bars are called "brown" because they tend to be dimly lit, contain wooden furniture, and have walls darkened by decades of cigarette smoke. Local barflies, eccentrics, and students generally form the clientele, and the atmosphere tends to be one of low-key drunken effervescence. People usually sit together around tables and talk, or sit alone watching other people talk. On Friday and Saturday nights, however, the crowd tends to be bigger. This raises the level of effervescence and makes it more complex. There is more intergroup mingling, faster drinking, perhaps some dancing and kissing, and different types of effervescence emerge, converge, or collide.

   Let me illustrate the atmosphere at brown bars, and how effervescent symbols are shared in this context, by zooming in on one night that I spent with my friend, Jim, in one of Copenhagen's oldest brown bars. We met at eight o'clock in the evening, found a table, and bought two beers and two shots of Fernet Branca. Jim lifted his shot glass and said, "Let's greet." I could feel how the liquor slowed down my mind and made me feel more present. A guy in the bar caught our attention. He was well dressed, thirtysomething, and had a moleskin notebook protruding from a pocket of his brown jacket. He appeared to be the artist type, but the miserable variant so typical of brown bars. He was trying to strike up conversations, but babbling incoherently to one patron after the other, until finally the bartender yelled at him, "NOW YOU GET OUT." And so he did without a word, slamming the door behind him. The bartender turned to us.

"Boys, if you take the same shit as him, I'll kick you out too," he said with a grin.

"What was he on?" I asked.

"No f-cking idea," answered the bartender. "Everything, I guess."

Clued by this incident, Jim and I immersed ourselves in a high-flying conversation about life. Should one try to fight the hardship? Flee from it? Cultivate acceptance? Or was it best to just give up and hope for the best? And the artist guy, was he really on drugs, as the bartender had claimed, or was he just crazy drunk? Jim took hold of a guy who walked by.

"Mathias! Good to see you, man!" he shouted.

Mathias was in his early thirties and dressed in casual clothes. He stayed for a short chat before returning to the back room. We soon followed and found him conversing with a friend. We sat down with them and had a round of beers, and then another, while discussing soccer and TV commercials for an hour or so. Jim suddenly broke out in laughter. He explained that he had come to think of how he recently met Mathias after several years with no contact. They had bumped into each other one early Sunday morning.

"You know, there you are on your way home, finding your old buddy walking the streets like some nutcase in his socks and freezing like hell," Jim said.

We all laughed, including Mathias, who explained that he had fallen asleep in a park and woke up to discover that his shoes were gone. Somebody must have stolen them.

This story perceptibly changed the mood around the table. Our discussions about soccer and commercials had also been lively, but they never went beyond the low-level effervescence of small talking. We were merely filling up the time with a steady flow of inconsequential words—about teams, players, matches, and actors—allowing us to express ourselves, listen to each other, and stay focused on the same activity. When Jim described his encounter with Mathias, the stakes and energies of the conversation increased because what he said could potentially have offended Mathias as well as his friend. However, all four of us reacted positively. We smiled and laughed and thereby gave the story our approval, although it portrayed one of us in a sad light.

Linguistic studies have found that transgressive talk, such as rudeness and drinking stories, may be a sign of intimacy in interaction (Jefferson, Sacks, and Schegloff 1987; Coupland and Jaworski 2003). Transgressive talk is more commonly shared among friends than strangers. Accordingly, by initiating such talk, a speaker may push a conversation in the direction of intimacy. I think that this is what happened when Jim told us about the essentially tragic situation in which he had found Mathias that early Sunday morning. The story abruptly brought an end to the small talk and turned our attention to the highly personal matter of Mathias walking the streets alone, drunk, shoeless, and freezing—as if he were a homeless person or "some nutcase," as Jim brusquely put it. The story was both frank and critical. However, it is not my impression that it was meant to hurt Mathias. Rather, the story depicted a flaw pertaining to all of us, not only Mathias: the occasional tendency to indulge in deep intoxication, despite the miseries that might result.

Laughter is a common reaction to stories, video clips, and other symbols of drunken degradation (Tutenges and Rod 2009). The type of laughter that such symbols provoke is clearly critical: it questions, challenges, and denounces the more or less out-of-control protagonists who violate various norms and rules (Bergson 1911). However, the laughter is rarely purely critical but often also signals more positive emotions such as joy, admiration, and praise. For a breaker of rules (especially when these are minor rules, such as taste and etiquette) is a Janus-faced agent: at once a villain who disturbs the flow of social life and a hero who disobeys the repressive demands of decency, common sense, and convention (Eco 1984, 2).

Bakhtin describes the ambiguities of humor in his discussion of "carnival laughter," which he defines as follows: "It is first of all, a festive laughter. Therefore it is not an individual reaction to some isolated comic event. Carnival laughter is the laughter of all the people. Second, it is universal in scope; it is directed at all and everyone, including the carnival's participants. The entire world is seen in its droll aspect, in its gay relativity. Third, laughter is ambivalent: it is gay, triumphant, and at the same time mocking, deriding. It asserts and denies, it buries and revives" (1984, 11–12).

The laughter provoked by the Mathias story was, in my understanding, a form of carnival laughter: collective, inclusive, and ambiguous. We laughed in unison, skeptically yet sympathetically, at a flaw common to all of us, thus acknowledging our shared human nature. In other words, the story about Mathias was a story about all of us. It connected us on an existential plane and made us laugh in a way that increased the intimacy of our group while allowing us to collectively confront and, perhaps, obtain a brief sense of reconciliation with the all too familiar situation of being on wobbly ground, out of control, and pitiful.

I therefore agree with Jackson's observation that "the comic is not the opposite of the tragic so much as a strategy for countermanding the tragic with distance and indirection" (2002, 182). Laughter can provide great relief in the face of tragedy, and the evocation of tragic scenarios may be a rhetorical maneuver to provoke laughter in an audience. In fact, there may be few other options but to laugh when somebody throws a bewilderingly sad story at you.

Other stories followed after the one Jim had told about Mathias. Some were merely snippets of stories, whereas others were long and complicated, including one about a man called Philip. Jim and I both knew him, so we collaborated on telling this story, weaving together the disparate pieces we had heard from various sources, including Philip himself. It began with an internet flirtation between Philip and a married woman from overseas. One day, the woman found an excuse to visit Denmark. However, when Philip went to the airport to pick her up, the first thing she did was check her emails, after which she said that she had to take care of a few things. They could meet later, she added, and she would have to stay overnight at some friends' house. Otherwise, her husband would suspect that she was having an affair, she explained. This all threw Philip into despair. He had hoped for romance and adventure, but what he got was reserve and practicalities. What followed was a long string of bad decisions and awkward situations; he tried to drink away his frustrations, later met with the woman in a fancy restaurant, took off too much of his clothing, was asked by a waiter to leave, got lost from the woman, drank some more, had a blackout, and woke up the next day in a hotel bathtub with a bloody bandage wrapped around his hand and his pockets empty of belongings.

This story made us laugh and shake our heads just as we had laughed and shaken our heads at the story about Mathias. Again, these are typical reactions to stories and other symbols of drunken degradation, reactions that I interpret as expressing a mix of feelings: disbelief over the nonsensical behavior of the storied protagonist, sadness over the imperfections of human life, appreciation that somebody has challenged the repressive power of rules, and relief from not being (or no longer being) as out of control as the protagonist. Much like folktales, stories about drunken effervescence generally convey multiple meanings and provoke diverse feelings (Jackson 1982). These stories do not advance any one message or morality; rather, they call into question established truths and facilitate discussions of complicated existential problems, such as the problem of losing and regaining control over oneself. The sharing of effervescent stories may, in this sense, be understood as a strategy to trigger emotionally uplifting investigations of existential dramas and dilemmas. Is it acceptable to have an affair with a married woman? What do you do when a person you are flirting with suddenly shifts from being passionately interested to being coldly uninterested? Where is the line between comical debauchery and tragic depravity? How does one deal with a friend who is out of control? These were but a few of the questions that were brought up by the Mathias and Philip stories.

Sharing personal stories is a moral event that can involve scrutinizing other people's behaviors, including former or projected selves (Presser 2010, 6). The storyteller and protagonist are never the exact same person, so even in first-person stories, the storyteller is standing apart and representing what the protagonist is doing (see also Linde 1993, 123). By implicitly or explicitly expressing critiques, storytellers may project themselves as moral beings with a moral understanding of the world. They may not present themselves as morally blameless or respectable, but storytellers typically frame themselves as somewhat superior to the protagonists. It can be comforting to point fingers and claim superiority over somebody else, even if that somebody is some version of yourself.

It is important to note that the stories we were sharing about Mathias, Philip, and others had certain dissimilarities with the events as they actually occurred. Inevitably, we storytellers got details wrong, omitted relevant information, or jumbled the chronology. This is how it is with storytelling. To tell a story is a process of reworking and reinventing past experiences so as to produce a certain effect in a certain social situation (Jackson 2002). As linguistic anthropologist Richard Bauman puts it, "Narratives are keyed both to the events in which they are told and to the events that they recount, toward narrative events and narrated events" (1986, 2). Narratives are, in this sense, never neutral but always selective and motivated. However, regardless of their accuracy, our stories were a success in that they lifted the level of energy and intimacy in our group. For what makes personal narratives successful is not so much their truth value, verifiability, or logical coherence but whether they achieve some personal or social end, such as generating effervescence. In the words of Collins, "personal narratives do not have to be true, they need mainly to be dramatic, to blow up the little mishaps of everyday life into adventures or comedies, minor adversities into martyrdoms and local scandals, in order to become good raw material for the dramatic performances on the conversational stage that make for a lively and engrossing conversation . . . the audience enters into the spirit of the performance by not questioning it but by taking it in a situational mood, whatever will build up the highest level of momentary collective effervescence" (2004, 85).

Collins's observations are true for all symbols of effervescent revelry, whether personal drinking stories, bad trip stories, fight stories, "stupid lists," "stupid hats," concert photos, or video clips of balconing. The social efficacy of these symbols is based on their capacity to move us, emotionally and intellectually, beyond the everyday world of rigid rules, reasonable decisions, and flat experiences. These symbols—when they are well made, well performed, and well received—give a glimpse and, indeed, a perceptible sense of worlds beyond, realms apart, or what philosopher Alfred Schütz and sociologist Thomas Luckmann call "extraordinary provinces of reality" (1973). The characteristics of each of these "provinces" vary according to the type of effervescence that they represent. Let me illustrate with three examples.

Symbols of drunken effervescence, such as the abovementioned "stupid list" and the Philip story, evoke and connect us with a province of reality inhabited by inebriated and more or less grotesque characters who challenge established truths, ridicule authorities, and make fools of themselves. These characters say the unsayable and do the unthinkable, and they say and do so in an altogether clumsy manner: revealing embarrassing secrets, insulting the wrong people, stripping in inappropriate situations, urinating on themselves, vomiting, crashing into things, and falling asleep in uncomfortable places and awkward positions. The ones who are represented by these symbols are generally drunk from alcohol only, but they sometimes also consume whatever other drugs they may get their hands on. However, it is above all the physical clumsiness of drunkenness that drives the protagonists, plots, and general moods of these symbols.

By contrast, *symbols of psychedelic effervescence* evoke and put us in contact with a province of reality that revolves around the use of psychedelic drugs (i.e., cannabis and LSD) and psychedelic events (i.e., psychedelic rock concerts and Goa trance festivals). Here, the familiar appears in mysterious guise, and the self-evident is warped into something utterly perplexing. The people represented by these symbols are not necessarily saying or doing anything out of the ordinary, nor are they particularly noisy, grotesque, or clumsy. Rather, psychedelic characters are extraordinary for their experiences: they are contacted by dead people, see monsters, hear voices, realize that the world is flat, merge with Mother Earth, and so on.

As for *symbols of violent effervescence,* these present and connect us with a province of reality filled with aggression, drama, and the display of force. What fuels and defines these symbols is not so much substances and substance-induced intoxication; rather, it is the powerful rush of verbal or physical confrontation between human agents. Individuals who are represented by these symbols typically come across as heroes who stand up for their friends, justice, or some principle—or they are villains who disrespect, assault, or abuse people.

Symbols of effervescence thus evoke and relate to specific types of effervescence. When a symbol of drunken effervescence is shared, for example, it may generate in the audience a sense not just of "collective effervescence" but, more exactly, of drunken effervescence. Affectively charged drinking symbols are, in this sense, mildly inebriating. They have the potential to bring about a bit of the disoriented group dynamics of actual drunkenness. This is why people so often share symbols of drunken effervescence just before drunken events or at their outset. Sharing these symbols is part of the process of achieving a desired state of drunkenness (Tutenges and Sandberg 2013). The same goes for symbols of psychedelic effervescence, melodramatic effervescence, violent effervescence, compassionate effervescence, sexual effervescence, and any other type of effervescence; these symbols also have mildly intoxicating properties, and it is common for people to share them prior to or in the beginning of effervescent events.

THE DURATION OF SYMBOLS

Effervescent experiences are of great significance not only for young people but for people of all ages. They can change people's relationships, thinking, and direction in life. As sociologist Alice Goffman puts it, effervescent social occasions "possess a comparatively high chance of prompting indeterminate occurrences that spill past the occasion's designated parameters to alter the trajectories of people going forward. In the relatively smooth fabric of everyday life, social occasions are potentially fateful situations" (2019, 55). Effervescent occasions certainly can be fateful, and they often provide excellent material for stories, pictures, and other symbols that can be saved and shared with others. Even decades later, effervescent occasions may be invoked and felt through the medium of symbols.

I witnessed several examples of the effects of effervescent symbols during an evening with my uncle Ole at his farm in Vendsyssel in the far north of Denmark. I had visited the farm every summer since my earliest childhood, and as always when the weather allowed for it, we spent the evening outside by a large bonfire, chewing on hot dogs and staring into the embers. A telephone rang. It was my uncle's friend Jens, who wanted to know if he could drop by. He arrived soon after with his wife, Yvonne, and their son, Thomas. Yvonne, Jens, and my uncle were all about seventy years old, and one could tell from their large, leathered hands that they had labored most of their lives. They talked about the weather. How much longer should they wait before harvesting? Would heavy rain come again this year and ruin the crops?

Jens changed the subject.

"Have you seen the photos of the sofa?" he asked me.

Ole went inside and came back with two photos. All eyes were on me as I inspected them. One showed Jens and Ole sitting together on a sofa, which was enveloped in smoke from a fire burning from below. The other showed Ole lying alone on the sofa, which by now had big flames running up the sides of it. It looked as if his crotch and boots had caught fire too.

"What the hell did you do that for?" I asked, laughing.

Ole admitted that the flames had injured his hand, but he had stayed longer on the couch than Jens, which made it all worth it. I passed the photos around and said that they should grow up. The photos had clearly changed the character and level of effervescence around the bonfire. Focus was no longer on the treacherous weather and small talk but on the melodramatic effervescence of the burning couch incident.

People from Vendsyssel have a reputation for being awfully taciturn and reserved. It is said that their feelings are sealed off behind crossed arms and stern faces. But there are many ways to express feelings, and the presentation of symbols is one of them. To me, the couch photos and the way they were narrated were essentially about love. The photos were also about melodramatic rivalry, toughness, and humor, featuring two adults acting like irresponsible teenagers. However, Jens and Ole did their stunt together. They behaved irresponsibly in unison, sitting side by side through fire and pain and thus demonstrating that they were willing to make a sacrifice for each other. Jens eventually had to leave the couch, but the main plot of the story was the joint transgression and strong bond between the two old friends.

Another story was brought up: a much older story that I had heard many times before. It began with Jens sending an anonymous, threatening letter to Ole, who soon found out where it came from. A couple of threatening letters went back and forth, until Jens one day stepped it up by sending Ole the severed ears of a piglet. Some time passed with no response. Then one late night, Jens heard the roar of an engine, spinning wheels, and gunshots from his yard. When Jens ventured outside, he found an envelope on the ground with two large pig ears in it and a letter saying that all adults would soon be executed but the kids spared. The thing is that Jens had a visitor that night who witnessed these events in sheer terror until somebody told her that it was all just for fun.

I was not there in person when Ole and Jens tortured themselves on the burning couch or when they exchanged threats. But as I was listening to their stories and seeing their photos, I felt emotionally connected with what they had been through. I was moved by what I heard and saw, and I am quite certain that the others around the bonfire were as well. These shared feelings indicate that the energized symbols from effervescent events may have an impact beyond the group of people who experienced the events firsthand. It is useful, therefore, to distinguish between two basic types of effervescent symbols: (1) symbols created in the midst of effervescent events, typically as a large and emotionally aroused group of people focus on the same object and invest it with their collective energies, thereby elevating it to the status of a group identity-marker; and (2) secondhand symbols that are evoked and revived postfestum in engrossing interactions, typically between people who have strong emotional ties (Collins 2004, 87).

While secondhand effervescent symbols point back to actual effervescent events, their energy does not come directly from the original events but from subsequent interactions about those events. So when Ole and Jens showed me the couch photos, I was not moved by remembrance of the couch incident (I had not been there to witness it) or by the photos in and of themselves (the quality was not very good). Rather, the photos moved me emotionally because of the way they were interactionally performed as we were sitting together around the bonfire, talking, laughing, and sympathetically attending to one another. Ole and Jens may have connected with the experience of actually sitting on the couch, whereas I (and presumably also Yvonne and Thomas) was connecting with the ongoing interactions that we were having. Today, when I look at the couch photos, I am filled by a bit of the warmth of sitting there by the bonfire.[5]

Importantly, Ole and Jens were able to lift the mood around the bonfire because they were presenting their symbols to an audience that was willing to help make these symbols come alive. Rather than passively receiving the symbols, Yvonne, Thomas, and I infused energy into them by asking probing questions, making encouraging comments, and laughing when fitting. All of us thus collaborated in amplifying the emotional energy and solidarity. We did so, I suppose, for immediate entertainment, but also because we considered the symbols worthy of commemoration and rejuvenation. These were symbols of a lifelong friendship—a friendship to which we gave our full emotional support.

CHAPTER 7

REVITALIZATION

Durkheim held that collective effervescence is something universally necessary for human beings. Without it, life would be an unmemorable flow of routinized work activities with no opportunity to connect fully with and tap into the life forces of other people. He was by no means antiwork but believed that too much focus on work and personal gain disconnects people from each other and saps their passions, leading to a life that is "monotonous, slack, and humdrum" (1995, 217). The remedy to these work-related ailments is to have periodic rituals that unite and excite people so that, ultimately, the rhythms of their bodies and minds become synchronized and everyone "is carried outside [themselves], pulled away from [their] ordinary occupations and preoccupations" (387). This is not merely a matter of escaping everyday life and blowing off steam. It is also about discovering who we are, where we belong, and what is important to us. Durkheim writes that once an effervescent ritual is over, "we return to profane life with more energy and enthusiasm, not only because we have placed ourselves in contact with a higher source of energy but also because our own capacities have been replenished through living, for a few moments, a life that is less tense, more at ease, and freer" (386).

Even funeral rites have certain revitalizing qualities; they can help participants regain a sense of purpose, meaning, vigor, and importantly, group membership.[1] Essentially, this is because funerals allow people to unite and connect over a common cause. It is common, for example, for people at funerals to walk in procession, hold hands, sing and cry together, and hug and caress one another—or burst into laughter to further connect and perhaps alleviate some of the sadness (Durkheim 1995, 403). The feeling of sadness may not be pleasant, but it is a feeling like any other and, as such, can be passed on from person to person and thereby unify them. The underlying reason or official purpose of a ritual is not essential for how intensely it is felt and how strongly it binds people together. What really matters is that the ritual participants come physically close and wholeheartedly engage in the same activity (Pickering 2009, 346).

To use a complicated but precise term, episodes of effervescence are generally of an agathokakological character. They are composed of both good and bad, and the dynamic interplay between these two opposites is a vital part of their draw and psychosocial impact. So if you ask people to describe the best party they have ever been to, the stories they tell are often brimming with drama and conflicting emotions. These very best of parties are not just "nice," "cozy," or "pleasant." Rather, to use a Durkheimian expression, they feature "wild intensity," whether in the melodrama of a daring flirtation, the sweaty sensuality of a dance party, or the dizzying head-banging at a heavy metal concert (1995, 403). Accidents and embarrassments may be part of the experience, but boredom and isolation not so.

THE CHRISTMAS FEAST

The Danish tradition of the Christmas feast is a good example of the agathokakological character of effervescence because it tends to inflict a great deal of pleasure and pain on those who participate. A Danish adult will typically attend several of these feasts with different groups of friends and colleagues over the month of December and sometimes into January. Every year, as the feasting season kicks off, the media start sending out a steady stream of reports about record-high alcohol sales, drunken brawls, celebrity scandals, and people who have fallen asleep outside in the cold.

The Christmas feast that occupies the most space in my field notes took place one December evening in the apartment of my friend Johannes. In what follows, I will describe this feast in some detail in order to illustrate the twists, turns, and ambiguous effects of effervescent revelry. Johannes had hosted this event many times before, and as usual, we were going to be a group of only men—ten in all—for a potluck-style dinner. Each of us was expected to bring a bag of beers and a dish to be shared. The eating would start around 6:00 p.m., but we were welcome to show up earlier for a beer and chat prior to the meal.

Everyone arrived well ahead of time—except for a fellow called Big D, who later confessed that he intentionally came late. He wanted to skip the first beers, he admitted, in the hope that this would prevent him from becoming too drunk. He had arranged for his wife to take care of their two-year-old son the next morning, but he knew from experience that his chances of sleeping off the debauch were microscopic. His son would find his way into the bedroom and execute a gruesome awakening with joyful squeals and leaps onto the bed.

We were all dressed in our finest clothes. Our friend Christopher even wore a suit and tie that probably dated back to his wedding. The food was also the best we could muster: assorted herring dishes, rye bread fresh from the oven, fish fillet, roast pork, Danish meatballs, boiled potatoes with brown sauce, red cabbage, rice pudding, and much more. Somebody had decided that I would be the only one to bring snaps and that it had to be exactly two bottles. Most people do not like the taste of this strong potato- and corn-based liquor, but during the Danish celebration of Christmas and Easter, it is almost obligatory to drink it. It is typically consumed ice-cold, in small glasses, and to the accompaniment of songs such as the "Haps-haps-haps now we all have snaps" song, which portrays snaps as an enhancer of sexual and culinary appetites. However, snaps also has a reputation for making people go out of their minds and for causing monstrous headaches the day after. Hence the decision that this year, we should have no more and no less than two bottles of snaps.

As could perhaps have been predicted, the two-bottles-only rule was flouted. At least two guests had come with extra bottles and discretely placed them in the freezer, and at some point as we ran out, Tobias went to the nearest kiosk for more because, as he explained, "After all, it is a Christmas feast."

Johannes brought in the first two dishes, but before digging in, a bottle of snaps was passed around. In accordance with custom, we all filled our glasses to the brim, raised them in salute, made eye contact around the table, and then simultaneously tossed back the cold liquor. Anders broke the silence with a loud exhalation followed by the announcement "Now I feel at home."

I also felt that way. First an ice-cold sensation in the mouth and then a warm feeling in the stomach, which spreads throughout the body and makes you more at ease and content.

We talked about the food. Tim said that the fish was from an old fishmonger's shop, which always served the best and freshest of fish. Somebody else admitted that he had bought his dish ready-made, which is slightly against the unwritten rules at special occasions such as a Christmas feast. But at this point, nobody cared where the food came from; it all tasted wonderful. Lots of friendly feelings circulated around the table as we ate, drank, and told stories about our lives and mutual acquaintances. I remember feeling blessed for having such great friends. I would say that at this point in time, the feast was primarily characterized by experiences of compassionate effervescence.

The effects of snaps change after a couple of glasses. At least to me, the experience no longer feels like being at home but rather is one of bloated disorientation and self-estrangement. I begin to move and talk clumsily. My thoughts become clouded. However, up to a certain point, my emotional activities are quite vivid and predominantly affectionate, perhaps because my snaps binges only occur at Christmas, when I am together with friends.

I think Big D was the first to throw up. I found the sink in the toilet clogged with vomit and Big D lying asleep in Johannes's bed. A little later, Erik was found sleeping in the same bed. Anders exclaimed, "Look at those giant trees, taken down before we even reached dessert!" The two fallen men were both larger and fitter than the rest of us, but they may have grown unused to heavy drinking due to their regular sports activities and paternal responsibilities.

Just before dessert, Erik came storming back into the living room with Christopher on his shoulders. When Erik bounced, Christopher was squashed up against the ceiling. All squeals and laughter and tumultuous dancing. After fifteen minutes of this, everyone was wide awake and back at the table. This must have been around 11:00 in the evening. We were now in a condition of very drunken but still compassionate effervescence.

Somebody suggested that we each take turns giving a short speech on a topic of our own choosing. I cannot recall the other speeches, but I distinctly remember what I was planning to say: I wanted to declare my friendship to everyone present and perhaps even say that I loved them. I got up and started talking, my voice thick with emotion. But before the end of my first sentence, Tobias jumped to his feet and angrily started to yell. His right arm was jerking back and forth, and his index finger pointed accusingly at me. I had no clue what he was yelling about, but it was clear that he was serious. I sat down again, baffled, and hoped it would soon pass so I could go on with my speech. The effervescence was still running high, but the experience was now tainted by elements of anger and frustration. The compassionate effervescence was gone; now we were left with a mix of drunken effervescence and violent effervescence.

Christopher tried to calm Tobias, but the angry finger and words continued firing in my direction for several minutes until, finally, Johannes told Tobias to shut up or leave. Tobias walked some meters away from the table and stood in silence with his back to the rest of us. The drama was still echoing in my body, but a sort of dampened or disappointed mood began to take over. I was acutely aware of the other people in the room and felt united with them. Perhaps even with Tobias. Everyone looked like I felt: not good. Perhaps the feast was, at this time, bordering on what might be called sad effervescence?

"So where were we?" Erik said to get things back on track.

Tobias then vomited on the floor and excused himself before collapsing on the couch. To my own surprise, I soon after found myself with a bucket and dishcloth in hand, cleaning up the vomit. Perhaps I wanted to signal that everything was all right and that we were still friends. Or perhaps I felt guilty about whatever I was being accused of and wanted to make up for it.

We resumed our talking and drinking and continued with this for a couple of hours. Around 1:00 or 2:00 in the morning, we were drained of effervescence. Shoulders were hunching, eyelids were drooping, and the conversation was petering out. The snaps binge had devolved into its lethargic phase, when both cognitive and emotional activities come to a standstill. Tobias spent the night on Johannes's couch. The rest of us went home.

I called Christopher the day after to hear how he was recuperating and what he thought about the feast. He said that he had enjoyed himself, but found it silly that we had consumed so much alcohol. Had we only limited ourselves to the planned two bottles of snaps, the night would have been longer and more enjoyable. Fewer of us would have become sick, and Tobias would not have launched into his senseless rant. We were all in our midthirties, yet at least five of us ended up vomiting. One would think we would know better, Christopher said.

We agreed that there is something inevitable to the snaps-drinking ritual. The bottle is passed around, and as if under a spell, everyone fills their glasses and then empties them just as quickly. At least in our group of friends, nobody ever suggests that we stop drinking or even slow down. It is very rare that somebody will skip a round, pour their glass half full, or take the shot in sips. This type of drinking is undergirded by social ideas about what it means to be a man, such as the notion that "to drink is to be masculine and to drink heavily is to be even more masculine" (Hunt, Moloney, and Evans 2010, 194). To back out of a snaps binge is just not an appropriate thing to do, not if you are a man among male friends at a Christmas feast.

A considerable amount of research on men's drinking emphasizes that it is important for men in many parts of the world to be able to "hold their drink," meaning to drink a lot and at a fast pace but without losing control over their ability to move with precision, speak authoritatively, hold their bladder, retain their bowels, and look coherent (see, e.g., Gefou-Madianou 1992). A real man is able to exhibit grace under the pressure of heavy drinking.

However, this portrayal of the controlled male drinker does not correspond well with the rather ungraceful and at times grotesque behavior that unfolds at Danish Christmas feasts. Here, emphasis is less on remaining in control than on losing it. There is little if any shame if a man moves clumsily, speaks gibberish, looks like a mess, or vomits (assuming the vomiting is done discretely and without leaving traces and smells). To urinate on oneself is very inappropriate, though not unheard of, whereas uncontrolled defecation will be met with disgusted disapproval. Moreover, in many friend groups, including the one that gathered at Johannes's home, there is no pride in being able to drink more or faster than the rest. What matters is to take part in the more or less synchronized drinking and continue till the bitter end.

There is a clear element of competition in many drinking practices, especially among adolescent males. This competition typically centers on who can consume the largest quantities of alcohol, who can drink fastest, who can seduce the most women, and who can perform the most spectacular stunts. However, this focus on competition and achievement tends to wane as adolescents enter their twenties and as they begin to form friendships that are solid and long-lasting (Thurnell-Read 2012). Over the years, the emphasis shifts from rivalry between friends to maintaining unity within friend groups.

One of the most powerful ways to enact and enhance group unity is through acts of self-sacrifice. This is the practice of giving away or destroying precious personal resources in order to prove loyalty to a person, group, or deity while demonstrating nonchalance in the face of danger, degradation, and even death (Pan 2012, 86). Snaps drinking at Danish Christmas feasts again provides a vivid example. Three basic forms of sacrificial destruction are common. First, the histrionic intake of liquor can involve quantities so large that they damage the body and mind. The adverse effects associated with this type of "episodic heavy drinking" include an increased risk of blackouts, violent confrontation, sexual assault, problems with the police, impaired driving, serious injury, and sudden death (Bellis, Hughes, and McVeigh 2005). Second, a snaps binge often lasts well into the night, and participants may require one or several days to fully recover. Precious time that could have been devoted to edifying weekend activities is squandered on revelry and its aftermath. Third, a snaps binge involves monetary outlays for the liquor and customary foods, and there may be additional expenses for the replacement or repair of damaged clothes, furniture, bicycles, and so forth. So when a group of people engage in a snaps binge, or in any other type of collective binge drinking, they violently sacrifice some of the most treasured resources in capitalist society. By sacrificing their own health, time, and money, they demonstrate that they place themselves at the service of the group and its sometimes brutal dictates. They also show that they are completely committed to the group and that their relationship is one of selfless amity rather than selfish utility (Bataille 1967, 94). This is the love of crashing and burning together, the solidarity of collective self-destruction.

Collective binge drinking may therefore be understood as a ritual of self-sacrifice because it involves the offering of personal values to a higher cause, in this case the group cause. But there are limits to what and how much binge drinkers are willing to offer. Their sacrifices are rarely what Bataille calls "sovereign" because there tends to be an element of holding back and some sense of self-preservation rather than a complete letting go. Bataille writes that "sovereignty is essentially the refusal to accept the limits that the fear of death would have us respect" (1993, 221) and that "the sovereign" is the one "who *is*, as if death were not" (1993, 222). Binge drinkers may be said to exhibit risk acceptance as well as death defiance, but they usually also take measures to protect themselves and their friends, for instance, by assisting the ones who become sick and calling for help if need be.

Bataille rarely makes direct reference to alcohol or drugs, but he does mention that a key motivation for drinking is to "escape from necessity" and experience moments of sovereign disregard for worldly concerns (1976, 249). I think this is true, although it is my impression that sovereignty is imagined more than lived among drinkers. Drinkers commonly pretend or fantasize themselves to be "as if death were not." They boisterously proclaim that they "don't give a damn about anything," that they "drink till they drop," and that they party "like there's no tomorrow." However, these fantasies rarely translate into truly death-defying action.

Fantasies of sovereignty also abound in popular music as well as in traditional folk songs and drunken proverbs. Consider these lines from a popular Danish drinking song:

Cheers! Cheers! Cheers!
We are the hearty herdsmen
Cheers! Cheers! Cheers!
We drink till we go down
Cheers! Cheers! Cheers!
Lift your glass my friend, you never know when you will go on rehab again

A similar logic is expressed in "A Drinking Song" by the Irish band the Divine Comedy:

We're drinking to life, we're drinking to death
We're drinking 'till none of our livers are left
We're winding our way down to the spirit store
We'll drink 'till we just can't drink any more [. . .]
We'll drink beyond the boundaries of sense
We'll drink 'til we start to see lovely pink elephants
Inside our heads, inside our beds, inside the threads of our pajama legs (1993).

These drinking songs convey a will to break out of the cage of healthy decisions and responsible living. There is a celebration of alcohol and the autonomy it bestows, but at the same time, there seems to be an implicit acknowledgment that intoxicated freedom may lead to new imprisonments in psychiatric hospitals, rehabilitation centers, churchyards, or the chains of addiction. One also senses an underlying current of critique—aimed at sanity, moderation, the parental generation, and so on—but this critique is tinged with irony. By depicting hell-bent intoxication and its fatal consequences, the songs point to the necessity for sobriety, or some degree of sobriety.

Another ambiguous ode to intoxication is "Rehab" by Amy Winehouse. This passage is particularly heartrending in light of her passing:

They tried to make me go to rehab I said, no, no, no
Yes, I've been black but when I come back you'll know, know, know

I ain't got the time

And if my daddy thinks I'm fine

He's tried to make me go to rehab, I won't go, go, go (2006).

Binge drinkers can often be heard singing along to such tunes of defiance, disorder, and death. But most of them ultimately choose life. They stop drinking when they feel that they have reached their limits. They take a taxi instead of driving home themselves. They swallow a handful of salt before going to sleep in the mistaken belief that this will reduce the hangovers. Sovereignty is an important part of binge drinking, but this sovereignty is more of a fantasy than a road map followed to the end.

Anders called me the day after the Christmas feast. He usually gets in touch after big drinking sprees in order to get details on what happened and to hear whether I think he did anything wrong. The problem is that heavy drinking significantly impairs his memory. When he wakes up the day after, he often worries that something has gone wrong and that he is the culprit. After having assured him that he had been his usual, amicable self, I asked him back what he thought about the Christmas feast. He replied that in spite of his physical and mental hangovers, it had all been worth it. He felt satisfied—happy, even.

"Things probably got kind of ugly toward the end, but hey, what of it? We almost never get together like this." Later he added, "Wouldn't it have been zzzzzzzzzzzz [snoring sound] if we had spent the evening seated around the table, nipping at our food and politely discussing the world situation?"

I pressed him to elaborate why it had been worth it.

"It's very intimate, isn't it?" he replied. "And so very different from what we normally do. You know what? I think it was enriching."

Anders's words point to the paradox of effervescence. On the one hand, it is rarely pretty, often risky, always disturbing. On the other hand, it is necessary for our survival as individuals and as a society. As Maffesoli makes clear in his chef-d'oeuvre, *The Shadow of Dionysus* (1985), collective effervescence, or what he calls "orgiasm," is an anthropological constant in human life. Whether we like it or not, we humans have always engaged in ritual activities that can transport us from mechanistic, self-centered existence toward volatile, group-centered existence. Religious, political, and academic voices frequently criticize these impulses for being unproductive, wasteful, sinful, barbaric, and dangerous. Maffesoli, however, insists that orgiasm is an indispensable source of social vitality because it enables members of a society to feel, fantasize, and freak out in communion. To suppress the orgiastic drive is both impossible and indeed potentially harmful. Maffesoli writes, "A city, a people, or a more or less limited group of individuals who cannot succeed in expressing collectively their wildness, their madness and their imaginary rapidly destructure themselves and, as Spinoza noted, these people merit more than any 'the name of solitude'" (1993, 8).

Much like Bataille, Maffesoli writes that orgiastic phenomena, including ecstasy and drunkenness, are a collective confrontation with the impassable problem of the limit—most notably, the limit of death (1993, 74, 137). The fear and frustration—but also fascination—with limits are ritually confronted, for example, when excited devotees gather around deadly forces such as the Hindu goddess Kali, "the black one," with her red eyes, bloody sword, and necklace made of skulls. Death in some form is also confronted during carnivals, like the one held in sixteenth-century Nuremberg, Germany, which featured a parade with "a giant devouring children, an old devil eating wicked wives . . . an oven for the baking of fools, a cannon to shoot ill-tempered women, a trap to catch fools, a galley with monks and nuns, and the wheel of fortune spinning fools" (Bakhtin 1984, 393–394). Other examples are Halloween, Shrovetide, New Year's parties, and concerts with death metal and rap music. During such events, death is all around in the form of skeletons, mummies, zombies, witches, ghosts, demons, devils, explosions, vandalism, and murderous lyrics.

The conjuring of death and destruction during effervescent events can also be understood as a strategy to collectively confront, scrutinize, and gain a sense of control over the uncontrollable. That which frightens us most is allowed to show up and express itself but in a manageable form of our own making. Here, the dreadful is not something that leaps at us unexpectedly; rather, *we* are the ones who do the leaping and the scaring when we walk the streets in monster costumes for Halloween, toss firecrackers at our neighbors on New Year's Eve, and scream insanities at a heavy metal concert. The tables are thereby turned on the dark forces that normally manipulate, diminish, and subdue us.

The role of humor is important to mention here because effervescent crowds often employ smiles and laughter to confront the dark forces in life. The darkness is made to appear deformed, diminished, or exaggerated to the point of absurdity. By making it laughable, it becomes less threatening and easier to deal with. In Denmark during Halloween, for example, private parties and kindergartens become haunted by all sorts of monsters, including cute ones equipped with deadly fangs, claws, and radiant baby-like eyes. Frankenstein looks mean with nasty stitches and bolts sticking out of his neck, but his head is sometimes so enormous that it seems unlikely that he will ever be able to capture and do harm to anyone. The skeletons, meanwhile, look like nervous wrecks with their rattling bones and eyes that are nearly popping out of their sockets in what seems to be terror. But they are already dead, so what are they afraid of? Laughter is a common reaction to sights like these, providing release from that which repels, confuses, and troubles us.

The monsters at events like Halloween can be interpreted as symbols of "life's darkest sides" (Santangelo 2013, 11). They are quintessentially tragic, doomed as they are to endless bloodthirst, madness, terror, hideousness, and death. They suffer and inflict suffering on those with whom they come into contact. The laughter that these monsters provoke should therefore not be misinterpreted as lightheartedness and superficial merriment. This is a laughter that is close to tears. It is ambiguous, cathartic, and comes in recognition that one is better off, after all, than the monsters.

Laughter is sometimes likened to winning because it involves a realization of superiority over somebody else or one's former or would-be self (Gruner 2000, 8). Accordingly, when a group of people laugh together, they generally feel good and better than those who are the target of their laughter. Laughter can thus draw people together and unite them against a perceived outsider. This unitive effect is amplified by the embodied ritual of sharing laughter: there is a coordination of breathing patterns, sound making, facial expressions, and bodily postures that eventually may trigger the process of rhythmic entrainment into states of effervescence (Collins 2004, 65). Shared laughter can therefore be deeply pleasurable and meaningful. As Collins writes, "Perhaps the strongest human pleasures come from being fully and bodily absorbed in deeply synchronized social interaction" (2004, 66). He adds that the symbols that represent laughter-filled events "hold deep connotations of pleasure for group members, and this helps make them sacred objects to defend, as well as reminders of group interactions that members would like to reestablish in future encounters" (2004, 66).

Danish Christmas parties do not feature the hellish hordes as Halloween parties do. There may be a few people wearing white beards and red hats, but otherwise, there are few costumes. Death nevertheless plays a part at Christmas parties, at least implicitly, through the heavy drinking that brings the participants to the verge of chaos and collapse—and sometimes beyond. At Johannes's Christmas feast, for instance, at least half of the participants drank so much alcohol that they vomited. One participant lost his temper and then his consciousness. Two participants fell asleep in the middle of dinner, and two participants "blacked out" a few hours after their arrival and only remembered the rest of the night in glimpses. The drinking at a Christmas feast can thus be a rather violent undertaking that drives the participants closer and closer toward the edge. But this does not mean that the participants are frustrated with their lives and want to end it all. In my interpretation, the collective staggering toward the edge is not a sign of some death wish but an expression of a fundamental curiosity toward aspects of reality that we normally do our best to ignore and forget about.

Consider a scenario that I have observed on several occasions: A person starts to vomit and other people turn or move in that direction to watch, express dislike, or take pictures of it. Similar reactions may occur when somebody passes out, falls, or starts a fight. Indeed, as Charles Baudelaire points out, many humans find delight in ugliness and have "the thirst for the unknown and the taste for the horrible" (2006, 121). These fancies may seem morbid, but they can have an affirmative element to them. After all, we humans are fallible mortals who are made of perishable matter. No matter how hard we try, we cannot save ourselves from failing, leaking, and making fools of ourselves. One strategy to deal with these imperfections is to try to shut them out of our consciousness. Another strategy is to embrace and make use of them. The latter strategy is the one pursued at Christmas feasts.

CHAPTER 8

AFTERWORD

Collective effervescence is, and always has been, a contested form of experience. Those in power—whether parents, politicians, priests, or corporate leaders—often view it with a mix of fascination and fear, and rightly so. For when people get together to stir up effervescence, when their energies are roused to the point that they forget themselves, they may realize their power as a group and engage in subversive behavior. A group consumed by an effervescent feeling wants to amplify, prolong, and spread this feeling. Anyone trying to block or diminish the feeling is likely to be met with opposition (Canetti 1978, 20).

Consider the way revelers reacted to the COVID-19 crisis. As the virus began its spread across the globe, authorities took drastic measures to keep people apart from one another. These measures included restrictions on physical proximity; bans on large social gatherings; and closures of schools, workplaces, and nightlife districts. Festive gatherings were seen as particularly problematic because of the tendency among revelers to approach strangers, get into close contact, and ignore health recommendations such as wearing a mask. Revelers were widely portrayed as "reckless," "reprehensible," and in need of firm control (Beer 2020). However, in spite of all the restrictions and negative attention, the pursuit of effervescent revelry continued, albeit in a more scattered manner. For example, there were media reports of foam parties in Bulgaria "in which holidaymakers wearing large swimming rings—apparently to enable them to physically distance from each other—dance in pools of flying foam" and engage in "close-contact drinking games" (Connolly 2020). Illegal rave parties were held with hundreds, sometimes thousands of participants in secluded locations such as forests and boats at sea. Many of these events were organized discreetly through personal networks and messaging apps in order to avoid police interference. As a reveler confided to a *New York Times* journalist, "It's like a military operation. . . . If people put half as much effort into solving coronavirus, we'd all be out of it by now" (Marshall, Rogers, and Méheut 2020).

The urge for effervescence is strong and irrepressible, even in times of a pandemic. It can be detrimental to health and long life but is, at the same time, essential to our humanity because it opens us to other people and makes us invest in our community (Ramp 1998, 141). Accordingly, as Collins argues, humans should not be understood as mere survival machines who are in perpetual search of safety, food, sex, wealth, and power; nor should humans be viewed as mere "pain-avoiders" who are "provoked into actions by frustrations and obstacles in the flow of habits" (2004, 373). We are also, at a fundamental level, seekers of effervescent events that provide us with the vitality we need to live our lives and the symbols with which we understand our world.

The stakes are high, therefore, when authorities get in the way of collective effervescence. Chris Shilling and Philip A. Mellor write in an article predating the COVID-19 crisis that "insufficient involvement in collectivities" may lead to "anomie and associated losses of energy, increases in melancholy, and the fading of threads attaching individuals to life" (2011, 23). The antidote to this is collective effervescence because this experience motivates "embodied subjects to overcome egoistic sensory appetites" and move beyond "their individual selves in order to become connected energetically to group life" (2011, 23).

Quantitative psychological research confirms that effervescence is vitally important to the microlevel of individual well-being as well as the macrolevel of social cohesion. One study by Shira Gabriel and colleagues suggests that experiences of effervescence may emerge in large crowds as well as smaller groups and that they are associated with "positive life outcomes such as feeling a sense of social connection, finding meaning in life, feeling awe, and being satisfied with life" (2020, 152). Another psychological study by Dario Páez and colleagues (2015) shows that there are causal pathways from collective effervescence to positive group outcomes, like strengthened collective identity and social integration. This study also found that higher levels of perceived emotional synchronization within a group are associated with "stronger emotional reactions, stronger social support, and higher endorsement of social beliefs and values" (2015, 711). A study of one of the world's largest religious gatherings, the "Magh Mela" in northern India, arrives at similar findings (Hopkins et al. 2016). However, the researchers behind this study emphasize that effervescence may evolve and express itself differently depending on the situation, group, and wider cultural context. Whereas the Magh Mela gives rise to feelings of spiritual connectedness, demonstrations and riots often involve "obstruction and violence that imposes the collective's will on an antagonistic out-group, notably the police" (Hopkins et al. 2016, 29; see also Drury and Reicher 2005). This is an important reminder that psychological insight and cultural sensitivity and contextualization are needed when studying effervescent events.

People differ in their preferences for collective effervescence. Some like high doses on a nightly basis, while others prefer low doses on rare occasions. There are those who love drunken effervescence, and many others who may find this disgusting. And certain individuals are drawn to psychedelic effervescence, which to other people seems the worst of nightmares. Generally speaking, however, collective effervescence is a vital part of human existence. It cannot be eradicated from social life, nor can it be completely controlled. This is why it is so important to understand it, embrace it, and make positive use of it—whether inside or outside of commercial, alcohol-focused venues.

In this book, my focus has been on the effervescence of revelry. The concepts I have presented are adapted to this particular context, but their applicability is broader. For effervescence is not only a thing of the night; it can be found thriving in other contexts, most importantly politics, sports, and religion. The experience is not the same across these contexts, but there are some striking similarities. Let me give some examples, beginning with a sinister one that we must remind ourselves of again and again: the annual rallies of the German Nazi party held in Nuremberg during the 1930s. Journalist and activist Barbara Ehrenreich describes these rallies as cunningly staged public rituals where hundreds of thousands of party members assembled to watch military parades, listen to rousing speeches, and rhythmically shoot up their right arm while shouting, "Sieg Heil" (2006, 181–182). The rallies lasted for several days and took place in pompous surroundings illuminated by antiaircraft searchlights and adorned with effervescent symbols such as the Nazi eagle and swastika. People who witnessed the rallies have described them as mystic, magic, delirious, unifying, and intoxicating. They were, in other words, brimming with a most powerful form of collective effervescence. Indeed, the Nazis' ritual mastery was so complete that historians argue that it was the primary driving force behind Hitler's rise to power and his success in convincing the German population to follow him into war. The example of the Nuremberg rallies illustrates the horrors that ensue when an extremist movement gains near control over the effervescent rituals in society (Bataille 1970).

Political parties today are still trying to recruit followers by organizing events that feature collective effervescence, such as election night parties and public speeches that are interspersed with musical performances, light shows, rhythmic applause, and cheering (Collins 2014). However, contemporary political events are generally designed to stir compassionate effervescence or drunken effervescence rather than the histrionically violent effervescence of the Nazi rituals. The historian William H. McNeill explains why: "Since World War II, widespread revulsion against everything associated with the Nazis has discredited mass muscular manifestations of political attachments" (1995, 149). The world, or most of it, still remembers the raging Nazi crowds of the 1930s and '40s. This memory dampens the effervescence at contemporary political events, especially those that are organized by established political parties (Ehrenreich 2006). That said, political events remain an important milieu for the experience of effervescence today.

Sporting events are another key forum for the experience of effervescence today. Arguably, the very raison d'être of these events is "having one's own emotions raised by a noisy crowd expressing the same thing" (Collins 2004, 55). Indeed, many sports fans prefer going to stadiums rather than watching games on television because this allows them to express collectively their team loyalty through rhythmic cheering, booing, singing, and jumping in the stands (McNeill 1995, 151). The excitement can be extremely intense, especially during peak moments when a team scores or wins a game. This may give rise to crying and bodily collapse on the side of the losing team while inspiring joyful noise-making and bodily contact on the side of the winners. In these moments, fans are pulled out of themselves and imbued with an embodied understanding of their group belonging and the nonbelonging of the opponent fans. This is collective effervescence in a nutshell.

Consider these words about fandom, expressed by a soccer zealot interviewed by sociologist Anthony King: "The boys—you're buzzing. You're on cloud cuckoo land" (1997, 333). Might this be a case of psychedelic-cum-compassionate effervescence? I think so, especially given that the fans in King's study refer to their ecstatic solidarity toward their team as "the crack," like the potent drug also called methamphetamine. Drawing on Durkheim, King writes that British soccer fans, whom he calls "the lads," reaffirm their relations with other fans through worship of the team: "The love for the team is a transposed love of the lads' own social group. The team, and the love invested in it, is a symbol of the values and friendships which exist between the lads" (1997, 333). This is true of all sports. Teams and their players are sacred symbols who embody values of significance to the community of supporters (Birrell 1981, 373).

Sociologist Marci D. Cottingham's study of fans of the Pittsburgh Steelers, an American football team, also illuminates the effervescence of sport spectatorship (2012). Here is a telling scene of joy, as described in her field notes:

> Late in the final quarter of the game the Steelers made a spectacular play, which resulted in much cheering, screaming, clapping, and waving. A man with a stern face in front of me, probably in his late twenties to early thirties, began to remove layers of clothing. Finally, he pulled his final shirt up over his head and stood cheering and screaming without a shirt in temperatures around 15 degrees Fahrenheit. After a second stellar play on behalf of the Steelers, the man beside him also took off his many layers of coats and shirts and the two clutched hands and screamed in earnest. (Cottingham 2012, 174)

The action on the field triggers what appears to be a compassionate form of effervescence among the Steelers fans. The fans are barred from physical contact with the players, and in this sense, the ritual is "stratified," with an unequal distribution of touch rights (Collins 2004, 57). The fans cannot make contact with the athletes, but they can make contact with each other, and so they do. Even strangers sometimes touch each other in the stands, typically when something good happens to their team. Importantly, in most sports, fans do little to hold back their feelings and often openly express them, thereby making such feelings stronger. As Páez and colleagues put it, "When expressed collectively, human feelings intensify. . . . Everyone drives everyone" (2015, 3).

Surprisingly, Collins argues that sport events "generate what might be considered an artificial ritual experience" and "bring together a community that has no other coherence, and no other purpose, than the experience of the peaks of ritual emotion itself" (2004, 59). By contrast, Cottingham (2012) demonstrates that the fans in her study form a strong community imbued with genuine solidarity that extends far beyond the stadium experience (see also Serazio 2012). This can be seen in the ways that fans venerate their teams in everyday life and even sometimes during important rites of passage, such as weddings and funerals. Also outside of the stadium, many fans tirelessly keep up with sporting news, wear their team's logo with pride, listen to team anthems, and boast about their preferred stars, thus drawing on and reenergizing their effervescent symbols.

Fandom is a form of group love (King 1997). However, it should not be "romanticized" one-sidedly as a beneficial force that pulls people together in mutual love and respect (Kennedy et al. 2019). The love of the group sometimes expresses and consolidates itself through disparaging talk and violence against perceived outsiders (Newson 2019). Some fan groups are deeply into violence (Buford 1993). They get their collective effervescence not so much from compassionate communion in the stands as from violent confrontations with opposing fans and the police. In these cases, the fans take center stage. As Collins writes, fan violence "is contrived to provide the entrainment and solidarity of fights, without being subordinate to the players. This violence emulates the combat structure of the game," with the fans "raised into heroes in their own right, usurping the place of the athletes" (2008, 316).

If we turn to the religious realm, we also find myriad institutions and events that provide effervescence on a large scale—and with good reason. Effervescence creates an awareness of institutions and events. By drawing people in, it can create dependency. Indeed, there is much to suggest that it is "the emotionally 'hot' forms of religion that are doing best" in the world today (Riis and Woodhead 2010, 1). Religious institutions can attract followers by offering them ways to transcend ordinary life and experience ecstatic union with the divine. Such experiences can be turning points in life trajectories (see Goffman 2019). As psychologist Marc Galanter argues in his book on cults, people become more open to social influence when they are "made to think, sense, and feel differently than usual, when someone or something disrupts their emotional balance. Such changes in subjective experience (or alterations in consciousness) can undermine the psychological matrix in which our views are rooted, so that we lose track of customary internal signposts" (1999, 60). Effervescent experiences may thus foster new values, beliefs, and allegiances.

Consider the case of "megachurches," which are commonly defined as Protestant churches with at least two thousand weekly attendees per church (Ellingson 2010, 247). Recent decades have seen a rapid proliferation of them, especially in North America and Asia. Besides their large size, megachurches are characterized by their wide range of services, such as fitness classes, day care, food courts, and spectacular worship events. Many megachurches are equipped with advanced audio-visual technology and have their own house band and charismatic pastors. Based on research in the United States, Wellman, Corcoran, and Stockly-Meyerdirk (2014) observe that the worship services in megachurches generate high levels of collective effervescence by bringing together large numbers of people and exposing them to elaborate shows of rousing music, lights, movement, and preaching. Cameras are also employed to "scan the audience and project images of people worshiping, raising their hands with closed eyes, crying, singing, or smiling" (2014, 660). These close-up images of individual church attendees inspire the audience to feel "a shared experience and mood, which contributes to the growing collective effervescence" (661). Attendees generally place great value on these experiences, which they refer to with forceful expressions such as "huge," "unreal," "a drug," and "the Holy Spirit" (661–662).

Christian megachurches specialize in providing what appears to be a mix of compassionate and psychedelic effervescence. Other religious institutions specialize in other types of effervescence, including ones that have not been named or discussed in this book. Sociologist Michal Pagis's study of vipassana meditation retreats provides an intriguing case in point (2015). Pagis writes that the participants at retreats are instructed to meditate most hours of the day as well as to abstain from speaking and reading. They generally meditate in a seated posture close to each other, observing their thoughts and sensations but without engaging with them. While many scholars and meditators portray this as an individual endeavor marked by noninteraction, Pagis argues that it is deeply social because it is learned in groups and centers on the cultivation of a common state of mind. The participants learn how to be together in a disengaged manner. They "share silence collectively" in the pursuit of "a heightened emotional experience of equanimity" (2015, 39, 42). Interestingly, many feel that they reach deeper levels of equanimity when they meditate in a group than when they meditate alone. Pagis argues that what is happening during successful group meditations is a form of "synchronized non-movement" (51) akin to what Collins calls rhythmic entrainment. The meditators do not directly attend to each other but nevertheless enter coordinated patterns of deep breathing and muscle-tension release through a process of "contagious relaxation" (51). Pagis thus argues that equanimity can be passed from body to body: it "does not merely emanate from the inside out, but also—as part of a social process—moves from the outside in" (54).

Although Pagis herself does not use the concept of effervescence, I read her work as an illustration of what could perhaps be termed *equanimous effervescence*. This is an experience characterized, first and foremost, by calmness and relaxation but also a sense of mutual awareness, bodily synchronization, and emotional attunement. The experience appears to be fleeting for many people, if not most. It can easily turn into a "feeling of expansive love" or what I have termed *compassionate effervescence* (Williamson 2010, 173). It may also switch into altered states that lack a sense of connection with other people, in which case the experience ceases to be within the category of collective effervescence. People typically learn to appreciate equanimous effervescence in a group context and, as is the case with other types of effervescence, its effects can be both long-lasting and wide-ranging. Some will begin to treat silence as a sacred symbol of their group (Pagis 2015, 47). Others will attribute their experience to a god or spiritual master (Healy 2010, 127), and still others will change their entire worldview—for instance, no longer viewing humans and other entities as separate but instead viewing everything as purposefully connected (Williamson 2010, 177).

My argument is not that equanimous effervescence is the end goal of all types of meditation or that all meditators appreciate this experience. Rather, I suggest that the concept of equanimous effervescence may be used as a sensitizing tool to examine a common type of experience that emerges when people engage in group meditation such as that practiced at vipassana retreats. Further research is needed, however, to verify whether the concept accords with empirical evidence and whether it is applicable beyond the context of group meditation. So it is with all the concepts I have presented in this book, including drunken effervescence, psychedelic effervescence, melodramatic effervescence, violent effervescence, compassionate effervescence, and sexual effervescence. Before new concepts can become part of an accepted theoretical framework, they have to undergo a long process of verification, debate, and refinement. Of course, most concepts do not survive this test of time and scholarly scrutiny.

Durkheim's writings on collective effervescence have stood the test. They have been debated and tested for more than a century and have been largely verified in a range of qualitative, quantitative, and mixed-methods studies (Draper 2019). There is still room for improvement, however, especially when it comes to understanding the phenomenology of effervescent experiences. As was pointed out already, in the 1920s, Durkheim did not specify exactly what collective effervescence is and how it varies across types of assembly (Richard 1994, 247–248). A similar problem pertains to Collins's interaction ritual theory: it presents

collective effervescence in an overly monolithic manner, as if it were one singular experience, irrespective of when, where, how, why, and among whom it
emerges. Hence my efforts in this book to present a more detailed account of
what effervescence is, how it is created, and how it is experienced from a first-
person perspective. In pursuing this project, I hope to have cleared the way for
the important work that needs to be done to deepen our understanding of collective effervescence and to develop better ways to live with it.

ACKNOWLEDGMENTS

This book has been long in the making, and I have received much help in the process. First, I would like to thank Flemming Balvig, Lars Holmberg, and Anne-Stina Sørensen. They got me started on researching intoxication back in 2001, when they hired me as a student assistant on the Ringsted Project. I collected ethnographic data among young revelers for their project and was later generously allowed to use these data for my own purposes. I would also like to thank Anna Bendtsen and Malene Flanding, who worked with me on conducting fieldwork in Ringsted. That experience was fun, and I learned a lot from it. After finishing the project, I continued collecting data in Ringsted for what became my master's thesis in anthropology at Copenhagen University. My supervisor was Michael Jackson, who then and ever since has guided and inspired my work. For this, I owe him my deepest gratitude. The Inge og Asker Larsens Fond funded the Ringsted Project, and the Danish Ministry of Justice funded part of the fieldwork for my master thesis.

Another study that informs this book is my PhD project on nightlife tourism, which I carried out from 2007 to 2010 while working at the Center for Alcohol and Drug Research (CRF) at Aarhus University. CRF funded this project. I would like to thank my former colleagues at CRF, especially Morten Hesse, who through his example has taught me a great deal about good colleagueship. Warm thanks are due, moreover, to my PhD supervisor, Margaretha Järvinen, and cosupervisor, Michel Maffesoli, for their generous advice and inspiration. My PhD project involved fieldwork at a Bulgarian resort called Sunny Beach. This fieldwork benefitted greatly from the research assistance of Ida Ravnholdt Poulsen, Pernille Bouteloup Koefod, Tine Reinholdt, and my wife, Sanna Schliewe. I owe them many thanks, especially Sanna, who has been a magnificent source of feedback and new ideas throughout my career.

The last study that informs this book is entitled "Safer Bars and Nightclubs" and was funded by Trygfonden (grant # 7-01-0705) and the Familien Hede

Nielsens Fond. It took place between 2011 and 2013 in the cities of Copenhagen, Aalborg, Nykøbing Falster, and Sønderborg. The data were collected by myself and a team of assistants, all of whom I am indebted to: Hallie Barrows, Trine Bøgkjær, Peter Ejbye-Ernst, Ask Greve Jørgensen, Lea Trier Krøll, Sergiy Matyushenko, Lars Nørr Mikkelsen, Merete Poulsen, Louise Saugman, Caspar Schliewe, Ida Thyrring, and Maj Witte.

There are a number of additional people and institutions to thank for their help along the way: Karen Hughes, Pamela Starbird, and Christian Borch for invaluable advice right when I needed it; Gro Dahle, Sveinung Sandberg, Anette Bringedal Houge, and Andreas Hessen Schei for housing me on numerous occasions; the Department of Sociology at Copenhagen University for office space during what I thought was the final stage of the writing process; the Department of Criminology and Sociology of Law at Oslo University for emotional support and funds for editing parts of this book; and my current workplace and colleagues at the Department of Sociology at Lund University for more emotional support and funds for editing other parts of this book.

Among the people who have given precious comments on drafts of chapters are Heith Copes, Eivind Grip Fjær, Camilla Winde Gissel, Michael Jackson, Margaretha Järvinen, Kristan Karlson, Marie Rosenkrantz Lindegaard, Katrín Sif Oddgeirsdóttir, Willy Pedersen, Sveinung Sandberg, Sanna Schliewe, Susie Scott, and Anneke Sools. Seth Sherwood has brilliantly commented on, proofread, and polished all the chapters. Peter Mickulas of Rutgers University Press provided vital support from the moment I submitted my book proposal. If mistakes have sneaked into the book, they are entirely mine. I owe them all a debt of gratitude.

Finally, I would like to express my heartfelt thanks to the many people who participated in my research, giving generously of their time, company, and insights.

The book contains excerpts from "The Road of Excess," *Harvard Divinity Bulletin* 41, nos. 1–2 (Winter/Spring 2013): 33–40; and "Stirring Up Effervescence: An Ethnographic Study of Youth at a Nightlife Resort," *Leisure Studies* 32, no. 3 (2013): 233–248. These are reprinted with permission of the President and Fellows of Harvard College and Taylor & Francis Ltd.

NOTES

CHAPTER 1 — INTRODUCTION

1. The term *narrative* is central in this book. I use it interchangeably with that of *story* to describe a form of communication that organizes events or experiences into a sequenced, meaning-making whole. In the words of cultural sociologist Philip Smith, "We can understand narratives as the stories we construct and exchange in the effort to make sense of the world . . . They display actions arrayed in chronological time and allow us to answer the journalist's questions: Who? What? When? Where? And How?" (2005, 18). Sociologist Lois Presser adds that narratives produce emotions and drive action in a more forceful manner than other discursive forms, such as chronicles, expositions, and reports: "They do more than guide and condone action. Stories beguile and engross us" (2018, 134).

2. Aspects of Durkheim's work are outdated. For example, he almost exclusively writes about men, and what little he writes about women tends to be both reifying and disparaging (Lehman 1994). Also, his idea that societies move through stages from the "primitive" and "simple" (e.g., Aborigine society) to the civilized and advanced (e.g., Western societies) is highly problematic (Jackson 2016, 9).

3. For a discussion of "sexually violent effervescence," see Tutenges, Sandberg, and Pedersen (2020).

4. It was sociologist Lea Trier Krøll who first made me aware of the existence and importance of melodramatic effervescence in nightlife settings.

5. The concepts of "emotional energy" and "collective effervescence" are sometimes confused, but they are not the same in the work of Collins. He explains, "I distinguish the collective effervescence of the situation itself from the EE that individuals feel in the aftermath of the situation. The former is a collective emotion, the excitement and energetic coordination of participants in their interaction; the latter is an individual emotion, felt by the individual as they are physically away from the social situation. The two emotions are related; as Durkheim said, the individual acquires a portion of the energy of the group, which can be carried for a time away from the group" (Baehr and Collins 2005, 9).

6. Durkheim's work is often associated with positivism, functionalism, and structuralism. However, *The Elementary Forms* also has affinities with phenomenology, particularly in its meticulous examination of religious experience and its insistence on setting aside "all preconceived ideas" and "commonsense notions" in order to understand "things as they are" (1995, 21, 22). It would be going too far to call the late Durkheim a phenomenologist, but *The Elementary Forms* contains powerful methods and concepts that can be used for studying the phenomenology of intoxication—that is, the actual here and now of intoxicating

experiences as these register in people's bodies and minds. For further phenomenological readings of Durkheim, see, for example, Tiryakian (1978) and Throop and Laughlin (2002).

7. For a more detailed study of the operations of nightlife venues, see Tutenges and Bøhling (2019).

8. As mentioned in the acknowledgments, my research has benefitted from the help of assistants, notably during fieldwork in Sunny Beach, Copenhagen, Aalborg, Nykøbing Falster, and Sønderborg. All assistants had either a BA or MA in social science studies, and prior to fieldwork, they received training in relevant methods, ethical guidelines, and safety procedures. Their job mainly consisted of collecting questionnaires, but some were also involved in other tasks, such as making observations, coding data, and coauthoring articles. The assistants thus did much more than generate data; they offered new perspectives and insights I would never have been able to come up with on my own. For example, observations made by Sanna Schliewe and Hallie Barrows illuminated some of the challenges that women confront in nightlife environments. Their input—combined with commentaries by peers (e.g., Radcliffe and Measham 2014; Bogren 2014; Fleetwood 2014b)—has pushed me to explore the themes of sexual objectification, sex work, and sexual violence in this book and elsewhere (Hesse and Tutenges 2011; Tutenges 2012; Tutenges, Sandberg, and Pedersen 2020).

9. For more information on the Ringsted Project, see Balvig, Holmberg, and Sørensen (2005).

10. Throughout the book, I refer to research participants with pseudonyms instead of their real names, and I have masked revealing personal details. I have done so in order to protect the participants' anonymity, which is important given the sensitive nature of what I am studying. Almost all the interviews were conducted in Danish. Everyone who took part in them was given detailed information about the research, and each gave their consent to be involved. It was not feasible to obtain informed consent from all the people who were observed. Some of the observed events had thousands of participants, and it would have been both impractical and intrusive to interrupt them in their revelry in order to inform them about my research. In such situations, we should not "mess with the vibe" of the ongoing party (García 2013, 9) but rather openly talk about the research with those who care to listen and make sure that everyone remains anonymous in all published material. For a more detailed discussion of my research methods, see Tutenges (2022).

CHAPTER 2 — WAYS TO EFFERVESCENCE

1. For a Danish-language analysis of the Ringsted Town Festival, see Tutenges (2004).

2. Anthropologist Alfred Gell (1980) writes in a study of the Muria people in central India that the cultivation of vertigo is key to their intoxicating practices. He writes that Muria socialization and childhood games "emphasise violent rocking, swinging, jiggling up and down, and balancing to a marked degree," testifying to a "profound cultural preoccupation with dizziness, which pervades subsequent religious experience" (1980, 239). Indeed, there are many ways to achieve and experience collective effervescence.

3. See Tutenges (2015) for a longer crowd theoretical analysis of pub crawls.

4. I generally write field notes in two stages. First, I scribble down a few words on paper while I am making observations. Then later, I turn the words into complete sentences while working on my laptop. The notes include descriptions of what I have observed, my emotional reactions in the field, tentative interpretations, and much more. All field notes and interview excerpts in this book have been translated from Danish into English.

5. Following Durkheim, collective representations may be understood as shared interpretative frameworks that influence the ways people make sense of and act in the world. Collective representations—including culturally recognized signs, symbols, beliefs, and

narratives—are charged with emotions and move people to behave in a socially appropriate manner (Schliewe and Tutenges 2021). It is typically, but not always, during moments of effervescence that representations become emotionally charged, as will be discussed in chapter 6.

6. The messages are quoted in an article by Josiam and colleagues (1998, 502).

7. Early crowd theorists also argued that the emotional outbursts during celebrations, riots, and other gatherings should not be understood merely as sudden spontaneous manifestations among unstable individuals who happen to be in the same place. As Le Bon points out, it may appear at first sight that mass excitement erupts with "startling suddenness," but this "is only a superficial effect, behind which must be sought a preliminary and preparatory action of long duration" (2001, 47). He mentions the example of the French Revolution, which was fueled by "the writings of the philosophers, the exactions of the nobility, and the progress of scientific thought. The mind of the masses, thus prepared, was then easily roused by such immediate factors as the speeches of orators" (2001, 47). Narrative scholars have since elaborated on this with a special focus on the unique capacity of narratives to arouse emotions, change public opinion, and inspire courses of action—including collective acts of violence (Presser 2018).

8. During the COVID-19 "lockdown," many people turned to livestreamed rituals, such as concerts, for entertainment, comfort, and hope. However, many of these rituals left participants frustrated and longing for physical proximity. For example, Femke Vandenberg and colleagues observe in a study of livestreamed raves that participants found it difficult to immerse themselves fully in the experience due to the absence of "visceral elements of a physical audience" (2020, 1). They conclude that these online raves succeeded in reminding participants of past effervescent experiences on the dance floor but seemed to fail in providing new experiences of effervescence.

CHAPTER 3 — UNITY

1. Many revelers have the impression that alcohol in large doses causes disinhibition, as if by some universal biochemical law. Hence the standard excuse for nightlife transgressions, "I was drunk," suggesting that what happened was exceptional and unrelated to the transgressor's true moral character. However, heavy drinking can lead to all sorts of behavior, depending on the cultural context. As anthropologists Craig MacAndrew and Robert B. Edgerton point out, "The presence of alcohol in the body does not necessarily conduce to disinhibition . . . drunken comportment is an essentially learned affair" (1969, 87–88). In other words, when drunken revelers permit themselves to act with disinhibition, they draw on an available cultural "script" for how to behave when drunk. For a comprehensive discussion of drunken disinhibition, see Fjær (2021).

2. Maffesoli has, with good reason, been criticized for focusing too narrowly on the positive aspects of effervescent assemblies. For example, Shilling and Mellor write that "Maffesoli overlooks the fact that sensual associations may not involve a 'keeping warm together', but may result in 'getting *burnt* together' and an enjoyment of '*burning others* together'" (1998, 203). A similar critique has been leveled against Durkheim (e.g., Graham 2007), although Durkheim repeatedly warns that the condition of collective effervescence is volatile and that it might harm oneself or others (see, e.g., Durkheim 1995, 213).

3. It is well known that heavy drinking may cause sexual impotence, including among young people. This constitutes an important "drinking dilemma" (Thurnell-Read 2016). On the one hand, alcohol may serve as a *social lubricant* that helps people become more bold, self-confident, outgoing, and sexually adventurous (Vander Ven 2011, 51–52). On the other hand, alcohol in large doses may function as a *social saboteur* that disrupts, thwarts, or otherwise impedes all attempts at interaction. Some male revelers try to solve this dilemma

by self-medicating with Viagra, which is a drug reputed to increase the blood flow to the male sexual organ. However, Viagra does not help much against the crushing fatigue that often strikes the overly drunken person who shifts from the effervescent atmosphere of a drinking venue to the tranquil atmosphere of a bedroom.

4. Stephen Lyng confirms that voluntary risk taking, or what he calls "edgework," is "more common among young people than older people and among males than among females" (1990, 872). He explains this gender difference in the following terms: "Males are more likely than females to have an illusory sense of control over fateful endeavors because of the socialization pressures on males to develop a skill orientation toward their environment. Insofar as males are encouraged to use their skills to affect the outcome of all situations, even those that are almost entirely chance determined, they are likely to develop a distorted sense of their ability to control fateful circumstances" (1990, 872–873). For a discussion of the cultural construction of gender identities, see Connell (2020) and Fleetwood (2014a).

5. Research that I and others have conducted in Norway suggests that the majority of sexual assaults that occur among youth in the context of nightlife constitute a dark form of effervescence, or what may be termed *sexually violent effervescence*, because they emerge out of emotionally turbulent interactions—which, on the victim's side, involve a sense of being caught up in a destructive flow of events that robs them of agency and leaves them harmed and confused (Tutenges, Sandberg, and Pedersen 2020; Stefansen, Frøyland, and Overlien 2020). After the assault, many victims find it difficult to recall it fully and describe what they have been through. Moreover, many are unsure whether the assault constituted a crime, whether they were responsible for it, and whether it is a problem worth mentioning. This confusion partly explains why so many victims of sexual violence refrain from reporting the crime to the police.

CHAPTER 4 — INTENSITY

1. O'Grady cautions that the nightlife ethnographer is faced with the problem of "researching a phenomenon where intrusion is not only inconvenient and impractical but effectively collapses and destroys the very object of attention" (2013, 18). She recommends that nightlife ethnographers accept the inherent messiness of revelry and that they embrace "the sense of embodied immersion" that is required of revelers (2013, 26). In so doing, the ethnographer may gain an embodied understanding of the revelry without destroying it (see also Kershaw and Nicholson 2011). This is certainly good advice, but it is hard to follow.

2. See the work of sociologist Ashley Mears (2020) for an exploration of conspicuous consumption and extreme gender inequality on the global VIP party circuit, which is frequented by superrich revelers and those who aspire to such "heights."

CHAPTER 5 — TRANSGRESSION

1. A key figure in cultural criminology, Keith Hayward, explains that "cultural criminology is a particular form of criminological theory that sets out to reinterpret criminal behaviour as a technique for resolving certain psychic conflicts—conflicts that in many instances are indelibly linked to various features of contemporary life. One might say that it represents a phenomenology of transgression fused with a sociological analysis of late modern culture. That said, cultural criminology should not be thought of as in any way oppositional to the more mainstream criminological enterprise. Rather it should be seen as a means of reinvigorating the study of crime" (2002, 91). This version of cultural criminology, with its emphasis on examining transgressions in cultural context, meshes well with the neo-Durkheimian

framework I am advancing in this book. However, up until now, the concept of collective effervescence has been strangely absent in the cultural criminological literature. For notable exceptions, see Dimou and Ilan (2018) as well as Binik (2020).

2. Different types of venues specialize in different types of effervescence. For example, many Goa trance festivals are packed with art featuring bright colors, swirling patterns, and mystic religious symbols. This art is part of the Goa trance machinery, which is meant to evoke and enhance psychedelic effervescence with its powerful transgressive sensations, visions, and ideas. The emphases are different in mainstream nightlife venues, where the focus tends to be on the promotion of drunken effervescence and the more conventional transgressions that accompany it, such as boisterousness, wastefulness, vulgarity, and extraversion.

3. Atrocious crimes sometimes also appear to be inspired and facilitated by role-playing. For example, there are numerous cases of school shootings where the perpetrators wore culturally recognizable costumes (e.g., a Darth Vader mask) during their crimes. I suspect that some of these perpetrators took on not just a costume but a different persona in order to make it easier for themselves to kill. As Collins demonstrates, "Violence is difficult, not easy" (2008, 449); but perhaps it can be made less difficult when done from behind a mask, a cloak, or from within a role. However, the link between crime and role-playing deserves more attention than what I am able to offer in this book.

4. Lyng's writings on edgework are key inspirations in cultural criminology. However, whereas Lyng mainly focuses on extreme sports, cultural criminologists tend to focus on criminal transgressions. Cultural criminologists have argued that many types of crime including vandalism, fighting, joyriding, graffiti writing, and drug use may be understood as edgework activities aimed not so much at moneymaking but more at merrymaking, expressivity, and exerting control over the uncontrollable. Accordingly, Mark Fenwick and Keith Hayward write that many crimes, although dangerous, "offer a mode of being in which individuals take control through a calculated act of decontrol. The seductiveness of crime is not only linked to the inherent excitement of the acts involved, but also to the more general feelings of self-realization and self-expression to which they give rise. It might be an unpalatable thought, but it is through such activities that individuals come alive" (2000, 49).

5. Roger Caillois observes that role-playing can be gratifying but warns that it may become corrupted if the role-players start believing that the roles they are playing are real or if their role-playing involves the use of alcohol or other drugs (2001, 49, 51). I partly agree with this. Substances that sometimes enable and ameliorate role-play experiences may also lead to harmful transgressions. Too many substances—and especially the continuous use of them—may, in the words of Caillois, lead to mere "stupidity," "organic disorder," and the deprivation "of the freedom to desire anything but [. . .] poison" (2001, 53). See also Milthorpe and Murphy (2019).

6. Details of the tattoo have been altered for anonymity.

CHAPTER 6 — SYMBOLIZATION

1. Christian von Scheve (2012) points out that modern psychological and neuroscientific research confirms Durkheim's proposition that symbols that are emotionally charged during effervescent events may keep their functions for a group after the event has ended. He explains that contact with emotionally "hot" symbols can activate emotional memories and specific, emotionally laden meaning, which relates to past experiences of effervescence. Something similar may happen to narratives. If an effervescent group focuses on the same narrative and imbues it with emotions (e.g., during a speech), the narrative becomes more compelling and committing for a period of time beyond the actual effervescent event.

2. Criminologists Heith Copes and Andy Hochstetler observe that it is common for criminal offenders to encourage each other verbally before perpetrating a crime. They describe

this as a process of "bucking up heads," which may involve sharing stories and statements about personal bravery, past criminal successes, and the ease of avoiding detection or arrest. Copes and Hochstetler explain that this kind of talk before the act creates "such an optimistic tone that hesitation by those who have claimed to be criminally capable is laughable" (2003, 291). Engrossing talk can thus fill a group with the motivation and emotional energy needed to carry out risky operations.

3. Presser and Sandberg define narrative criminology as "any inquiry based on the view of stories as instigating, sustaining, or effecting desistance from harmful action. We study how narratives inspire and motivate harmful action, and how they are used to make sense of harm" (2015, 1). This emerging tradition has clear affinities with cultural sociology in that both are concerned with processes of meaning making and the way narratives "allocate causal responsibility for action, define actors and give them motivation, indicate the trajectory of past episodes and predict consequences of future choices, suggest courses of action, confer and withdraw legitimacy, and provide social approval by aligning events with normative cultural codes" (Smith 2005, 18; see also Presser 2016). Narrative criminology also overlaps with cultural criminology, although the former has a "methodological commitment to studying discourse" (Presser and Sandberg 2015, 13), while the latter is committed to exploring "the visceral immediacy and experiential thrill of crime and transgression" (Aspden and Hayward 2015, 239).

4. There is mixed evidence for the effectiveness of information, education, and warning campaigns. Providing information and education about alcohol, for example, does not lead to sustained behavioral changes (Burton et al. 2017). However, when it comes to cigarettes, pictorial health warnings on cigarette packaging seem to reduce smoking (Thrasher et al. 2011).

5. Stories read in solitude can generate very strong reactions in readers. These reactions may resemble the condition of effervescence, but full-blown effervescence requires the energy rush of being copresent with other people and partaking in mutually attuned synchronized interactions, such as those of an engrossing storytelling session.

CHAPTER 7 — REVITALIZATION

1. Cultural psychologists Brady Wagoner and Ignacio Brescó observe that funerals and other "grief rituals" are experienced "not only as an individual's emotional reaction to loss but also publicly, in the first-person plural—that is, *we* grieve for the loss of *our* group's members. This is particularly apparent in today's world after terrorist attacks, school shootings and the death of national figures. After such events, national days of mourning are often declared and people feel the need to meet in public spaces and express themselves with other members of the community" (2021). Grief rituals can serve to strengthen in-group solidarity, trigger collective memories, and resurrect shared symbols.

REFERENCES

ABTA. 2012. "Booze and Balconies Don't Mix." https://www.abta.com/sites/default/files/news-article/document/Booze_and_balconies_dont_mix.pdf.

Alexander, Jeffrey C., Ronald N. Jacobs, and Philip Smith, eds. 2012. *The Oxford Handbook of Cultural Sociology*. Oxford: Oxford University Press.

Allen, Nicholas J., W. S. F. Pickering, and William W. Miller, eds. 1998. *On Durkheim's Elementary Forms of Religious Life*. London: Routledge.

Armstrong, Elizabeth A., Laura T. Hamilton, Elizabeth M. Armstrong, and Lotus J. Seeley. 2014. "'Good Girls': Gender, Social Class, and Slut Discourse on Campus." *Social Psychology Quarterly* 77 (2): 100–122. https://doi.org/10.1177/0190272514521220.

Aspden, Kester, and Keith J. Hayward. 2015. "Narrative Criminology and Cultural Criminology." In *Narrative Criminology: Understanding Stories of Crime*, edited by Lois Presser and Sveinung Sandberg, 235–259. New York: New York University Press.

Avramenko, Richard. 2013. "Freedom from Freedom: On the Metaphysics of Liberty in Dostoevsky's 'Crime and Punishment.'" In *Dostoevsky's Political Thought*, edited by Richard Avramenko and Lee Trepanier, 159–180. Plymouth, Mass.: Lexington.

Baehr, Peter, and Randall Collins. 2005. "Review Forum: The Sociology of Almost Everything: Four Questions to Randall Collins about Interaction Ritual Chains." *Canadian Journal of Sociology Online* (January–February): 1–11.

Bakhtin, Mikhail. 1984. *Rabelais and His World*. Bloomington: Indiana University Press.

Balvig, Flemming, Lars Holmberg, and Anne-Stina Sørensen. 2005. *Ringstedforsøget. Livsstil og Forebyggelse i Lokalsamfundet*. Copenhagen: Jurist-og Økonomforbundets Forlag.

Bargeman, Bertine, and Greg Richards. 2020. "A New Approach to Understanding Tourism Practices." *Annals of Tourism Research* 84:1–11. https://doi.org/10.1016/j.annals.2020.102988.

Bataille, Georges. 1967. *La Part Maudite*. Paris: Les Éditions de Minuit.

———. 1970. "La Structure Psychologique du Fascisme." In *Œuvres Complètes*, vol. 1, *Georges Bataille*, 339–371. Paris: Gallimard.

———. 1976. *Œuvres Complètes*. Vol. 8. Paris: Gallimard.

———. 1979. "The Psychological Structure of Fascism." *New German Critique* 16:64–87.

———. 1985. "The Sacred Conspiracy." In *Visions of Excess: Selected Writings 1927–1939*, edited by A. Stoekl, 178–181. Minneapolis: University of Minnesota Press.

———. 1986. *Erotism*. San Francisco: City Lights.

———. 1993. *The Accursed Share: An Essay on General Economy*. Vols. 2–3. New York: Zone.

Bateson, Gregory. 2000. *Steps to an Ecology of Mind: Collected Essays in Anthropology, Psychiatry, Evolution, and Epistemology*. Chicago: University of Chicago Press.

Baudelaire, Charles. 2006. *Intimate Journals*. New York: Dover.

Beauvoir, Simone de. 1949. *Le Deuxième Sexe*. Vols. 1–2. Paris: Gallimard.

Becker, Howard. 1997. *Outsiders*. London: Simon & Schuster.

Beer, Tommy. 2020. "'Reckless' and 'Reprehensible' Frat Party Linked to Coronavirus Outbreak at UNH." *Forbes*, September 7. https://www.forbes.com/sites/tommybeer/2020/09/07/reckless-and-reprehensible-frat-party-linked-to-coronavirus-outbreak-at-unh-here-are-the-latest-college-coronavirus-updates/?sh=a5d7986b3a0c.

Bellis, Mark, Karen Hughes, Jim McVeigh, Rod Thomson, and Chris Luke. 2005. "Effects of Nightlife Activity on Health." *Nursing Standard* 19 (30): 63–71. https://doi.org/10.7748/ns2005.04.19.30.63.c3838.

Belk, Russel. 2000. "May the Farce Be with You: On Las Vegas and Consumer Infantalization." *Consumption, Markets and Culture* 4 (2): 101–124. https://doi.org/10.1080/10253866.2000.9670352.

Bergson, Henri. 1911. *Laughter: An Essay on the Meaning of the Comic*. London: Macmillan.

Binik, Oriana. 2020. *The Fascination with Violence in Contemporary Society*. New York: Springer International.

Birrell, Susan. 1981. "Sport as Ritual: Interpretations from Durkheim to Goffman." *Social Forces* 60 (2): 354–376. https://doi.org/10.2307/2578440.

Blake, Joseph A. 1978. "Death by Hand Grenade: Altruistic Suicide in Combat." *Suicide and Life-Threatening Behavior* 8 (1): 46–59.

Bogle, Kathleen A. 2008. *Hooking Up: Sex, Dating, and Relationships on Campus*. New York: New York University Press.

Bogren, Alexandra. 2014. "Sign of the Times? Gender, Sexuality, and Drinking Stories." *International Journal of Drug Policy* 25 (3): 359–360. https://doi.org/10.1016/j.drugpo.2014.04.003.

Borch, Christian. 2012. *The Politics of Crowds: An Alternative History of Sociology*. Cambridge: Cambridge University Press.

Bourdieu, Pierre. 2001. *Masculine Domination*. Palo Alto, CA: Stanford University Press.

Boyns, David, and Sarah Luery. 2015. "Negative Emotional Energy: A Theory of the 'Dark-Side' of Interaction Ritual Chains." *Social Sciences* 4 (1): 148–170. https://doi.org/10.3390/socsci4010148.

Briggs, Daniel. 2013. *Deviance and Risk on Holiday: An Ethnography of British Tourists in Ibiza*. London: Palgrave Macmillan.

Brown, Rebecca. 2013. "A Picture Tells a Thousand Stories: Young Women, Mobile Technology, and Drinking Narratives." In *Emerging Perspectives on Substance Misuse*, edited by W. Mistral, 59–79. Oxford: Wiley-Blackwell.

Bruner, Edward M. 1986. *Experience and Its Expressions: The Anthropology of Experience*. Urbana: University of Illinois Press.

Buford, Bill. 1993. *Among the Thugs*. New York: Vintage Departures.

Burton, Robyn, Clive Henn, Don Lavoie, Rosanna O'Connor, Clare Perkins, Kate Sweeney, Felix Greaves, et al. 2017. "A Rapid Evidence Review of the Effectiveness and Cost-Effectiveness of Alcohol Control Policies: An English Perspective." *Lancet* 389 (10078): 1558–1580. https://doi.org/10.1016/s0140-6736(16)32420-5.

Bøhling, Frederik. 2014. "Crowded Contexts: On the Affective Dynamics of Alcohol and Other Drug use in Nightlife Spaces." *Contemporary Drug Problems* 41 (3): 361–392. https://doi.org/10.1177/009145091404100305.

Caillois, Roger. 2001. *Man, Play and Games*. Chicago: University of Illinois Press.

Canetti, Elias. 1978. *Crowds and Power*. New York: Continuum.

Chatterton, Paul, and Roger Hollands. 2003. *Urban Nightscapes: Youth Cultures, Pleasure Spaces and Corporate Power*. London: Routledge.

Collins, Randall. 1988. "The Micro Contribution to Macro Sociology." *Sociological Theory* 6 (2): 242–253. https://doi.org/10.2307/202118.

————. 2004. *Interaction Ritual Chains*. Princeton, N.J.: Princeton University Press.

————. 2008. *Violence: A Micro-sociological Theory*. Princeton, N.J.: Princeton University Press.

————. 2014. "Interaction Ritual Chains and Collective Effervescence." In *Collective Emotions*, edited by C. Scheve, 299–311. Oxford: Oxford University Press.

Connell, Raewyn. 2020. *Masculinities*. London: Routledge.

Connolly, Kate. 2020. "Germany's Covid-19 Fears Grow over 'Reckless' Partygoers." *The Guardian*, July 29. https://www.theguardian.com/world/2020/jul/29/germany-covid-19 -fears-grow-over-reckless-partygoers.

Conroy, Dominic, and Richard de Visser. 2014. "Being a Non-drinking Student: An Interpretative Phenomenological Analysis." *Psychology & Health* 29 (5): 536–551. https://doi .org/10.1080/08870446.2013.866673.

Copes, Heith, and Andy Hochstetler. 2003. "Situational Construction of Masculinity among Male Street Thieves." *Journal of Contemporary Ethnography* 32 (3): 279–304.

Cottingham, Marci D. 2012. "Interaction Ritual Theory and Sports Fans: Emotion, Symbols, and Solidarity." *Sociology of Sport Journal* 29 (2): 168–185. https://doi.org/10.1123/ssj.29 .2.168.

Coupland, Justine, and Adam Jaworski. 2003. "Transgression and Intimacy in Recreational Talk." *Narratives, Research on Language & Social Interaction* 36 (1): 85–106. https://doi .org/10.1207/s15327973rlsi3601_5.

Cox, Harvey. 1969. *The Feast of Fools*. Cambridge, Mass.: Harvard University Press.

Cullen, Fin. 2011. "'The Only Time I Feel Girly Is When I Go Out': Drinking Stories, Teenage Girls and Respectable Femininities." *International Journal of Adolescence and Youth* 16 (2): 119–138. https://doi.org/10.1080/02673843.2011.9748051.

Dawkins, Clinton Richard. 1989. *The Selfish Gene*. New York: Oxford University Press.

Deleuze, Gilles. 1992. "Postscript on the Societies of Control." *October* 59 (Winter): 3–7.

Dimou, Eleni, and Jonathan Ilan. 2018. "Taking Pleasure Seriously: The Political Significance of Subcultural Practice." *Journal of Youth Studies* 21 (1): 1–18. https://doi.org/10 .1080/13676261.2017.1340635.

The Divine Comedy. 1993. "A Drinking Song." Compact disc. Track 10 on *Promenade*. Setanta Records.

Dostoevsky, Fyodor. 2003. *Crime and Punishment*. London: Penguin.

Douglas, Mary. 1987. *Constructive Drinking*. London: Routledge.

Draper, Scott. 2019. *Religious Interaction Ritual: The Microsociology of the Spirit*. Lanham, Md.: Rowman & Littlefield.

Drury, John, and Steve Reicher. 2005. "Explaining Enduring Empowerment: A Comparative Study of Collective Action and Psychological Outcomes." *European Journal of Social Psychology* 35 (1): 35–38. https://doi.org/10.1002/ejsp.231.

Duff, Cameron. 2008. "The Pleasure in Context." *International Journal of Drug Policy* 19 (5): 384–392. https://doi.org/10.1016/j.drugpo.2007.07.003.

Duffett, Mark. 2015. "Elvis' Gospel Music: Between the Secular and the Spiritual?" *Religions* 6 (1): 182–203. https://doi.org/10.3390/rel6010182.

Durkheim, Émile. 1979. *Suicide: A Study in Sociology*, translated by J. A. Spaulding and G. Simpson. New York: Free Press.

————. 1994. "Contribution to Discussion 'Religious Sentiment at the Present Time.'" In *Durkheim on Religion*, edited by W. S. F. Pickering, 181–189. Atlanta: Scholars Press.

————. 1995. *The Elementary Forms of Religious Life*. New York: Free Press.

————. 2017. *Les Règles de la Méthode Sociologique*. Paris: Flammarion.

Easthope, Antony. 1992. *What a Man's Gotta Do: The Masculine Myth in Popular Culture*. London: Routledge.

Eco, Umberto. 1984. "The Frames of Comic 'Freedom.'" In *Carnival!* edited by T. A. Sebeok, 1–9. Berlin: Mouton.

Ehrenreich, Barbara. 2006. *Dancing in the Streets: A History of Collective Joy*. New York: Holt.

Elias, Norbert. 2000. *The Civilizing Process*. Oxford: Blackwell.

Ellingson, Stephen. 2010. "New Research on Megachurches." In *The New Blackwell Companion to the Sociology of Religion*, edited by Bryan S. Turner, 245–266. Oxford: Blackwell.

Fenwick, Mark, and Keith Hayward. 2000. "Youth Crime, Excitement and Consumer Culture: The Reconstruction of Aetiology in Contemporary Theoretical Criminology." In *Youth Justice: Theory and Practice*, edited by Jane Pickford, 31–50. London: Cavendish.

Ferrell, Jeff, Keith Hayward, and Jock Young. 2015. *Cultural Criminology: An Invitation*. 2nd ed. London: Sage.

Fileborn, Bianca. 2016. *Reclaiming the Night-Time Economy: Unwanted Sexual Attention in Pubs and Clubs*. London: Palgrave Macmillan.

Fine, Gary Alan. 2002. *Shared Fantasy: Role Playing Games as Social Worlds*. Chicago: University of Chicago Press.

Fjær, Eivind Grip. 2012. "The Day after Drinking: Interaction during Hangovers among Young Norwegian Adults." *Journal of Youth Studies* 15 (8): 995–1010. https://doi.org/10.1080/13676261.2012.693594.

———. 2021. "Party Morals." PhD diss., University of Oslo. https://www.sv.uio.no/iss/forskning/aktuelt/arrangementer/disputaser/2022/abstract.pdf.

Fjær, Eivind Grip, Willy Pedersen, and Sveinung Sandberg. 2015. "'I'm Not One of Those Girls': Boundary-Work and the Sexual Double Standard in a Liberal Hookup Context." *Gender & Society* 29 (6): 960–981. https://doi.org/10.1177/0891243215602107.

Fleetwood, Jennifer. 2014a. *Drug Mules: Women in the International Cocaine Trade*. Hampshire, U.K.: Palgrave Macmillan.

———. 2014b. "A Feminist, Narrative Analysis of Drinking Stories." *International Journal of Drug Policy* 25 (3): 351–352. https://doi.org/10.1016/j.drugpo.2014.03.011.

Frank, Arthur W. 2010. *Letting Stories Breathe: A Socio-narratology*. University of Chicago Press.

Gabriel, Shira, Esha Naidu, Elaine Paravati, C. D. Morrison, and Kristin Gainey. 2020. "Creating the Sacred from the Profane: Collective Effervescence and Everyday Activities." *Journal of Positive Psychology* 15 (1): 129–154. https://doi.org/10.1080/17439760.2019.1689412.

Galanter, Marc. 1999. *Cults: Faith, Healing and Coercion*. Oxford: Oxford University Press.

García, Luis-Manuel. 2013. "Doing Nightlife and EDMC Fieldwork: Guest Editor's Introduction." *Dancecult: Journal of Electronic Dance Music Culture* 5 (1): 3–17. https://doi.org/10.12801/1947-5403.2013.05.01.01.

Gardaphé, Fred. 2014. "'What'ya Mean I'm Funny?' Ball-Busting Humor and Italian American Masculinities." In *Gender and Humor*, edited by Delia Chiaro and Raffaella Baccolini, 240–252, London Routledge.

Garrett, Bradley. 2013. *Explore Everything: Place-Hacking the City*. London: Verso.

Gauthier, François. 2004. "Rapturous Ruptures: The Instituant Religious Experience of Rave." In *Rave, Culture and Religion*, edited by Graham St John, 65–84. London: Routledge.

———. 2005. "Orpheus and the Underground: Raves and Implicit Religion—from Interpretation to Critique." *Implicit Religion* 8 (3): 235–283.

Gefou-Madianou, Dimitra, ed. 1992. *Alcohol, Gender and Culture*. London: Routledge.

Gell, Alfred. 1980. "The Gods at Play: Vertigo and Possession in Muria Religion." *Man* 15 (2): 219–248.

Gennep, Arnold. 1960. *The Rites of Passages*. London: Routledge.

Goffman, Alice. 2019. "Go to More Parties? Social Occasions as Home to Unexpected Turning Points in Life Trajectories." *Social Psychology Quarterly* 82 (1): 51–74. https://doi.org/10.1177/0190272518812010.

Goffman, Erving. 1990. *The Presentation of Self in Everyday Life*. London: Penguin.

Graham, Tyler E. 2007. "The Danger of Durkheim: Ambiguity in the Theory of Social Effervescence." *Religion* 37 (1): 26–38.

Grazian, David. 2005. *Blue Chicago: The Search for Authenticity in Urban Blues Clubs*. Chicago: University of Chicago Press.

———. 2007. "The Girl Hunt: Urban Nightlife and the Performance of Masculinity as Collective Activity." *Symbolic Interaction* 30 (2): 221–243. https://doi.org/10.1525/si.2007.30.2.221.

———. 2008. *On the Make: The Hustle of Urban Nightlife*. Chicago: University of Chicago Press.

Gruner, Charles R. 2000. *The Game of Humor: A Comprehensive Theory of Why We Laugh*. New Brunswick, N.J.: Transaction.

Grønnestad, Trond E., Hildegunn Sagvaag, and Philip Lalander. 2020. "Interaction Rituals in an Open Drug Scene." *Nordic Studies on Alcohol and Drugs* 37, no. 1 (February): 86–98. https://doi.org/10.1177/1455072519882784.

Hadfield, Phil. 2009. *Nightlife and Crime: Social Order and Governance in International Perspective*. Oxford: Oxford University Press.

———. 2015. "The Night-Time City. Four Modes of Exclusion: Reflections on the Urban Studies Special Collection." *Urban Studies* 52 (3): 606–616. https://doi.org/10.1177/0042098014552934.

Hall, Stuart, ed. 1997. *Representation: Cultural Representations and Signifying Practices*. London: Sage.

Hayward, Keith. 2002. "The Vilification and Pleasures of Youthful Transgression." In *Youth Justice: Critical Readings*, edited by John Muncie, Gorden Hughes, and Eugene McLaughlin, 80–94. London: Sage.

Healy, John Paul. 2010. *Yearning to Belong: Discovering a New Religious Movement*. Farnham, U.K.: Ashgate.

Heider, Anne, and Steven R. Warner. 2010. "Bodies in Sync: Interaction Ritual Theory Applied to Sacred Harp Singing." *Sociology of Religion* 71 (1): 76–97. https://doi.org/10.1093/socrel/srq001.

Henriksson, Carina, and Norm Friesen. 2012. Introduction to *Hermeneutic Phenomenology in Education: Method and Practice*, edited by Norm Friesen, Carina Henriksson, and Tone Saevi, 1–14. Rotterdam, Netherlands: Sense.

Hesse, Morten, and Sébastien Tutenges. 2010. "Predictors of Hangover during a Week of Heavy Drinking on a Holiday." *Addiction* 105 (3): 476–483. https://doi.org/10.1111/j.1360-0443.2009.02816.x.

———. 2011. "Young Tourists Visiting Strip Clubs and Paying for Sex." *Tourism Management* 32 (4): 869–874. https://doi.org/10.1016/j.tourman.2010.08.002.

Hesse, Morten, Sébastien Tutenges, Sanna Schliewe, and Tine Reinholdt. 2008. "Party Package Travel: Alcohol Use and Related Problems in a Holiday Resort: A Mixed Methods Study." *BMC Public Health* 8 (351). https://doi.org/10.1186/1471-2458-8-351.

Hobbs, Dick, Philip Hadfield, Stuart Lister, and Simon Winlow. 2003. *Bouncers: Violence in the Night-Time Economy*. Oxford: Oxford University Press.

Holmquist, J. 2006. "Student Essay: An Experience in Acronyms." In *The Curious Reader: Exploring Personal and Academic Inquiry*, edited by Bruce Ballenger and Michelle Payne, 115–122. New York: Pearson.

Hopkins, Nick, Stephen D. Reicher, Sammyh S. Khan, Shruti Tewari, Narayanan Srinivasan, and Clifford Stevenson. 2016. "Explaining Effervescence: Investigating the Relationship between Shared Social Identity and Positive Experience in Crowds." *Cognition and Emotion* 30 (1): 20–32. https://doi.org/10.1080/02699931.2015.1015969.

Horsfall, Sara Towe. 2016. "Music as Ritual: A Hotline to the Collective Conscious." In *Music Sociology: Examining the Role of Music in Social Life*, edited by Sara Towe Horsfall, Jan-Martijn Meij, and Meghan Probstfield, 51–59. London: Routledge.

Hunt, Geoffrey, and Judith C. Barker. 2001. "Socio-cultural Anthropology and Alcohol and Drug Research: Towards a Unified Theory." *Social Science & Medicine* 53 (2): 165–188. https://doi.org/10.1016/s0277-9536(00)00329-4.

Hunt, Geoffrey, Molly Moloney, and Kristin Evans. 2009. "Epidemiology Meets Cultural Studies: Studying and Understanding Youth Cultures, Clubs and Drugs." *Addiction Research & Theory* 17 (6): 601–621. https://doi.org/10.3109/16066350802245643.

———. 2010. *Youth, Drugs, and Nightlife*. London: Routledge.

Jackson, Michael. 1982. *Allegories of the Wilderness: Ethics and Ambiguity in Kuranko Narratives*. Bloomington: Indiana University Press.

———. 1989. *Paths toward a Clearing: Radical Empiricism and Ethnographic Inquiry*. Bloomington: Indiana University Press.

———. 1996. "Phenomenology, Radical Empiricism, and Anthropological Critique." In *Things as They Are: New Directions in Phenomenological Anthropology*, edited by Michael Jackson, 1–50. Bloomington: Indiana University Press.

———. 1998. *Minima Ethnographica: Intersubjectivity and the Anthropological Project*. Chicago: University of Chicago Press.

———. 2002. *The Politics of Storytelling: Violence, Transgression and Intersubjectivity*. Copenhagen: Museum Tusculanum.

———. 2013. *Lifeworlds: Essays in Existential Anthropology*. Chicago: University of Chicago Press.

———. 2015. *Harmattan: A Philosophical Fiction*. New York: Columbia University Press.

———. 2016. *The Work of Art: Rethinking the Elementary Forms of Religious Life*. New York: Columbia University Press.

Jackson-Jacobs, Curtis. 2009. *Tough Crowd: An Ethnographic Study of the Social Organization of Fighting*. PhD diss., University of California, Los Angeles. https://curtisjacksonjacobs.files.wordpress.com/2011/03/dissertation_full.pdf.

Jefferson, Gail, Harvey Sacks, Emmanuel Schegloff. 1987. "Notes on Laughter in the Pursuit of Intimacy." In *Talk and Social Organisation*, edited by Graham Button and John Lee, 152–205. London: Multilingual Matters.

Jenks, Chris. 2003. *Transgression*. London: Routledge.

Johnson, Peter. 2013. "'You Think You're a Rebel on a Big Bottle': Teenage Drinking, Peers and Performance Authenticity." *Journal of Youth Studies* 16 (6): 747–758. https://doi.org/10.1080/13676261.2012.744816.

Jørgensen, Morten Hulvej, Tine Curtis, Pia Haudrup Christensen, and Morten Grønbæk. 2007. "Harm Minimization among Teenage Drinkers: Findings from an Ethnographic Study on Teenage Alcohol Use in a Rural Danish Community." *Addiction* 102 (4): 554–559. https://doi.org/10.1111/j.1360-0443.2006.01697.x.

Josiam, Bharath M., John S. Perry Hobson, Uta C. Dietrich, and George Smeaton. 1998. "An Analysis of the Sexual, Alcohol and Drug Related Behavioural Patterns of Students on Spring Break." *Tourism Management* 19 (6): 501–513. https://doi.org/10.1016/s0261-5177(98)00052-1.

Kahn-Harris, Keith. 2007. *Extreme Metal: Music and Culture on the Edge*. Oxford: Berg.

Katz, Jack. 1988. *Seductions of Crime: Moral and Sensual Attractions in Doing Evil*. New York: Basic Books.

———. 2002. "Start Here: Social Ontology and Research Strategy." *Theoretical Criminology* 6 (3): 255–278. https://doi.org/10.1177/136248060200600302.

Kavanaugh, Philip R., and Tammy L. Anderson. 2008. "Solidarity and Drug Use in the Electronic Dance Music Scene." *Sociological Quarterly* 49 (1): 181–208. https://doi.org/10.1111/j.1533-8525.2007.00111.x.

Kennedy, Liam, Derek Silva, Madelaine Coelho, and William Cipolli. 2019. "'We Are All Broncos': Hockey, Tragedy, and the Formation of Canadian Identity." *Sociology of Sport Journal* 36 (3): 189–202. https://doi.org/10.1123/ssj.2019-0006.

Kershaw, Baz, and Helen Nicholson. 2011. *Research Methods in Theatre and Performance*. Edinburgh: Edinburgh University Press.

Kertzer, David I. 1989. *Ritual, Politics, and Power*. New Haven, Conn.: Yale University Press.

Kierkegaard, Søren. 1983. *Kierkegaard's Writings*. Vol. 6, *Fear and Trembling/Repetition*. Princeton: Princeton University Press.

King, Anthony. 1997. "The Lads: Masculinity and the New Consumption of Football." *Sociology* 31 (2): 329–346. https://doi.org/10.1177/0038038597031002008.

King, Rosamund S. 2011. "New Citizens, New Sexualities: Nineteenth-Century Jamettes." In *Sex and the Citizen Interrogating the Caribbean*, edited by Faith Smith, 214–223. Charlottesville: University of Virginia Press.

Lamont, Michèle, and Thévenot Laurent, eds. 2000. *Rethinking Comparative Cultural Sociology: Repertoires of Evaluation in France and the United States*. Cambridge: Cambridge University Press.

Leary, James P. 1976. "Fists and Foul Mouths: Fights and Fight Stories in Contemporary Rural American Bars." *Journal of American Folklore* 89 (351): 27–39. https://doi.org/10.2307/539544.

Le Bon, Gustave. 2001. *The Crowd: A Study of the Popular Mind*. Kitchener, Canada: Batoche.

Lehmann, Jennifer M. 1994. *Durkheim and Women*. Lincoln: University of Nebraska Press.

Liebst, Lasse Suonperä. 2019. "Exploring the Sources of Collective Effervescence: A Multilevel Study." *Sociological Science* 6 (2): 27–42. https://doi.org/10.15195/v6.a2.

Linde, Charlotte. 1993. *Life Stories: The Creation of Coherence*. New York: Oxford University Press.

Lindholm, Charles. 2003. "Culture, Charisma, and Consciousness: The Case of the Rajneeshee." *Ethos* 30 (4): 357–375. https://doi.org/10.1525/eth.2002.30.4.357.

Lindsay, Jo. 2009. "Young Australians and the Staging of Intoxication and Self-Control." *Journal of Youth Studies* 12 (4): 371–384. https://doi.org/10.1080/13676260902866520.

Lyng, Stephen. 1990. "Edgework: A Social Psychological Analysis of Voluntary Risk Taking." *American Journal of Sociology* 95 (4): 851–886. https://doi.org/10.1086/229379.

———. 2004. *Edgework: The Sociology of Risk Taking*. New York: Routledge.

MacAndrew, Craig, and Robert B. Edgerton. 1969. *Drunken Comportment: A Social Explanation*. Chicago: Aldine.

Maffesoli, Michel. 1985. *L'ombre de Dionysos*. Paris: Librairie des Méridiens.

———. 1993. *The Shadow of Dionysus: A Contribution to the Sociology of the Orgy*. Albany: State University of New York Press.

———. 1996a. *The Contemplation of the World: Figures of Community Style*. Minneapolis: University of Minnesota Press.

———. 1996b. *Le Temps des Tribus: Le Déclin de l'individualisme Dans les Sociétés Postmodernes*. Paris: La Table Ronde.

Malbon, Ben. 1999. *Clubbing Dancing, Ecstasy and Vitality*. London: Routledge.

Maloney, Patricia. 2013. "Online Networks and Emotional Energy." *Information, Communication & Society* 16 (1): 105–124. https://doi.org/10.1080/1369118x.2012.659197.

Marshall, Alex, Thomas Rogers, and Constant Méheut. 2020. "At Europe's Illegal Parties, the Virus Is the Last Thing on Anyone's Mind." *New York Times*, August 7. https://www.nytimes.com/2020/08/07/arts/music/illegal-parties-coronavirus-europe.html.

Marx, Karl. 2008. "Contribution to the Critique of Hegel's Philosophy of Right." In *On Religion*, by Karl Marx and Friedrich Engels, 41–58. Mineola, N.Y.: Dover.

Mason, Peter. 1998. *Bacchanal! The Carnival Culture of Trinidad*. Philadelphia, Pa.: Temple University Press.

Mauss, Marcel. 1979. *Sociology and Psychology: Essays*. London: Routledge.

Mauss, Marcel, and Henri Beuchat. 2008. "Essai Sur Les Variations Saisonnières: Des Sociétés Eskimos: Étude De Morphologie Sociale." In *Sociologie et Anthropologie*, edited by Marcel Mauss, 389–478. Paris: Presses Universitaires de France.

McFarland, Daniel A., Dan Jurafsky, and Craig Rawlings. 2013. "Making the Connection: Social Bonding in Courtship Situations." *American Journal of Sociology* 118 (6): 1596–1649. https://doi.org/10.1086/670240.

McNeill, William Hardy. 1995. *Keeping Together in Time: Dance and Drill in Human History*. Cambridge, Mass.: Harvard University Press.

McRobbie, Angela. 1994. "Youth Culture and Femininity." In *Postmodernism and Popular Culture*, edited by Angela McRobbie, 155–176. London: Routledge.

Mears, Ashley. 2020. *Very Important People: Status and Beauty in the Global Party Circuit.* Princeton: Princeton University Press.

Melechi, Antonio. 1993. "The Ecstasy of Disappearance." In *Rave Off: Politics and Deviance in Contemporary Youth Culture*, edited by Steve Redhead, 29–40. Aldershot, U.K.: Avebury.

Mellor, Philip A., and Chris Shilling. 1997. "Confluent Love and the Cult of the Dyad: The Pre-contractual Foundations of Modern Contractarian Relationships." In *Sex These Days: Essays on Theology, Sexuality and Society*, edited by Jon Davies and Gerard Loughlin, 51–78. Sheffield, U.K.: Sheffield Academic.

Merleau-Ponty, Maurice. 1964. *Sense and Non-sense.* Evanston, Ill.: Northwestern University Press.

Milbank, John. 2011. "Darkness and Silence: Evil and the Western Legacy." In *Evil in Contemporary Political Theory*, edited by Bruce Haddock, Peri Roberts, and Peter Sutch, 10–41. Edinburgh: Edinburgh University Press.

Milthorpe, Naomi, and Eliza Murphy. 2019. "Reading the Party: Festivity as Waste in Evelyn Waugh's 1930s Fiction." *Journal of Festive Studies* 1 (1): 36–51. https://doi.org/10.33823/jfs.2019.1.1.20.

Moran, Dermot. 2000. *Introduction to Phenomenology.* London: Routledge.

Newson, Martha. 2019. "Football, Fan Violence, and Identity Fusion." *International Review for the Sociology of Sport* 54 (4): 431–444. https://doi.org/10.1177/1012690217731293.

Nietzsche, Friedrich Wilhelm. 1969. *On the Genealogy of Morals.* New York: Random House.

———. 2006. *Thus Spoke Zarathustra: A Book for All and None.* New York: Cambridge University Press.

O'Grady, Alice. 2012. "Spaces of Play: The Spatial Dimensions of Underground Club Culture and Locating the Subjunctive." *Dancecult* 4 (1): 86–106. https://doi.org/10.12801/1947-5403.2012.04.01.04.

Olaveson, Tim. 2004a. "'Connectedness' and the Rave Experience: Rave as New Religious Movement?" In *Rave Culture and Religion*, edited by Graham St John, 85–106. London: Routledge.

———. 2004b. "'Non-stop Ecstatic Dancing': An Ethnographic Study of Connectedness and the Rave Experience in Central Canada." PhD diss., University of Ottawa. https://ruor.uottawa.ca/handle/10393/29150.

Páez, Dario, Bernard Rimé, Nekane Basabe, Anna Wlodarczyk, and Larraitz Zumeta. 2015. "Psychosocial Effects of Perceived Emotional Synchrony in Collective Gatherings." *Journal of Personality and Social Psychology* 108 (5): 711–729. https://doi.org/10.1037/pspi0000014.

Pagis, Michal. 2015. "Evoking Equanimity: Silent Interaction Rituals in Vipassana Meditation Retreats." *Qualitative Sociology* 38 (1): 39–56. https://doi.org/10.1007/s11133-014-9295-7.

Pan, David. 2012. *Sacrifice in the Modern World: On the Particularity and Generality of Nazi Myth.* Evanston, Ill.: Northwestern University Press.

Pedersen, Willy. 2006. *Bittersøtt: Ungdom, Sosialisering, Rusmidler.* Oslo: Universitetsforlaget.

Pedersen, Willy, Sébastien Tutenges, and Sveinung Sandberg. 2017. "The Pleasures of Drunken One-Night Stands: Assemblage Theory and Narrative Environments." *International Journal of Drug Policy* 49:160–167.

Pérez-Bovet, Jordi, Carol Lorencio, Abdo Taché, Pablo Pujol Valverde, and Secundino Martín Ferrer. 2015. "Traumatic Brain Injury Caused by 'Balconing.'" *British Journal of Neurosurgery* 29 (1): 41–45. https://doi.org/10.3109/02688697.2014.952269.

Pickering, W. S. F. 2009. *Durkheim's Sociology of Religion Themes and Theories.* Cambridge: James Clarke.

Pini, Maria. 1997. "Women and the Early British Rave Scene." In *Back to Reality? Social Experience and Cultural Studies*, edited by Angela McRobbie, 152–169. Manchester: Manchester University Press.

Pink, Sarah. 2015. *Doing Sensory Ethnography*. Los Angeles: Sage.

Presdee, Mike. 2004. "Cultural Criminology: The Long and Winding Road." *Theoretical Criminology* 8 (3): 275–285. https://doi.org/10.1177/1362480604044609.

Presser, Lois. 2010. *Been a Heavy Life: Stories of Violent Men*. Urbana: University of Illinois Press.

———. 2013. *Why We Harm*. New Brunswick, N.J.: Rutgers University Press.

———. 2016. "Criminology and the Narrative Turn." *Crime, Media, Culture: An International Journal* 12 (2): 137–151. https://doi.org/10.1177/1741659015626203.

———. 2018. *Inside Story: How Narratives Drive Mass Harm*. Oakland: University of California Press.

Presser, Lois, and Sveinung Sandberg, eds. 2015. *Narrative Criminology: Understanding Stories of Crime*. New York: New York University Press.

Radcliffe, Polly, and Fiona Measham. 2014. "Repositioning the Cultural: Intoxicating Stories in Social Context." *International Journal of Drug Policy* 25 (3): 346–347. https://doi.org/10.1016/j.drugpo.2014.02.007.

Ram, Kalpana, and Christopher Houston. 2015. *Phenomenology in Anthropology: A Sense of Perspective*. Bloomington: Indiana University Press.

Ramp, William. 1998. "Effervescence, Differentiation and Representation in *The Elementary Forms*." In *On Durkheim's Elementary Forms of Religious Life*, edited by Nicholas J. Allen, W. S. F. Pickering, and William Watts Miller, 136–148. London: Routledge.

Rappaport, Roy A. 1999. *Ritual and Religion in the Making of Humanity*. Cambridge: Cambridge University Press.

Richard, Gaston. 1994. "Dogmatic Atheism in the Sociology of Religion." In *Durkheim on Religion: A Selection of Readings with Bibliographies*, edited by W. S. F. Pickering, 228–276. Atlanta: Scholars Press.

Riis, Ole, and Linda Woodhead. 2010. *A Sociology of Religious Emotions*. Oxford: Oxford University Press.

Rivera, Lauren A. 2015. "Go with Your Gut: Emotion and Evaluation in Job Interviews." *American Journal of Sociology* 120 (5): 1339–1389. https://doi.org/10.1086/681214.

Rossheim, Matthew E., and Dennis L. Thombs. 2018. "Estimated Blood Alcohol Concentrations Achieved by Consuming Supersized Alcopops." *American Journal of Drug and Alcohol Abuse* 44 (3): 317–320. https://doi.org/10.1080/00952990.2017.1334210.

Rossner, Meredith. 2013. *Just Emotions: Rituals of Restorative Justice*. Oxford: Oxford University Press.

Saldanha, Arun. 2007. *Psychedelic White: Goa Trance and the Viscosity of Race*. Minneapolis: University of Minnesota Press.

Sandberg, Sveinung. 2015. "Terrorism as Cultural Bricolage: The Case of Anders Behring Breivik." In *Framing Excessive Violence: Discourse and Dynamics*, edited by Daniel Ziegler, Marco Gerster, and Krämer Steffen, 177–196. Basingstoke, U.K.: Palgrave Macmillan.

Santangelo, Paolo. 2013. *Zibuyu, "What the Master Would Not Discuss," according to Yuan Mei (1716–1798): A Collection of Supernatural Stories*. Boston: Brill.

Schliewe, Sanna, and Sébastien Tutenges. 2021. "Moral Holidays: The Cases of Expatriates and Nightlife Tourists." In *Theorising Liminality: Between Art and Life*, edited by Brady Wagoner and Tania Zittoun, 71–84. New York: Springer.

Schütz, Alfred, and Thomas Luckmann. 1973. *Structures of the Life-World*. Evanston, Ill.: Northwestern University Press.

Serazio, Michael. 2012. "The Elementary Forms of Sports Fandom: A Durkheimian Exploration of Team Myths, Kinship, and Totemic Rituals." *Communication & Sport* 1 (4): 303–325. https://doi.org/10.1177/2167479512462017.

Shakespeare, William. 2002. *The Complete Works of William Shakespeare*. New York: Race Point.

Shilling, Chris, and Philip Mellor. 1998. "Durkheim, Morality and Modernity: Collective Effervescence, Homo Duplex and the Sources of Moral Action." *British Journal of Sociology* 49 (2): 193–209. https://doi.org/10.2307/591309.

———. 2001. *The Sociological Ambition: Elementary Forms of Social and Moral Life.* London: Sage.

———. 2011. "Retheorising Emile Durkheim on Society and Religion: Embodiment, Intoxication and Collective Life." *Sociological Review* 59 (1): 17–41. https://doi.org/10.1111/j .1467-954X.2010.01990.x.

Smith, Philip. 2005. *Why War? The Cultural Logic of Iraq, the Gulf War, and Suez.* Chicago: University of Chicago Press.

———. 2020. *Durkheim and After: The Durkheimian Tradition, 1893–2020.* Cambridge: Polity.

Spaaij, Ramon. 2006. *Understanding Football Hooliganism: A Comparison of Six Western European Football Clubs.* Amsterdam: Amsterdam University Press.

Stefansen, Kari, Lars Roar Frøyland, and Carolina Overlien. 2020. "Incapacitated Sexual Assault among Youths: Beyond the Perpetrator Tactics Framework." *Journal of Youth Studies*, 24 (10): 1373–1387. https://doi.org/10.1080/13676261.2020.1844172.

St John, Graham. 2018. "Civilised Tribalism: Burning Man, Event-Tribes and Maker Culture." *Cultural Sociology* 12 (1): 3–21. https://doi.org/10.1177/1749975517733162.

Tarde, Gabriel. 2007. *L'opinion et la Foule.* Paris: Éditions du Sandre.

Tan, Qian Hui. 2013. "Flirtatious Geographies: Clubs as Spaces for the Performance of Affective Heterosexualities." *Gender, Place & Culture* 20 (6): 718–736. https://doi.org/10 .1080/0966369x.2012.716403.

Thompson, Hunter S. 2005. *Fear and Loathing in Las Vegas: A Savage Journey to the Heart of the American Dream.* London: Harper Perennial.

Thrasher, James F., Matthew C. Rousu, David Hammond, Ashley Navarro, and Jay R. Corrigan. 2011. "Estimating the Impact of Pictorial Health Warnings and 'Plain' Cigarette Packaging: Evidence from Experimental Auctions among Adult Smokers in the United States." *Health Policy* 102 (1): 41–48. https://doi.org/10.1016/j.healthpol.2011.06.003.

Throop, C. Jason, and Charles. D. Laughlin. 2002. "Ritual, Collective Effervescence and the Categories: Toward a Neo-Durkheimian Model of the Nature of Human Consciousness, Feeling and Understanding." *Journal of Ritual Studies* 16 (1): 40–63.

Thurnell-Read, Thomas. 2011. "'Common-Sense' Research: Senses, Emotions and Embodiment in Researching Stag Tourism in Eastern Europe." *Methodological Innovations Online* 6 (3): 39–49. https://doi.org/10.4256/mio.2011.005.

———. 2012. "What Happens on Tour." *Men and Masculinities* 15 (3): 249–270. https://doi .org/10.1177/1097184x12448465.

Tiryakian, Edward A. 1978. "Durkheim and Husserl: A Comparison of the Spirit of Positivism and the Spirit of Phenomenology." In *Phenomenology and the Social Sciences: A Dialogue,* edited by Joseph Bien, 20–43. Boston: Martinus Nijhoff.

Tutenges, Sébastien. 2004. "Beruselse." *STOF* 4:35–37.

———. 2009. "Safety Problems among Heavy-Drinking Youth at a Bulgarian Nightlife Resort." *International Journal of Drug Policy* 20 (5): 444–446. https://doi.org/10.1016/j .drugpo.2008.11.004.

———. 2012. "Nightlife Tourism: A Mixed Methods Study of Young Tourists at an International Nightlife Resort." *Tourist Studies* 12 (2): 131–150. https://doi.org/10.1177/ 1468797612454250.

———. 2013. "Stirring Up Effervescence: An Ethnographic Study of Youth at a Nightlife Resort." *Leisure Studies* 32 (3): 233–248. https://doi.org/10.1080/02614367.2011.627372.

———. 2015. "Pub Crawls at a Bulgarian Nightlife Resort: A Case Study Using Crowd Theory." *Tourist Studies* 15 (3): 283–299. https://doi.org/10.1177/1468797615597856.

———. 2022. "Nightlife Ethnography: A Phenomenological Approach." In *The Oxford Handbook of Ethnographies of Crime and Criminal Justice,* edited by Sandra Bucerius, Kevin Haggerty, and Luca Berardi, 408–426. Oxford: Oxford University Press.

Tutenges, Sébastien, and Frederik Bøhling. 2019. "Designing Drunkenness: How Pubs, Bars and Nightclubs Increase Alcohol Sales." *International Journal of Drug Policy* 70:15–21. https://doi.org/10.1016/j.drugpo.2019.04.009.

Tutenges, Sébastien, and Morten Hesse. 2008. "Patterns of Binge Drinking at an International Nightlife Resort." *Alcohol and Alcoholism* 43 (5): 595–599. https://doi.org/10.1093/alcalc/agno39.

Tutenges, Sébastien, and Morten Hulvej Rod. 2009. "'We Got Incredibly Drunk . . . It Was Damned Fun': Drinking Stories among Danish Youth." *Journal of Youth Studies* 12 (4): 355–370. https://doi.org/10.1080/13676260902866496.

Tutenges, Sébastien, and Sveinung Sandberg. 2013. "Intoxicating Stories: The Characteristics, Contexts and Implications of Drinking Stories among Danish Youth." *International Journal of Drug Policy* 24 (6): 538–544. https://doi.org/10.1016/j.drugpo.2013.03.011.

Tutenges, Sébastien, Sveinung Sandberg, and Willy Pedersen. 2020. "Sexually Violent Effervescence: Understanding Sexual Assault among Youth." *Sexualities* 23 (3): 406–421. https://doi.org/10.1177/1363460719830342.

Vaadal, Kristine. 2019. "Navigating Nightlife: Women's Discourses on Unwanted Attention in Nightlife Settings in Norway." *Gender, Place & Culture* 27 (7): 1023–1043. https://doi.org/10.1080/0966369x.2019.1654982.

Valsiner, Jaan, ed. 2012. *The Oxford Handbook of Culture and Psychology.* Oxford: Oxford University Press.

———. 2014. *An Invitation to Cultural Psychology.* Los Angeles: Sage.

Vandenberg, Femke, Michaël Berghman, and Julian Schaap. 2020. "The 'Lonely Raver': Music Livestreams during COVID-19 as a Hotline to Collective Consciousness?" *European Societies* 23 (1): S141–S152. https://doi.org/10.1080/14616696.2020.1818271.

Vander Ven, Thomas. 2011. *Getting Wasted: Why College Students Drink Too Much and Party So Hard.* New York: New York University Press.

von Scheve, Christian. 2012. "Collective Emotions in Rituals: Elicitation, Transmission, and a 'Matthew-Effect.'" In *Emotions in Rituals and Performances: South Asian and European Perspectives on Rituals and Performativity,* edited by Axel Michaels and Christoph Wulf, 78–92. London: Routledge.

Wagoner, Brady, and Ignacio Brescó. 2021. "Collective Grief: Mourning Rituals, Politics and Memorial Sites." In *Experiencing the Death of the Other: Cultural, Existential, and Phenomenological Dimensions of Bereavement,* edited by Allan Køster and Ester Holte Kofod, 197–213. London: Routledge.

Weber, Max. 1968. *On Charisma and Institution Building: Selected Papers,* edited by Schmuel Noah Eisenstadt. Chicago: University of Chicago.

Weil, Andrew. 1998. *The Natural Mind: An Investigation of Drugs and the Higher Consciousness.* Boston: Houghton Mifflin.

Weininger, Elliot B., Annette Lareau, and Omar Lizardo, eds. 2018. *Ritual, Emotion, Violence: Studies on the Micro-sociology of Randall Collins.* New York: Routledge.

Wellman, James K., Katie E. Corcoran, and Kate Stockly-Meyerdirk. 2014. "'God Is like a Drug . . .': Explaining Interaction Ritual Chains in American Megachurches." *Sociological Forum* 29 (3): 650–672. https://doi.org/10.1111/socf.12108.

Williamson, Lola. 2010. *Transcendent in America: Hindu-Inspired Meditation Movements as New Religion.* New York: New York University Press.

Winehouse, Amy, vocalist. 2006. "Rehab." Compact disc. Track 1 on Amy Winehouse, Back to Black. Island Records.

INDEX

ABOUT THE AUTHOR

SÉBASTIEN TUTENGES is an associate professor at the Department of Sociology at Lund University and the editor-in-chief of *Nordic Journal of Criminology*. He has previously worked as postdoc at Oslo University and associate professor at Aarhus University. He has a master's degree in anthropology from Copenhagen University and a PhD in sociology, also from Copenhagen University. His research is broadly concerned with risk-taking behaviors. In particular, he is interested in how people experience and make meaning of intoxication, violence, and extremism. These interests have resulted in years of studying young people in a variety of risk-prone environments, including nightclubs, music festivals, drug markets, and seaside resorts in Spain and Bulgaria. Tutenges has published a wide range of book chapters and articles, including in *Addiction, Alcohol & Alcoholism, American Journal on Addictions, BMC Public Health, British Journal of Criminology, European Addiction Research, International Journal of Drug Policy, Leisure Studies, Tourism Management, Tourist Studies*, and *Journal of Youth Studies*.